About the Speaker

OXFORD STUDIES IN THEORETICAL LINGUISTICS

GENERAL EDITORS: David Adger, Queen Mary College London; Hagit Borer, University of Southern California

ADVISORY EDITORS: Stephen Anderson, Yale University; Daniel Büring, University of California, Los Angeles; Nomi Erteschik-Shir, Ben-Gurion University; Donka Farkas, University of California, Santa Cruz; Angelika Kratzer, University of Massachusetts, Amherst; Andrew Nevins, Harvard University; Christopher Potts, University of Massachusetts, Amherst; Barry Schein, University of Southern California; Peter Svenonius, University of Tromsø; Moira Yip, University College London

For a complete list of titles published and in preparation for the series, see pp 231–32.

About the Speaker

Towards a Syntax of Indexicality

ALESSANDRA GIORGI

OXFORD
UNIVERSITY PRESS

OXFORD

UNIVERSITY PRESS

Great Clarendon Street, Oxford, OX2 6DP,
United Kingdom

Oxford University Press is a department of the University of Oxford.
It furthers the University's objective of excellence in research, scholarship,
and education by publishing worldwide. Oxford is a registered trade mark of
Oxford University Press in the UK and in certain other countries

Published in the United States of America by Oxford University Press
198 Madison Avenue, New York, NY 10016, United States of America

British Library Cataloguing in Publication Data
Data available

Library of Congress Cataloging in Publication Data
Data available

ISBN 978–0–19–957189–5

Contents

General Preface

The theoretical focus of this series is on the interfaces between subcomponents of the human grammatical system and the closely related area of the interfaces between the different subdisciplines of linguistics. The notion of 'interface' has become central in grammatical theory (for instance, in Chomsky's recent Minimalist Program) and in linguistic practice: work on the interfaces between syntax and semantics, syntax and morphology, phonology and phonetics, etc., has led to a deeper understanding of particular linguistic phenomena and of the architecture of the linguistic component of the mind/brain.

The series covers interfaces between core components of grammar, including syntax/morphology, syntax/semantics, syntax/phonology, syntax/pragmatics, morphology/phonology, phonology/phonetics, phonetics/speech processing, semantics/pragmatics, intonation/discourse structure as well as issues in the way that the systems of grammar involving these interface areas are acquired and deployed in use (including language acquisition, language dysfunction, and language processing). It demonstrates, we hope, that proper understandings of particular linguistic phenomena, languages, language groups, or inter-language variations all require reference to interfaces.

The series is open to work by linguists of all theoretical persuasions and schools of thought. A main requirement is that authors should write so as to be understood by colleagues in related subfields of linguistics and by scholars in cognate disciplines.

A reoccurring theme in the interaction between grammer and meaning concerns the extent to which utterance context is reflected in syntactic representation. In this new volume, Alessandra Giorgi argues that the temporal coordinates of the speaker of an utterance are encoded in the complementizer layer of syntactic structure and that the relation between grammer and pragmatic context is, to a certain extent, bidirectional. This novel theory provides explanations of some surprising constraints on a disparate range of phenomena connected to types of temporal interpretation and their associated syntactic effects.

David Adger
Hagit Borer

Acknowledgements

I feel it is very difficult properly to acknowledge everybody who gave me ideas, suggestions, and hints for the writing of this book, especially because writing it took a long time and in one way or another all my colleagues, students, and friends participated in this, for me, lengthy and complex enterprise.

Hence, I thank here the linguists with whom I discussed some of the specific topics studied in this book, for their comments and suggestions: Guglielmo Cinque, Denis Delfitto, Jacqueline Guéron, Jim Higginbotham, and Fabio Pianesi.

This list is however by no means exhaustive and I wish to thank all my colleagues in my department in Venice, my friends in the Department of Linguistics at UCLA, where I have spent some happy months in recent years, and all the scholars and students around the world who attended my talks and classes, and asked questions and raised problems. I also thank the reviewers for their insightful comments, and the editors of the series, for trusting me.

I dedicate this book to my son Enrico, who presumably will never read it, but if he did, would find it excruciatingly boring, and justly so.

List of Abbreviations

C	Complementizer
CD	Complementizer Deletion
CL	clitic
C-layer	Complementizer-layer
DAR	Double Access Reading
DP	Determiner Phrase
FID	Free Indirect Discourse
IMPF	imperfect
IMPF IND	imperfect indicative
IND	indicative
IND IMPF	indicative imperfect
IND PRES	indicative present
INF	information(al)
LDA	long distance anaphor
LF	Logical Form
NP	Noun Phrase
PAST SUBJ	past subjunctive
PRES COND	present conditional
PRES IND	present indicative
PRES SUBJ	present subjunctive
SoT	Sequence of Tense
SUBJ	subjunctive
SUBJ PAST	subjunctive past
SUBJ PRES	subjunctive present
T	Tense
T-layer	Temporal layer
UG	Universal Grammar
vP	v Phrase
VP	Verb Phrase
V2	Verb Second

1

Introduction

1.1 The issue

In this book I investigate the relationship between syntax and context. In particular, I propose that in the syntactic representation of the sentence a syntactic *layer*—i.e., a sequence of positions functionally related—is especially devoted to play such a role at the interface. I identify this set of positions with the Complementizer-layer and argue that the temporal—and arguably spatial as well—coordinates of the speaker are represented in its left-most projection, which I dub here *C-speaker*.

It is widely recognized that the meaning of a sentence requires a 'context' to be computed. This is a very general phenomenon and in particular it concerns the items called *indexicals*, i.e., 'linguistic expressions whose meaning remains stable while their reference shifts from utterance to utterance.'[1] Pronouns such as *I* and *you* are the prototypical indexical items. Other examples include demonstratives, such as *this* or *that*, temporal and spatial locutions, such as *this room*, or *last month, here, now, yesterday, tomorrow*, etc. All these items can be assigned a reference only if we know who is talking, when, and where.

The literature in philosophy and in semantics about these issues is very rich and a discussion of its content would be far beyond the

---

[1] Cappelen and Lepore (2002: 271). Recently a definition of *indexical* such as the one by Cappelen and Lepore has been challenged by scholars like Schlenker (2003), who argue that indexicals can indeed change their meaning—i.e., adopting Kaplan's (1989) terminology they can be *monsters*—at least in certain languages. I will not consider this issue here, because it seems to me it would lie outside a discussion concerning the *syntax* of indexicality, but I will keep to a view according to which there are no *monsters*, following Kaplan's tradition. See also Higginbotham (2003).

scope of this book. There are however some relevant considerations that can be discussed with respect to indexicality even taking a purely syntactic perspective, like the one taken in this book.

There is an obvious question that we might ask as soon as we consider indexical phenomena: how does the syntax interact with the context? The first naive answer might be: it does not, there is no real interaction. The syntax computes structures and interactions among *constituents*, and then, *after*—metaphorically, not necessarily temporally—the syntactic computation has been done, the structure is interpreted and only at that point does the context come into play. Under this perspective, the context would not be a necessary component of syntax.

In this light, *this book* is a noun phrase and does not differ from any other noun phrase, as far as the rules of grammar are concerned. The fact that it includes a demonstrative does not concern the syntax, but some other module of language.

Even if this perspective might certainly be the right one, there are indexical components in language that cannot be as easily put aside, and *outside* syntax. What I mean is not that a *specific* context should be represented on the syntax. The main thesis of this book is that in the syntax there is a position—or better to say a *layer*, i.e., a set of contiguous positions—devoted to the interface between the syntax and the extra-sentential context, whatever it might be.

Note that the studies developed so far on this issue were already on this path. Rizzi's (1997) seminal work on split-Comp already implicitly shows that the left periphery of the clause is projected out of functional items which typically play a discourse role: *Topic*, signalling old information, *Focus*, signalling new information, and the Complementizer positions named *Force* and *Fin(ite)*, also playing a role in the contextual interface.

In this book I propose a precise hypothesis to this extent, claiming that the left-most peripheral position is specifically devoted to the representation of the speaker's temporal and spatial coordinates.

In order to exemplify, consider for instance the temporal interpretation of sentences. *John ate a sandwich* is a well-formed sentence in English, as far as its grammar is concerned, and it includes an indexical item, namely a past tense. The eating event is located in the past with respect to the utterance event, i.e., with respect to the speaker's temporal location. The same holds for a present tense: *John is eating an apple*, or for a future: *John will eat an apple*. In this case, indexicality becomes part of verbal morphology. This however might be considered just an accident, due to the peculiar morpho-syntactic structure of the language in question. In certain languages, such as Navajo, Chinese, and Haitian Creole, for instance, there are no morphemes devoted to the expression of tense, and still, the sentences are interpreted as past, present, or future, much as they are in Italian and English.[2]

The crucial point relevant to this discussion is constituted by the temporal location of the embedded eventuality in sentences such as example (1):

(1)   John said Mary is pregnant

In languages such as English and Italian, this sentence has a peculiar interpretation—see Abusch (1997)—called *Double Access Reading*. In order for the sentence to be felicitous, the pregnancy of Mary must hold both at the time John spoke about it and at the time the speaker utters the sentence. In Chapter 2 I will consider this phenomenon, with further details. Here, I would like to point out that in sentence (1) both the main verbal form and the embedded one are interpreted with respect to the context as defined by the speaker's temporal location—i.e., *both* verbal forms have an indexical component.

Note that this consideration is not trivial, in that it cannot be simply said, as a general rule, that the embedded verbal form is interpreted *as if it were in isolation*, i.e., simply with respect to the speaker's temporal location. Consider, for instance, the following case:

(2)   John said Mary ate an apple

[2] On Navajo and Chinese, see Smith (1997, 2007) and Smith and Erbaugh (2005). On Haitian Creole aspect and tense, see Giorgi and Pianesi (2001a). The temporal interpretation is considered as derivative with respect to the aspectual one. For a comparative discussion see Giorgi (2008).

In sentence (2) the eating must precede the saying. That is, by means of (2) the speaker reports the following sentence by John:

(3) 'Mary ate an apple'

Whereas she cannot be reporting the following one:[3]

(4) 'Mary will eat an apple'

Even if the eating event located in the future by John could lie in the past with respect to the speaker, it is not possible to report (4) by means of (2). For instance, if John utters sentence (4) on 3 December and Mary indeed eats the apple on the 4th, I still cannot report John's saying on the 5th by means of (2). The embedded event must be temporally located with respect to the main one. It cannot be interpreted as if it were a past form in isolation.

This is true with respect to sentence (1) as well: the embedded eventuality must hold *now, and* it must hold at the time John said it. The indexical interpretation of the present verbal form is not enough to yield the correct interpretation. Therefore, in a language like English, on one hand it is necessary to hypothesize that the embedded verbal form has, or at least can have, an indexical component as in example (1) above, on the other this is not sufficient to obtain the correct interpretation of an embedded form.

The interpretation assigned to sentence (1) in English, and Italian as well, as in many other languages, however, is not a universal fact. The same sentence, with an embedded present tense, in a language such as Romanian—Russian, Japanese, Chinese, etc.—does not have this interpretation. Consider for instance the following Romanian examples:[4]

---

[3] In this case, the speaker has to use, both in English and Italian, the so-called future-in-the-past:

i. John said Mary **would eat** an apple

I will discuss this verbal form in Chapter 4, section 7.

[4] I wish to thank all my Romanian students, visiting Venice through our Erasmus programme, who participated in the course Theoretical Linguistics in the academic years 2006–7 and 2007–8, for discussing these and related data. In particular, I thank Iulia Zegrean for her kindness in answering all my questions. Every misusage of the evidence is my fault entirely.

(5)   Maria e insarcinata.
      Maria is(PRES IND) pregnant

(6)   (Acum 2 ani) Gianni a spus ca Maria e insarcinata.
      Two years ago John said that Maria is(PRES IND) pregnant

The present tense is the form used in main sentences to express simultaneity with the utterance time. But in Romanian, the equivalent of sentence (1), i.e., (6), has the same meaning as sentence (7) in English:

(7)   (two years ago) John said Mary was pregnant

In sentence (7), as in the Romanian example in (6) above, Mary's pregnancy holds at the time of the saying, but, contrasting with (1), the pregnancy does not have to hold at utterance time. This is shown by the fact it is possible to add the temporal specification *two years ago*, which is totally incompatible with an embedded present tense in English:

(8)   *Two years ago, John said that Mary is pregnant

Both in English and Romanian a present tense in a main clause is interpreted indexically, but in an embedded clause the indexical component disappears in Romanian, whereas it is retained in English. Why is there such a cross-linguistic difference? How is it possible to capture it?

Let's go back to the naive hypothesis given above, the one according to which the syntax and the context do not talk to each other, i.e., the indexical component comes into play in a module of language separated from the syntax. To account for the phenomena just presented, we would be compelled however to endow this non-syntactic, indexical, module with syntactic notions, at least with notions such as *main* and *embedded clause*. For instance the indexical module of English would contain the following rule:[5]

(9)   If the verbal form of the embedded clause is a present tense, then the embedded eventuality must be located with respect to the speaker's temporal location, as it is in isolation.

---

[5] Note that as I briefly mentioned above, rule (9) is necessary, but is not enough to account for the interpretation of the embedded verbal form in English, given that *is* must also be interpreted as expressing simultaneity with the main event of saying.

Whereas in Romanian and Japanese rule (9) would be absent, and replaced by the following:

(10) If a present verbal form appears in a main clause, then the eventuality must be located with respect to the speaker's temporal location. If the present tense is associated with a verbal form appearing in an embedded clause, then the eventuality is not located with respect to the speaker's temporal location.

Rules such as (9) and (10) are necessary, otherwise the presence or lack of the Double Access interpretation associated with (1) could not be captured.

It is possible in this respect to observe two important facts. The first is that the existence of rule (9) vs. (10) seems totally unjustified and arbitrary. Why should languages differ and why should they differ in exactly that way?

As for the second fact, as I remarked above, in these rules it is necessary to refer to syntactic notions, such as *main* and *embedded* clause. It therefore appears impossible to account for the interactions of sentences with the context *a priori*, without resorting to a syntactic 'level'. But, then, if a syntactic analysis is necessary, *exactly* what is the role of syntax with respect to phenomena such as the temporal interpretation of sentences?[6]

And so we are back to the original question, which can be addressed at this point with the basic remark that there is after all a relationship between syntax and indexicality and that *how* this relationship is established is an interesting issue of investigation. This is the topic of this book.

The issue is relevant both with respect to the general topic of the architecture of syntax and from the point of view of a cross-linguistic analysis. I will largely consider the first aspect, with some reference to cross-linguistic differences illustrated by a comparison between English and Italian, and occasionally Chinese and Romanian.

---

[6] In Abusch's (1997) terminology—see also Schlenker (2004)—one might say that in English the embedded present tense is *de re*, whereas in Romanian it is not. Independently of a discussion about the *pro* and *contra* of this proposal, let me point out that this idea would not help in clarifying the issue concerning the relationships between syntax and indexicality. See also Chapter 2 for further details.

1.2 The proposal

The proposal I argue for in this book is the following:

(11)   There is a syntactic position in the left-most periphery of the clause, and precisely in the Complementizer-layer, that encodes the temporal— and presumably spatial as well—coordinates of the speaker.

This position contains the *features* identifying the utterance event and exhibits different properties according to its syntactic environment— as is usually the case with syntactic phenomena—so that it is possible to account for intra- and cross-linguistic differences. I will illustrate theoretical and empirical arguments to this end.

Similar proposals have already emerged occasionally in the literature, in particular, but not exclusively, in the literature on temporal phenomena, for example Giorgi and Pianesi (2001a), Bianchi (2003, 2006), and Sigurðsson (2004, 2007). My proposal is a development of the one by Giorgi and Pianesi—even if there are several important differences—and differs in relevant ways from Bianchi's and Sigurðsson's, as will be discussed later in the book.

Perhaps the main distinguishing feature of the account I propose here concerns the relevance attributed to interpretive facts. As in Giorgi and Pianesi (1997) and subsequent work, I claim that the temporal interpretation of a sentence—and perhaps other interpretive aspects as well—is read off the syntax. Therefore, a difference in the temporal interpretation of the sentence *is* a difference in the syntactic structure. This hypothesis, though it may obviously be wrong, seems to me to have a strong heuristic power. Moreover, it is clearly the simplest possible starting point: there is no *deus ex machina* creating one particular interpretation instead of another. All we have is a syntactic structure and a context. The interpretation of the sentence arises from these components and nothing else.

In this introduction, and in this book, I am mostly talking about the *temporal* interpretation of clauses and about the necessity of hypothesizing the presence of the speaker's *temporal* location in the syntax—precisely in the left-most position of the C-layer. The natural questions therefore might be: are there other phenomena, besides those connected to the temporal interpretation, which might be relevant to the purpose of the hypothesis developed here? The answer is 'yes', and I briefly consider the distribution of long-distance anaphors in a tenseless language such as Chinese, in Chapter 4. I will show that the hypothesis that in Italian and English takes care of the temporal interpretation of embedded clauses, in Chinese contributes to explaining the distribution of anaphoric items such as *ziji* (self).[7] Besides this brief remark, however, I only consider questions relating to the temporal interpretation. The matter of whether the present hypothesis might be relevant in other domains as well is left for further research.

The other issue, namely, whether the *spatial* location of the speaker is represented in the C-layer, together with the *temporal* one—*hic et nunc*—is also left vague. I think there is evidence that this is indeed the case, as might be expected. For instance, in Halkomelem Salish, as analysed by Ritter and Wiltschko (2004, 2005, 2008), it seems that the temporal interpretation is based on the speaker's *spatial* coordinate and not on her temporal one. The relevance of the speaker's spatial location also emerges in the analysis of some phenomena concerning Free Indirect Discourse, discussed in Chapter 6. In general, however, I limit my remarks to the speaker's temporal location.

1.3 The background

The theoretical background of this work is constituted by the analysis of temporal relations provided in the generative framework of the 1990s, together with the minimalist proposals by Chomsky (1995, 2001, 2005).

I assume, following the seminal intuitions by Zagona (1988) and Stowell (1996), and much in the spirit of Giorgi and Pianesi (1997), that the temporal relations are represented in the syntax. Even if I do not propose here a multi-layered representation like the one

---

[7] See also Giorgi (2006, 2007).

made explicit in Stowell (1996), I follow his, and Zagona's, basic intuition that tenses are relational predicates, as also proposed in Higginbotham (2002, 2004, 2006).[8] According to the proposal adopted here, therefore, tenses are relational predicates represented in T. In languages distinguishing indicative and subjunctive, such as Italian, it is possible to capture the difference between the two by hypothesizing that the subjunctive is not a relational tense, in that it does not express a *tense* at all. The idea I will develop is that the subjunctive realizes an *agreement* relation with the superordinate form, with some interesting exceptions, however, which will prove useful in making the whole proposal more precise.

The core of the hypothesis argued for in this book is that, when appearing in subordinate clauses, relational tenses—in Italian in particular, and in DAR languages in general—require a special Complementizer, in that the eventuality, besides requiring anchoring to the superordinate event, must be located with respect to the speaker's temporal coordinate. This Complementizer has peculiar syntactic properties, which distinguish it from the Complementizer introducing a subjunctive, i.e., non-relational verbal forms. As I said above, it encodes the speaker's temporal and spatial coordinates, permitting—and requiring—evaluation of the verbal form with respect to the speech event even in embedded clauses.

The presence of the speaker-related features in the left-most position of the C-layer shows up not only indirectly, when analysing Double Access Reading phenomena, but also directly, when considering the distribution of certain first-person verbal forms, such as *credo* (I think), which—under specific syntactic conditions— will be analysed as epistemic heads. These heads will be shown, in certain clauses, to occupy exactly the speaker-related position in the Complementizer-layer I hypothesize.

Technically, the subordinate clauses not requiring the Complementizer endowed with the speaker-related features will simply

---

[8] For further developments of the same proposal, see also Zagona (1994, 1995, and 1999). For a slightly different development, see Guéron (1993, 2004) and Guéron and Hoekstra (1995).

be accounted for by means of applications of *Merge* and *Agree*. Conversely, the clauses endowed with the speaker-related position will also internally merge T in C, much in the spirit of Pesetsky and Torrego (2001), so that the correct interpretation will be triggered.[9]

In the literature about temporal phenomena it is possible to find reference to systematic exceptions to the general framework sketched by the various scholars. For instance, in dependence of a superordinate future verbal form, and in 'special' contexts, such as those found in narration, it is well known that the distribution of tenses is not the one normally expected.

In this book I address several of these 'difficult' issues. In particular, I will consider the distribution of the Italian imperfect indicative, the properties of the so-called future-in-the-past, the dependencies from a main future, and the properties of Free Indirect Discourse—a particular literary style, which looks like a counter-example to every possible generalization in terms of syntactic structure and DAR.

I will show that the framework I propose can account for these facts quite elegantly, and in a natural way. The same general picture is adopted for the simple cases discussed in Chapters 2–4: two possible options are available for a speaker of English or Italian; either the C-layer includes the speaker-related position or it does not. The temporal location of the speaker, however, might be affected by several factors, for instance the presence of certain operators or specific fictional devices. These factors yield the 'anomalies' mentioned above, but the general framework does not need to be altered. In particular, Chapter 6, on Free Indirect Discourse, provides a very strong argument in favour of my hypothesis. The leading idea is that the speaker's coordinates are syntactically represented, and, as such, might be subject to syntactic manipulation.

As I mentioned above, I will briefly sketch an analysis of the speaker's projection in Chinese, a language not exhibiting the same morphological complexity observed in Italian. A final important question must be raised, however: What can be said about languages

---

[9] For further discussion, see also Pesetsky and Torrego (2004a, 2004b, and 2006).

such as Romanian, which are as rich in verbal morphology as Italian, but do not exhibit any DAR? I will leave this issue for further research and offer here only some speculations with respect to it.[10]

1.4 The organization of this book

There are six further chapters in this book. In Chapter 2 I address the differences between indicative subordinate contexts and subjunctive ones, mostly with reference to complement clauses. I show that many interpretive and (purely) syntactic phenomena can be explained by means of a simple hypothesis: in some cases the left-most position of the Complementizer-layer is endowed with the speaker's temporal and spatial coordinates.

In Chapter 3 I consider the distribution of first-person, subjectless verbal forms such as *credo* (I think) in Italian, and show that there is evidence for claiming that the hypothesized speaker-related position is made visible by these items under certain syntactic conditions.

In Chapter 4 I examine the properties of the Italian imperfect—not in general, but only as far as the hypothesis developed in this work is concerned—and of the future-in-the-past. I show that in spite of their peculiar behaviour, their distribution is expected under the present proposal. In this chapter I also show that in a tenseless language such as Chinese, the properties of the distribution of Long Distance Anaphors, which I have discussed elsewhere, can be taken as evidence in favour of the analysis developed here.

In Chapter 5 I discuss the dependencies from a future verbal form and in Chapter 6 Free Indirect Discourse examples. Finally, in Chapter 7, I add a few closing remarks.

---

[10] I proposed some reflections about this point in Giorgi (2007). Note however that the empirical evidence is quite complex, and only native speakers can actually deal with it. This is the main motivation for not addressing the issue in this monograph.

2

The Speaker's Projection

2.1 Introduction

In this chapter I address some questions concerning the interpretation of an embedded verbal form in Italian. In this language, as in several other Romance and Germanic languages, the embedded verbal form exhibits a variety of morphological endings. Besides having the possibility of appearing with the same set of endings used in main clauses—i.e., the *indicative*—the embedded verb can appear with verbal endings which are not compatible with main assertions—i.e., the subjunctive and the infinitive. The main difference between subjunctive and infinitive is that the subjunctive is a finite form licensing a lexical subject. Here I will mostly consider the alternation indicative/subjunctive and show that it might be expressed by introducing in the embedded clause the representation of the temporal and spatial location of the *speaker*, which I will call from now on *the speaker's coordinates*.

I will compare Italian and English, where English does not distinguish between indicative and subjunctive in the same way Italian does. I will show that, in spite of the superficial differences, the representation of speaker's coordinates in embedded clauses holds in English as well and helps explain many facts concerning Sequence of Tense properties.[1]

---

[1] On English subjunctive, see among the others Portner (1997) and Stowell (2008). In the cases I am going to consider here, however, English subordinate clauses do not exhibit an alternation in the verbal form, whereas Italian does, hence the two sets of phenomena do not overlap. For this reason, I will not deal here with the English data and will instead refer the reader to the cited references.

The fact that the two languages show similar abstract properties, in spite of the morphological differences, is especially interesting because it permits us to draw some theoretical conclusions on the mechanisms underlying the temporal interpretation and the way it is realized in natural language.

2.2 The Double Access Reading

2.2.1 *The issue*

In this section I briefly describe the phenomenon known as Double Access Reading. I will not give a full discussion of the literature dealing with the topic, but will only summarize the points which are relevant to the present discussion.

The classical problem discussed by the scholars interested in the semantics of temporal relations concerns the interpretation of a present tense under a past form. This issue is only an 'iceberg point' for a more complex question, which is actually at the core of the temporal interpretation of embedded clauses, namely, the type of temporal anchoring strategy adopted by the different languages. The question concerns the interpretation to be attributed to sentences like the following:

(1)   John said that Mary is pregnant

(2)   Gianni ha detto che Maria è incinta

In languages like English and Italian this sentence means that the pregnancy of Mary overlaps both the time of the utterance and the time of John saying it—and obligatorily so. In these languages, the sentence cannot mean that Mary was pregnant at the time John said it, but that she is no longer pregnant at the utterance time. By contrast, in languages such as Romanian and Chinese, this meaning is available. In these languages the sentence is interpreted as the following ones in English and Italian, respectively:[2]

---

[2] Note also that in non-DAR languages the interpretation past-under-past of sentence (3)—i.e., the one in which the pregnancy of Mary precedes the saying—which is present in English, is not available. For some English speakers though this interpretation seems harder to obtain.

(3)   John said that Mary was pregnant

(4)   Gianni ha detto che Maria era incinta

In (3) and (4) the pregnancy does not necessarily extend to the present moment, even if this could be the case, in the absence of further specification. As a corollary, the following sentence is deviant in English (and Italian):

(5)   #Two years ago, John said that Mary is pregnant

(6)   #Due anni fa, Gianni ha detto che Maria è incinta

We know that pregnancy in human beings lasts nine months; therefore a sentence entailing that Mary's pregnancy lasted at least two years is deviant. However, it is well formed in the languages belonging to the other group.

Let me emphasize the fact that in sentences such as (3) in English—with the simultaneous reading—and (4) in Italian, the state *might* be holding at the utterance time. This is so, simply because states are, or at least might be, persistent, and in absence of any further temporal specification—as in sentences (3)–(4)—they might still be holding at the time the sentence is uttered. Therefore, even in non-DAR languages, in a sentence such as (3) it might be pragmatically plausible to suppose that the pregnancy is still holding *now*—i.e., at utterance time—but it is not necessary, as in DAR languages. The DAR is an *obligatory* interpretation, to the extent that examples (5) and (6) are not well formed in English and Italian.

So far I have distinguished between two language groups: DAR languages, where the embedded eventuality is *doubly* evaluated; and non-DAR ones, where it is temporally located only with respect to the main event.

No language has been discussed in the literature belonging to a third group, which should be possible, at least in principle, namely a language in which the *only* time to be considered for the interpretation of the embedded clause is the utterance time. For instance, in no language does a sentence such as (7) mean something like (8):

(7)   Two years ago John said that Mary is pregnant

(8)   Two years ago John said that Mary *be* pregnant *now*, at the time *I, the speaker,* am speaking

In other words, in no language does a complement clause have exactly the same range of interpretations it has in isolation: sentence (7) cannot mean that Mary is pregnant *now*—which is the meaning of the sentence '*Mary is pregnant*' used as a main clause—but that when John said it, she was not.

The conclusion that can be drawn from this observation is that the temporal location of the embedded eventuality cannot be identified exclusively on the basis of the indexical reference, and temporal anchoring to the main clause is obligatory. As a consequence only two language types can possibly exist. In non-DAR languages, the pregnancy holds at the time John—*the subject*—is speaking, whereas in DAR languages it holds *both then and now*.[3]

The same generalization also holds for the following example, where the embedded form is a past tense:

(9)   John said that Mary left

(10)   Today is the 27th, John *say* on the 24th that Mary *leave* on 25th

In no language does a sentence such as (9) mean something like (10). That is, it is not possible for a past tensed event to be interpreted as past only with respect to the utterance time.[4]

In the literature, it is possible to find suggestions that address at least some aspects of the problem I am considering here. For instance, with

---

[3] See also Enç (1986, 1987). For completeness, consider again the following English sentence, which will be better analysed in section 2.2.2 below:

i.   John said that Mary was sleeping

In English, the sleeping time is perceived as being either past (backwards shifted reading) or simultaneous to the sayer's. The Russian counterpart of (i) only gives a backward shifted reading. That is, we find again the situation discussed above: English forces the consideration of both the utterance time and the time of the superordinate event, whereas only the latter seems to matter for Russian. Again, what is missing is a language in which the embedded past tense is interpreted as in matrix clauses—that is, as a mere indexical—allowing them to report about a *dictum* of John which for instance locates the sleeping simultaneously in John's future and the speaker's past.

[4] In Chapters 4 and 5 I will discuss some cases in English and Italian, which seem, under certain circumstances, to have a reading such as the one provided in (10). I will argue that those contexts are to be analysed in a DAR perspective as well and do not constitute an exception, but on the contrary, provide further support to the theoretical proposal of this book.

respect to the impossibility of sentence (9) being appropriate to express the temporal relations in (10), Ogihara (1995a, 1995b, 1996) and Higginbotham (1995) argue that the temporal orientation of the embedded clause expressing the content of a propositional attitude must be isomorphic to the content it expresses. In other words, a past verbal form, such as *left*, cannot be used to express a future relation. This way, the unavailability of the temporal relations expressed in (10) is accounted for. That reading, in fact, would express the future-oriented speech uttered by John—'Mary **will** leave on the 25ᵗʰ'—by locating the *leaving* in the speaker's past by means of the simple past *left*. Pursuing this line of reasoning, the lack of a pure indexical reading of the embedded present tense of (1) is accounted for in a similar way: the sentence would express a present-time perspective by the utterer, and a future perspective by the subject.

Let me point out that, as noted by Higginbotham in a later work (2002), the temporal isomorphism constraint might exhibit some problems. For instance, it requires some further working out to account for the acceptability of the following sentence (Higginbotham's (23)):

(11)   Maria will say on Sunday that Mario was here on Saturday

Suppose that the speaker expresses that content on *Friday*. Then the reported speech is past-oriented, from the standpoint of the subject (Mario), but future-oriented from the standpoint of the speaker. As such, it doesn't comply with temporal isomorphism, even if it turns out to be perfectly acceptable. I will not discuss these examples here, but will come back to this kind of problem in Chapter 5. Consider also that the principle in question looks rather stipulative and it is not clear why it should exist at all.[5]

Another relevant proposal to rule out (10) as a possible interpretation for a sentence such as (9) is discussed in Abusch (1997). Noticing the unavailability of the future-oriented reading of (1), she proposes

---

[5] A reviewer notes that the temporal isomorphism constraint also seems problematic for the grammatical version of (10) using *would*, instead of *will*, where *would* is interpreted as *will* + past.

that this is due to a 'metaphysical' asymmetry between past and future times. Future temporal locations are intrinsically indeterminate, and this is reflected in a linguistic interpretive constraint to the effect that the local *now*, in Abusch's terminology, is an *upper limit* for tense reference. She proposes therefore the *Upper Limit Constraint*; such a principle applied to (9) would have the effect of ruling out the interpretation in which the embedded eventuality follows the relative now—i.e., the time of the *saying*—of the superordinate clause.

Irrespective of the merits or limitations of these proposals, the main point is that their perspective is different from the one developed by Giorgi and Pianesi (2001a, 2004a) and discussed here. The perspective, originally developed by Giorgi and Pianesi, is that the unavailability of mere indexical readings of tenses in embedded clauses is not a typological problem, but on the contrary, it reflects properties of the syntax/semantic interface. In other words, a grammar permitting indexical temporal reference in the embedded clause is an *impossible* grammar. Those properties arguably also explain the very existence of Sequence of Tense.[6]

Simplifying, the impossibility for tenses to behave as mere indexicals in embedded contexts is due to the fact that this would amount to making the expressed content a property of the speaker, whereas the speaker must share this responsibility with the subject.

Giorgi and Pianesi (2000, 2001a, 2004a) mainly discussed the necessity of representing the subject's temporal coordinates in clauses embedded under attitude predicates. This move permitted explanation of the obligatoriness of temporal anchoring and the contrast between attitude predicates, such as *believe* and *wish*, and non-attitude ones, for instance fictional predicates like *dream* and *imagine*, both in Italian and in English.

---

[6] Let me point out for completeness that Giorgi and Pianesi's perspective is closer to Ogihara's and Higginbotham's position than to Abusch's. This is by virtue of their more or less explicit appealing to *subjects* (the speaker, the one whom a given context is ascribed, etc.). This is compatible with Giorgi and Pianesi's idea that all the behaviour of tenses in subordinate context is determined by the need to accommodate the different perspectives a speaker has about the content she ascribes to a given subject, with respect to that of the subject itself.

They also suggested that DAR phenomena were related to the representation of the speaker's coordinates in the embedded clause. Though in their analysis the existence of DAR languages—such as English and Italian—next to non-DAR ones—such as Romanian and Chinese—was not accounted for, still their idea that the indexical context had to be represented in the left periphery of the clause is a crucial one, and I will develop it in the following pages.

In this chapter I will provide syntactic and interpretive arguments in favour of the syntactic representation of the speaker's temporal (and spatial) coordinates in the C-layer. In Chapter 3 I will provide arguments in favour of a typology of language, able to distinguish on principled grounds between DAR and non-DAR languages.

2.2.2 *There is no* optional *Double Access Reading*

In this brief section I want to point out that the position I am taking here is that DAR is exclusively an obligatory phenomenon. This point will also be stressed elsewhere in the book, but it is important, for the discussion to go through, to bear it clearly in mind. In a language such as Romanian, as I pointed out above, there is no DAR, in the sense of its *obligatoriness*. Consider again sentence (6) in the introduction, reproduced here for simplicity:

(12)   (Acum due ani) Gianni a spus ca Maria e insarcinata
         Two years ago John said that Maria is(PRES IND) pregnant

When the temporal locution *acum due ani* (two years ago) is not present, it is *possible* for this sentence to be felicitous in a situation in which Maria is pregnant *now*, i.e., at the time of the utterance. This does not mean that the sentence is *optionally* a DAR one, but simply that certain states—hence, pregnancy—might be *persistent*, at least for a certain interval, and therefore that, since the sentence does not provide any cue, in this case we do not know for a fact whether Maria is still pregnant or not.

The crucial point, and the crucial difference from Italian and English, is that in Romanian the embedded present tense is perfectly compatible with the temporal locution in question, showing that it does not matter how far away the *saying* is located, since the embedded state does not have to hold *now* even if it could. This is similar to what happens in the English sentence (7) from the introduction:

(13)   (two years ago) John said Mary was pregnant

In this case, if the temporal locution is not there, the embedded eventuality is *compatible* with a reading in which Mary is pregnant *now*. For a more detailed analysis of past tense combined with stative predicates, and of the Italian equivalent forms, see also Chapter 4 below.

2.2.3 *The Double Access Reading and Sequence of Tense*

Let's consider now the basic data concerning the distribution of verbal forms in English under verbs of saying in the past form.

Consider the following pairs in Italian and English, which I will treat as equivalent:[7]

(14)   John said that Mary left

(15)   Gianni ha detto che Maria è partita

(16)   John said that Mary will leave

(17)   Gianni ha detto che Maria partirà

(18)   John said that Mary would leave

(19)   Gianni ha detto che Maria sarebbe partita

In sentences (14)–(15) the embedded past is interpreted as locating the eventuality of leaving before the saying. In (16) and (17) the

---

[7] In what follows the Italian present perfect is considered as equivalent to the English simple past. In Italian there is however a simple past—in this case *partì* (left). The distribution of the present perfect and the simple past in Italian is very different from in English. In English they are really two different *tenses*, exhibiting different properties and obeying different constraints. In Italian, in many contexts, they seem to be largely equivalent forms—even if this is undoubtedly an oversimplification—and their distribution varies according to the dialectal and regional linguistic background of the speakers. Even if the two forms are not perfectly equivalent—see Giorgi and Pianesi (1997, ch. 3 and references cited there)—here I will abstract away from the differences, given that they do not seem relevant to the end of this discussion. To translate the English simple past, I will therefore adopt the present perfect, which is the form mostly—even if not uniquely—present in my variety of Italian.

embedded future locates the leaving after the utterance time, whereas in (18) and (19) the future-in-the-past locates it after the saying, but not necessarily after the utterance time.[8]

The question that must be considered at this point is whether the temporal location of the embedded event in (14) through (19) is ruled by the same principles ruling its location in sentences (1) and (2). The answer depends on the theory one develops for the DAR. If one wants to attribute the peculiar effect found in (1)–(2) to the properties of the present tense as such, then the principles of SoT ruling (14)–(19), where other temporal forms appear, must be different ones.[9]

I will discuss first the theory considering the present tense effect as a *special* one, due to the present tense itself, and then an alternative theory—namely, the *Generalized DAR theory* originally proposed by Giorgi and Pianesi (2001a).

Under the first theory, it could be claimed that the present tense obeys some specific principles yielding the DAR effects observed in (1) and (2). Whatever these principles might be, then the distribution and interpretation of an embedded past tense and an embedded

---

[8] The future-in-the-past is expressed in English by means of a periphrastic form including the auxiliary *would* which is often analysed as *will* + *ed*, i.e., a *past-future* auxiliary. In Italian the same meaning is realized by means of the perfect conditional. The other Romance languages are not like this, however. In Spanish, for instance, the simple conditional plays the same role. We are not going to investigate here what the correspondence between such, apparently, very different forms might be, but we are going to take for granted that at the relevant level, they are interpreted alike.

[9] An important issue is constituted by the differences in anchoring between eventive predicates and stative ones. Eventive predicates can only be ordered as preceding the superordinate event as is the case in example (14) in the text. English stative predicates, by contrast, can be interpreted both as preceding and as simultaneous with respect to the superordinate event. As noted by a reviewer, a sentence such as (ii) is in fact ambiguous. Note however that in Italian such a sentence would be translated by means of an embedded imperfect of the indicative:

i.   Gianni ha detto che Maria era(IMPF IND) incinta

ii.   John said that Mary was pregnant

On the properties of the imperfect in Italian and the corresponding forms in English, see Chapter 5 below. For a general analysis of the anchoring of stative vs. eventive predicates, see also Giorgi and Pianesi (1997, ch. 3).

future must follow different principles. According to Schlenker (2004), following Abusch (1997, see also Stowell 1996), for instance, the present tense is 'special' being *de re*.[10]

There are some considerations that might cast doubt on this proposal. The first one is conceptual: this view introduces a substantial difference between DAR and non-DAR languages. Non-DAR languages, in fact, must be claimed to have a non-*de re* present tense. By using a present tense—for instance in a sentence such as *Mary is happy*—a language like Romanian must be taken to express a different *meaning* than English or Italian. This might well be the case, but there is no independent evidence in favour of this view.

The second consideration has to do with the epistemological structure of the theory. In particular, if the present tense alone, due to its own intrinsic properties, exhibits the DAR, then the distribution and interpretation of an embedded past tense and an embedded future must follow from different principles. For instance, the past tense might be claimed to obey a general anchoring principle to the effect that the anchoring point of the embedded past is not the utterance time—as in *Mary left* taken as a main clause—but the time of the main eventuality—i.e., the time of the saying.

As for the embedded future, in the literature, which mostly considers Germanic languages, it is often regarded as a present *modal* form yielding a future interpretation. According to this perspective, its distribution obeys the same principles ruling embedded modals as in the following case:

(20)   Mary believes that John can sing

Such a view concerning the future cannot however be trivially generalized to Romance languages, which, on the contrary, do have a *real* morphological future. In all Germanic languages the

---

[10] Let me also comment that it is not crystal clear what *de re* exactly means as applied to a *tense*. The authors adopting this view leave it mostly to the intuition of the reader. Let me stress that it is crucial, for their argument to go through, that the *tense* itself, and *not* the eventuality with which it is associated, be interpreted *de re*. Though one might easily work out the technical operations scoping out the *de re* part, still it is not clear what lies beyond the technicality.

future tense is periphrastic, being constituted by a modal and a non-finite form. In many Romance languages, by contrast, it appears as a synthetic verbal form, with no transparent modal components.

Consequently, in this theory, some further *ad hoc* hypotheses must be proposed to the effect that the future of Italian-like languages, even if different with respect to its morphosyntax, should be considered equivalent to an English-like modal form.

Following this view, therefore, four different principles should be hypothesized to yield the correct Sequence of Tense for the embedded clauses above. In fact one should hypothesize a principle affecting the present tense in embedded contexts, an *ad hoc* anchoring principle concerning past-under-past forms, a hypothesis about the nature of Germanic future, and a further hypothesis about the morphosyntax of Italian-like future forms.

The other possibility would be to argue that the effects found with the present tense in (1)–(2) are not due to some principles of grammar at work only with the present tense, but that, on the contrary, the principles of SoT are the same for all the verbal forms appearing in the embedded contexts. The interaction between the morphosyntactic properties of the verbal forms and the rules of grammar determining the temporal location of the embedded event gives rise to the whole paradigm in (14)–(19). Such a hypothesis is more appealing than the one proposing a different principle for each tense, and I will develop it in the chapters that follow.[11]

---

[11] See Fleischman (2009) for a discussion of the future in Romance and its diachronic development. Note that the *consecutio* in dependence from the future verbal form is in some respects the same as the one from a present verbal—as opposed to a past, as I will better discuss in section 2.3.1 below. In spite of this apparent similarity with the present tense, however, I show in Chapter 5 that the future has properties of its own, which differentiate it from the other tenses. Consider also that the issue concerning bi-partition of tenses vs. tri-partition might be somewhat misleading, given that the real empirical problem concerns the difference in the interpretation between examples (14) and (16). In (14) the embedded event must be past with respect to the main event—and redundantly with respect to *now*. In (16) it must be future *both* with respect to the main event and to *now*, crucially contrasting with example (18).

Let me now provide an empirical argument in favour of the double evaluation of the embedded tense. Suppose that on 28 May John says, 'Mary is happy' and that Mary continues happy for the next two days. On 30 May I can then felicitously utter the following sentence:

(21)   John said that Mary is happy

This sentence would be a faithful report of the situation: the happiness of Mary is understood as extending from the time of the saying up to *now*. With exactly the same interpretation I might utter:

(22)   On the 28th of May, John said that Mary is happy

In this case, it is simply made explicit that the day of the saying has to be located on 28 May and that the state of happiness extends from the 28th up to *now*.

Consider however that the following sentence is *not* a possible option, in that it would not be a faithful report of the situation:

(23)   *John said that on the 28th of May Mary is happy

Given that the utterance event—*now*—is located on 30 May, it is impossible to utter (23) felicitously.[12]

This piece of evidence is important because it shows that the DAR effect cannot stem out of a *single* evaluation of the embedded eventuality. As is clear from the grammatical status of example (21) above, in fact, it is possible to understand the sentence as mentioning a state of happiness attributed to Mary, extending from 28 May up to *now*. Therefore, on one hand, it is true that Mary is happy on 28 May, but, on the other, it is possible to locate the embedded state on that day only *derivatively*, by means of the location of the saying event, as in (22). On the contrary, locating the state *explicitly* on that day gives rise to ungrammaticality. In the next section I will provide a step-by-step derivation for such cases.

---

[12] The following sentence is grammatical:

i.   John said that today, the 30th of May, Mary is happy

According to this sentence, however, John must have uttered 'Mary is happy' on the same day.

2.2.4 *A proposal on Sequence of Tense*

The hypothesis concerning DAR languages that I will argue for in this book is the following:[13]

(24)   The eventuality embedded inside a complement clause must be evaluated twice. Once with respect to the subject's—attitude bearer's—temporal coordinate and once with respect to the speaker's temporal coordinate.

In other words, in DAR contexts, the embedded event must be located once with respect to the superordinate event and once with respect to the utterance event. Therefore, a past, present, or future embedded verbal form will turn out to be past, present, or future with respect to the main event *and* with respect to the utterance time.[14]

As will become clearer in this book, the mechanism adopted to this end is theta-identification. Note that theta-identification can be recursively applied, as in the cases of *secondary predication*, such as the following one:[15]

(25)   John left angry

Both *angry* and the argument of *leave* are theta-identified with *John*.

The head of the tense projection, T, is a bi-argumental predicate of the following form:

(26) $e_1 R e_2$

R, which stands for *Relation*, is to be interpreted either as *precedes*, *follows*, or *overlaps with*, depending on the particular temporal form/morpheme associated with the verb. The first term of the predicate e_1 is identified with the embedded event by means of theta-identification; the second one, e_2, is a variable whose reference is determined locally.

---

[13] Note that I am claiming here that the *same* morpheme is located twice with respect to the superordinate event and the Speech event, as I will show below in this section. Crucially, I am not hypothesizing the presence of two morphemes, one of which is covert.

[14] Giorgi and Pianesi (2001a).

[15] On the notion of predication see the seminal work by Williams (1980). On secondary predication see among others Legendre (1997).

Giorgi and Pianesi (1997) proposed that the present tense is a default value and not an actual predicate represented in T, the only predicate being *precedence*. Both *follow* and *overlap* could be dispensed with. The proposal advocated here is in principle compatible with that view. For simplicity, in this chapter I consider the present tense as well as a predicate, *overlap*, represented in T and will not discuss the issue any further, given that it is not immediately relevant for the questions discussed in this book. The same applies to the *follow* relation, which could be reduced to the *precedence* one.

The original proposal that the embedded event must be located with respect to the superordinate one is due to Higginbotham (1995). According to his proposal, the main attitude predicate must be represented in the embedded clause. Giorgi and Pianesi (2001a) argued that this is the basis of the anchoring conditions. Namely, an event, complement of an attitude predicate, must be anchored to the superordinate one, as a general property of Universal Grammar.[16]

In this book, I will not consider this point any longer and will take it for granted. The focus of this chapter and Chapter 3 is mostly on identification of the second variable. The proposal is that this variable is identified twice: the first time in a lower position, and the second in a higher position in the C-layer.

To make this view more precise, I propose here that, from a syntactic point of view, the anchoring to the superordinate event is implemented through the representation in the T-layer of the feature Φ of the event corresponding to the main attitude—i.e., the saying, thinking, etc. episode. Such a feature represents the temporal, and spatial, coordinates of the subject of the main clause—i.e., the bearer of the attitude. It can be thought of as an index that in the semantics is *expanded* to include all the variables necessary for the interpretation.

According to this perspective, the closest second argument, e_2, is the event defined by Φ in the T-layer. Therefore, the result is the establishing of a relation between the embedded event and the superordinate one.

---

[16] For further discussion, see also Higginbotham (2002).

The relation can be *precede, follow,* or *overlap.* Let *e* be the subordinate event, and *e'* the event of the main clause. The precedence relation accounts for past — *e' precedes e* — and future — *e follows e'* — interpretation. The overlapping relation — $e \approx e'$ — is the one required by the present tense.

The following diagram gives a representation of the past tense relation:

(27)   T(e1,e2)
         /   \
     e2(Φ)   T (e1, e')
              /   \
            T   V(e1)
     precede (e, e')   /   \
                     V   e1

The same representation would hold with the predicates *follow* and *overlap,* giving rise to a future and present tense interpretation respectively.

This first step holds in both DAR and non-DAR languages. The machinery needed is minimal, the basic mechanism being exactly identical to theta-marking and theta-identification. So far, in fact, English/Italian and Romanian/Japanese do not differ. The differences between the two language groups concern the second step of the temporal interpretation, namely, the relationship between T and C.[17]

The bi-argumental temporal predicate in T, in fact, as suggested recently by many scholars, is then related to the C-layer. Giorgi and Pianesi (2001a), following Pesetsky and Torrego (2001), proposed that in the highest C-projection a feature τ requires movement/ internal merge of T to C and that in Italian such a movement takes place when the verb is in the indicative mood.[18]

---

[17] For an application of the same model to long distance binding, see Giorgi (2006, 2007).

[18] On T-to-C, see also Pesetsky and Torrego (2004a, 2004b, 2006). In light of subsequent developments in the Minimalist approach to the theory of grammar, it might be proposed that (multiple) Agree is at work, where T and C must agree. I will discuss below apparent exceptions in English and the behaviour with respect to the anchoring mechanism of moods other than the indicative in Italian.

The only difference with respect to the previous step is that the second argument in this case is identified with the *speaker's* coordinate, which I will call here U, where U is reminiscent of *utterance*. Therefore, at this step the second event of the bi-argumental relation is the utterance event itself, U. The resulting configuration is as follows:

(28)   C $(e1, e2)$
          /   \
    $e2 (U)$ C $(e1,e')$
                   / \
                  C   .....
            precede $(e1,e')$

This process takes place in DAR languages and is responsible for the interpretation of the embedded event, or state, as past, future, or simultaneous with the utterance event. The utterance event is defined on the basis of the speaker's temporal coordinate, exactly as past-ness or simultaneity with the superordinate event is defined on the basis of the subject's temporal coordinate.

According to the view just sketched, the embedded verbal form in DAR languages must be evaluated twice. The second argument of the tense predicate is in fact a variable identified locally with the superordinate event, defined by means of Φ, and again with the utterance event, defined by means of U. Technically, it is possible to look at the temporal morphology as bearing an uninterpretable unvalued feature, which is then valued in C.

The difference between DAR and non-DAR languages according to this perspective is that in DAR languages not only does the embedded T agree with C, but the main V agrees as well with them. In other words, the superordinate verb requires—and in some cases does not require—DAR to take place in the embedded clause.

This is the difference I will argue for in Chapter 6 with respect to Italian and Chinese, whereas for languages such as Romanian a more complex picture must be sketched.

In order to exemplify the proposal above, let me go through a simple derivation concerning assembly of the items relevant to temporal interpretation of the embedded clause (details omitted). Consider a sentence in a DAR language such as the following Italian example:

(29)   Gianni ha detto che Maria ha telefonato
        Gianni said that Maria called

(30)   Gianni ha detto che Maria telefonerà
        Gianni said that Maria called

As I argued above, in example (29) the calling event must precede both the saying and the utterance event, and, as a mirror image, in example (30) it must follow both the saying event and the utterance one. At the first step, the Tense predicate—*e* precedes/follows *e'*, noted as *R*—is merged with V—i.e., the event *e1* of *calling*—and the first member of the temporal relation is theta-identified with *e1*:

(31)   T (e1, e')
          /   \
        T   V (e1)
      R (e1, e')

At the next step, the temporal coordinate of the *sayer*, i.e., the temporal location of the event of *saying by Gianni*, e2 (Φ)—recall that following Higginbotham (1995) and Giorgi and Pianesi (2001a), it is represented in the embedded clause—is merged in the tree. The resulting structure is the following:

(32)   T (e1, e2Φ)
          /   \
     e2 (Φ)   T (e1, e')
                  /   \
                T   V (e1)
              R (e1, e')

At this point T is moved to C—internal merged—giving rise to the following structure:

(33)   C(e1, e')
          /   \
        C   T (e1, e2Φ)
     R(e1, e')   /   \
        e2 (Φ)   T (e1, e')
         /   \
        T   V(e1)
     ~~R(e1, e')~~

The temporal coordinate of the speaker, e2 (U), is now merged into the structure, and again theta-identification takes place between e' and e2:

(34)   C (e1, e2 U)
         /   \
     e2 (U)   C (e1, e')
                  /   \
                C   T (e1, e2Φ)
            R (e1, e')   .....

As a final result, both T and C must be interpreted, giving rise to a double evaluation of the past/future tense: once in T with respect to Φ—i.e., the features of the *sayer* Gianni—and once in C with respect to U—i.e., the features of the speaker. This derivation is just an example and does not take into account many relevant details. The chapters that follow should clarify at least some of them.

   Let us go back now to the paradigm illustrated above in examples (21)–(23). These phenomena follow from the hypothesis proposed here. Let's hypothesize that the event combines with the temporal location present in its clause, giving rise in this case to the event of *being happy on 28 May*.

   Consider first that under the alternative hypothesis, i.e., that the temporal morphology is interpreted only once, a sentence such as (23) should be perfectly grammatical even in DAR languages: the state should simply be taken to extend from the utterance time to 28 May. But this does not fit with the actual status of the sentence, which is bad.

Alternatively, let's hypothesize that the embedded tense is evaluated twice. In the ungrammatical example (23), *being happy on 28 May* is therefore evaluated in T, as overlapping with the subject's coordinates Φ. Since the saying event does indeed take place on 28 May, the first evaluation goes through. As a second step, the embedded eventuality must also be interpreted as overlapping with respect to the speaking event, defined on the basis of U. According to the given scenario, however, the utterance event does *not* take place on 28 May, being placed on the 30th. The second evaluation therefore gives rise to ungrammaticality in DAR languages.[19]

Notice also that sentence (22) is grammatical, given that the eventuality that is located on 28 May is not the *being happy*, but the *saying*.

Summarizing, the DAR effect is due to a double interpretation of the temporal morpheme: it is evaluated in T with respect to the subject's temporal coordinate, Φ, and in C with respect to the speaker's temporal coordinate, U. According to my hypothesis, the syntactic item responsible for the interpretation of an embedded verbal form with respect to the utterance time is located in the C-layer.

A piece of evidence in favour of this idea comes from the analysis of differences in the syntactic realization of the C. One would expect in fact that differences in the realization of the Complementizer correlate—at least in some cases—with a DAR/non-DAR interpretation of a complement clause. In the following section I will illustrate

---

[19] In non-DAR languages the equivalent of sentence (23) is grammatical. For completeness, consider also that the basic sentence might seem quite odd:

i.   John is happy on the 28th of May

I think however that this is so because of an informational failure. The 'normal' way to express the sentence would be:

ii.   John is happy today

The mentioning of the actual date becomes meaningful only if a *reason* is provided to this extent by the context, as for instance in the following case:

iii.   After a long period of unhappiness, on the 28th of May I am eventually happy again!

The day in question is indeed the day on which the utterance is located and the sentence is perfectly acceptable.

this point, comparing clauses featuring an indicative mood with those with a subjunctive verbal form.[20]

Two important questions that do not have an answer so far: Should the syntactic representation of the speaker's coordinates be considered universal? What makes languages different from each other?

In section 2.4 below I will return to questions connected with the technical implementation of the proposal.

2.3 The subjunctive

2.3.1 *Temporal dependencies with the subjunctive*

In some languages—for instance Italian, Romanian, Spanish, Catalan, German, Icelandic, and Modern Greek—besides an indicative mood there is a so-called *subjunctive* form. The subjunctive mood usually consists of a *present* and a *past*, with peculiar personal endings. In some languages, such as Romanian and Modern Greek, the subjunctive is distinguished from the indicative by means of a particle preceding a verbal form (almost) identical to the indicative. Moreover, in many languages the subjunctive exhibits a higher degree of syncretism in the expression of person morphology, a fact not yet completely understood. Bianchi (2003) considers the subjunctive as a fully inflected verbal form, exactly like the indicative. She argues that the indicative and the subjunctive pattern together, as opposed to the infinitive. On one side, this is obviously true in Italian, given that subjunctive and indicative clauses can have lexical subjects and infinitive clauses cannot. This point becomes particularly relevant when considering obviation phenomena. From the point of view of Sequence of Tense, however, the subjunctive patterns much more like the infinitive than like the indicative, given that both do not exhibit

---

[20] See also Giorgi and Pianesi (2004a). A reviewer also points out that the crucial point in the derivation described above is that the tense is in a sentence complement of the main clause and not in an adjunct clause.

DAR phenomena. My proposal is that, though presumably related, the two phenomena—obviation and the absence of DAR—cannot be reduced to a single property and should to a certain extent be kept separate.[21]

The subjunctive is a dependent mood, in that it cannot be used in main clauses, and when used in non-dependent contexts it has a *modal* meaning—i.e., it cannot express assertions—and it is typically used in exclamative contexts, desideratives, optatives, and in certain forms of positive and negative imperatives. Consider for instance the following examples:

(35)   Gianni mangia un panino
       Gianni is eating(IND PRES) (lit: eats) a sandwich

(36)   *Gianni mangi un panino
       Gianni is eating(SUBJ PRES) (lit: eats) a sandwich

(37)   Gianni vuole che Mario parta
       Gianni wants that Mario leaves(SUBJ PRES)

(38)   Gianni credeva che Maria partisse
       Gianni believed that Maria left(SUBJ PAST)

A sentence such as (36) can be used only if modal, for instance as an imperative:[22]

(39)   Che Gianni mangi un panino!
       That Gianni eats(SUBJ PRES) a sandwich!

Interestingly, in sentence (39) there is a sentence-initial Complementizer. In the same vein, consider also the following example:

(40)   Che ti prenda un colpo!
       Lit: That to you-CL takes(SUBJ PRES) a stroke!
       'Might you have a stroke!'

The analysis of these contexts is not the focus of the present work. Let me simply remark that, putting aside 'modal' usages, a subjunctive

---

[21] For a recent discussion of Italian subjunctive obviation and its possible relation with SoT data, see Costantini (2005, 2006). For a general introduction to obviation phenomena, see Farkas (1992b) and Kempchinsky (1985, 2009). For a general overview of the state-of-the-art, see also Quer (2009).

[22] On these issues see, among others, Zanuttini and Portner (2003), Portner (1997).

verbal form is not admitted in main clauses, but only in subordinate ones.[23]

In examples (37) and (38), the subjunctive appears in a complement clause. It can also appear in clauses in subject position—preverbally or postverbally—as in the following cases:

(41)   Che Gianni sia malato, è una disdetta
          That Gianni is(SUBJ PRES) sick is a misfortune

(42)   Che Gianni fosse il vincitore sorprese tutti
          That Gianni was(SUBJ PAST) the winner surprised everybody

(43)   È una disdetta che Gianni sia malato
          It is a misfortune that Gianni is(SUBJ PRES) sick

(44)   Sorprese tutti che Gianni fosse il vincitore
          It surprised everybody that Gianni was(SUBJ PAST) the winner

The rules governing the appearance of the subjunctive forms are the same as above, independently therefore from the syntactic role played by the clause. In what follows I will describe the peculiarities of the distribution of this mood in Italian—and in Romance in general.[24]

As can already be seen in the previous examples, an embedded present subjunctive appears when the main verbal form is a present tense, and an embedded past subjunctive appears when the main verbal form is a past tense. This kind of Sequence of Tense is reminiscent of the classical Latin *consecutio temporum et modorum* (sequence of tenses and moods).

---

[23] I will not consider in this work the distribution of the subjunctive mood in relative clauses:

i.   Un uomo che fugga davanti al pericolo è un codardo
       A man who runs(SUBJ PRES) in front of danger is a coward

The distribution of the subjunctive in these clauses is determined by a variety of factors, for instance indefiniteness, that are not under investigation here. Therefore, I will put this issue aside.

[24] I will leave aside the analysis of the Romanian subjunctive, which seems to follow a set of rules only partially overlapping with the ones adopted by the other Romance languages. Given the complexity of the judgements in question, the issue must be addressed by a native speaker.

A past form cannot be dependent on a present tense and conversely a present form cannot be dependent on a past one:[25]

(45)   *Gianni spera che Maria partisse
        Gianni hopes that Maria left(SUBJ PAST)

(46)   *Gianni sperava che Maria parta
        Gianni hoped that Maria leaves(SUBJ PRES)

In example (45), the embedded verb is in the past subjunctive, whereas in (46) it appears in the present tense. In both cases, the tense of the embedded form does not match that of the main one, and the structure is not grammatical. There are however some (apparent) exceptions to this generalization, which I will consider in section 2.4.3 below.

Notice also that the past-ness of the embedded verbal form cannot automatically be translated into a past relation with respect to the utterance time. Consider for instance the following examples:

(47)   Gianni sperava che Maria partisse ieri/oggi/domani
        Gianni hoped that Maria left(SUBJ PAST) yesterday/today/tomorrow

The leaving event can be placed at any time with respect to the utterance time, as indicated by the indexical temporal expressions, which are all compatible with the embedded past subjunctive.[26]

Sentence (47) means that Gianni had a hope concerning a past, present, or future event. Notice that the temporal adverbs are indexical ones—i.e., they identify a certain time with respect to the *speaker*.

---

[25] Even in Latin the rules of *consecutio* were not without exceptions, even if quite rigid, particularly in the written non-classical style. See for instance Molinelli (2000).

[26] Notice that in this case, since *partire* (leave) is an achievement predicate, it is always interpreted as following the main predicate, even in the absence of a future temporal specification. In the case of a stative, by contrast, the interpretation is a simultaneous one:

i.   Gianni sperava che Maria partisse
     Gianni hoped that Maria left(SUBJ PAST)

ii. Gianni sperava che Maria fosse felice
     Gianni hoped that Maria was(SUBJ PAST) happy

In (i) the leaving is located in the future with respect to the subject coordinate. In (ii) it is located in its present. These differences in interpretation are due to aspectual properties, which I will not discuss here. For simplicity, I will take in these cases the simultaneous reading to be the *standard* interpretation. On aspectual issues concerning the anchoring conditions, see among others, Giorgi and Pianesi (2001a).

This shows that the temporal location of the speaker and the subjunc-tive temporal morphology on the verb are not dependent on each other, as is the case with the indicative. The same phenomenon is observed with an anaphoric temporal modifier:

(48)   Gianni credeva che Maria partisse il giorno prima/dopo
        Gianni thought that Maria left(PAST SUBJ) the day before/the next day

Again, the leaving event can be placed by means of the adverbs either in the past or in the future, even if the form is always a *past* subjunctive.

With the indicative, on the contrary, the temporal adverb and the verbal form must be coherent: if one expresses past-ness, the other one has to express it as well, and analogously with respect to futurity. [27]

(49)   Gianni ha detto che Maria è partita ieri/*domani
        Gianni said that Maria left(IND) yesterday/*tomorrow

(50)   Gianni ha detto che Maria partirà domani/*ieri
        Gianni said that Maria will leave tomorrow/*yesterday

The temporal relation between the embedded event and the event of the main clause is simultaneity, as can easily be seen with embedded stative predicates. Consider for instance the following examples:

(51)   Gianni crede che Maria sia felice
        Gianni believes that Maria is (SUBJ PRES) happy

(52)   Gianni credeva che Maria fosse felice
        Gianni believed that Maria was(SUBJ PAST) happy

[27] In the following examples I use the present perfect form of the indicative, instead of the simple past one, both in main clauses and in subordinate ones—i.e., *ha detto* (lit: has said) instead of *disse* (said) and *ha telefonato* (lit: has called) instead of *telefonò* (called). In Italian, especially the central and northern varieties, the present perfect serves approximately the same function as the simple past in English. See also fn. 7 above. With stative verbs, such as *credere* (believe) and *desiderare* (wish)—i.e., verbs expressing an attitude of the subject towards a certain content—the past form usually chosen is the imperfect of the indicative: *credeva* (believed) and *desiderava* (wished). The present perfect (*ha creduto, ha desiderato*) and the simple past (*credette, desiderò*) convey the meaning that the psychological state, or attitude, of the subject doesn't hold any more. This effect is presumably to be connected with the aspectual and actional properties of the predicates. Concluding this brief remark, these questions are intriguing and complex ones, but are not crucial for the issue considered in this paper, so I will not further consider them. See Giorgi and Pianesi (1997) for a comparative discussion about Romance vs. Germanic languages.

In Italian, *believe* predicates have a subjunctive in the subordinate clause. In both examples, the state of happiness is taken to hold at the time of the believing.[28]

Anteriority can be expressed by means of the periphrastic perfective form, as in the following cases:

(53)   Gianni crede che Maria abbia telefonato
Gianni believes that Maria has(PRES SUBJ) called

(54)   Gianni credeva che Maria avesse telefonato
Gianni believed that Maria had(PAST SUBJ) called

In this case, the leaving event might be prior to the utterance time. The appropriate morphology—a present or a past ending—appears on the auxiliary, followed by the past participle. The past participle carries the value of *perfectivity*—or *resultant state*—as it does in isolation. In this case, therefore, anteriority is derivative on aspectual properties (perfectivity), and not directly obtained by means of a *temporal* morpheme.[29]

To conclude, the presence of the past subjunctive does not seem to be connected with a *past* interpretation, either with respect to the utterance time or with respect to the superordinate predicate. The same holds with respect to the present subjunctive. In both cases, the default temporal interpretation of the embedded eventuality—i.e., in the absence of a temporal locution providing a temporal location—is simultaneity with respect to the main clause, and there is no *a priori* ordering with respect to the utterance event.

This paradigm contrasts with the indicative one in Italian-like languages. In particular, in subjunctive clauses, the utterance event seems to play no role in this process and the presence of a *past* morpheme on the subjunctive verbal form seems to have no pastness entailment whatsoever.

---

[28] For a cross-linguistic analysis of the distinction subjunctive/indicative in embedded clauses, see Giorgi and Pianesi (1997), Schlenker (2004), Roussou (2009), Kempchinsky (2009), Giorgi (2009).

[29] See Giorgi and Pianesi (1997) for an analysis of the perfect form in Italian, compared with the English one.

Therefore, it can be concluded that the present or past morphology appearing on the verbal form is a pure agreement morpheme and that—at least so far—the only feature which matters is the tense of the superordinate clause. In section 2.4.3 below, however, I will show that this is too simplistic a view and that things are more complex, both empirically and theoretically. For the time being, however, let me state the following generalization:

(55)   The temporal morpheme of a subjunctive verbal form appearing in a complement clause agrees with the tense of the superordinate one.

The issue to be addressed next concerns the syntactic representation of the temporal properties of the subjunctive embedded clauses. What is needed is a representation of the anchoring of the embedded verbal form to the superordinate one; there is no need of the representation of the speaker's temporal coordinate, given that they are not relevant in this case. In other words, the subjunctive is not a form inducing the DAR, as far as it is correct to represent the DAR as the evaluation of a verbal form with respect to two sets of temporal coordinates: the subject's and the speaker's. The speaker's coordinate is not taken into account in this case.[30]

Consistently with what I proposed above, one might suggest that the difference lies in the C-layer. In what follows, I am going to argue that this is exactly the relevant consideration.[31]

---

[30] The subjunctive in non-DAR languages, for instance Romanian, does not exhibit the same pattern as in Italian. In particular in a past-under-past structure, the interpretation of the embedded event with respect to the matrix clause is not a simultaneous one, but only a past one. That is, the embedded event is interpreted as a *real* past with respect to the superordinate one. Again, I will not address this issue in this work.

[31] A reviewer asks about the possibility of licensing indexical temporal expressions, such as *oggi* (today) in subjunctive complement clauses, given that the speaker's temporal location is supposed not to be syntactically represented. The answer is that a temporal morpheme in a language such as Italian is a predicate, whose arguments must be theta-identified in the syntax. A temporal expression such as *oggi* (today), on the contrary, can be taken to be immediately referential, hence no syntactic processing is necessary. The situation might be different in languages such as Chinese, where there is no morphology expressing temporal relations. On temporal locutions see also Chapter 5 below. For an analysis of indexicality in Chinese, see Chapter 4 section 6.

2.3.2 *The subjunctive and the DAR*

Let's now consider in more detail the properties of the embedded subjunctive. As pointed out above, the embedded verb must appear in the past or present form, depending upon the form of the superordinate verb: present under present and past under past. The temporal interpretation assigned to the event of the embedded clause is simultaneity with the main predicate—for instance, with respect to the interpretation of sentences (51) and (52) Maria's happiness holds at the time Gianni believed it.[32]

These considerations point to the conclusion that subjunctive morphology does not instantiate a relational tense—i.e., a temporal relation between two events—but only a sort of *temporal agreement* with the superordinate verbal form.

As a consequence, with respect to the DAR, there is no *a priori* possibility for it to arise in embedded subjunctive complements, given that the embedded event does not undergo an independent temporal evaluation at all.

Prima facie, therefore, one might conclude that the DAR is a property of the indicative and not of the subjunctive. I will argue however that this is not a precise characterization of what happens, given that in some cases we can detect DAR properties with subjunctive clauses as well. I will show that the morphosyntax of the subjunctive, together with the properties of the C-layer, gives rise to the complex phenomenology of the DAR.

As a starting point, recall that, trivially, the existence of the DAR has nothing to do with the truth of the embedded contexts. In particular, both in the case in which the embedded clause appears with an indicative and in the case in which it appears with a subjunctive, the speaker is *not* endorsing the truth of the embedded clause. Both sentences can be continued with a disclaimer, as for instance in the following examples:

---

[32] In this case as well, the simultaneous interpretation can be said to be the *default* one, given that it is the one obtained in absence of any further specification. If temporal adverbs intervene, the interpretation will vary according to the temporal specification carried by the adverbial modifier. I will discuss this point below.

(56)   Gianni ha detto che Maria ha telefonato, ma non è vero
       Gianni said that Maria called(IND), but it is not true

(57)   Gianni crede che Maria abbia telefonato, ma non è vero
       Gianni believes that Maria has (SUBJ) called, but it is not true

Furthermore, some factive verbs select the subjunctive mood, as in the following examples:

(58)   Gianni rimpiange che Maria abbia vinto
       Gianni regrets that Maria has(SUBJ) won

In this case, contrary to (56) and (57), the truth of the embedded clauses is actually presupposed. The conclusion is therefore that the truth of a certain proposition is independent from the morphology on its predicate and is not connected with the presence of a certain mood—i.e., indicative vs. subjunctive.[33]

To conclude, let me capitalize on the following observations: a) the truth of an embedded clause is not at stake here and does not distinguish between the indicative and the subjunctive; b) the location in time of the speaker is relevant for the indicative verbal morphology, but not for the subjunctive one, as shown by the compatibility with time modifiers illustrated above.

Notice also that, coherently with the observations discussed so far, even in the case of factive complements, the subjunctive exhibits no compatibility requirement with respect to temporal expressions:

(59)   A Gianni dispiaceva che Maria partisse ieri/oggi/domani
       Gianni was sorry that Maria left(PAST SUBJ) yesterday/today/tomorrow

The truth of the embedded clause is presupposed, but the location in time of the event with respect to the speaker—as specified by the indexical adverbs—has no relevance.

Let me now illustrate a last point. The so-called *past* subjunctive is also triggered by present tense verbs, which however appear with a non-indicative morphology, such as the conditional one. Consider the following pattern:

---

[33] In this sense, the notion of *realis* vs. *irrealis*, often adopted to describe the properties of the indicative vs. the subjunctive mood, seems to be incoherent, in that it is reminiscent of the true/false dichotomy, which however seems to be inappropriate in these cases. See also Quer (2009) and papers published there.

(60)   Gianni vuole che Maria parta/*partisse
        Gianni wants(PRES) that Maria leaves(PRES SUBJ)/*left (PAST SUBJ)

(61)   Gianni vorrebbe che Maria partisse/*parta
        Gianni would like(PRES COND) that Maria left(PAST SUBJ)/*leaves (PRES
        SUBJ)

The main verbal form *vorrebbe* in example (61) is a present one. *Vorrebbe* (would want, lit: *want-pres.cond.*) in fact is simultaneous with the utterance event and expresses a present wish by the speaker, even if it appears in a modal form—i.e., in the *conditional mood*, thanks to the morphological ending *-ebbe*. Simplifying somewhat, this means that the wish is *removed* with respect to the real world. The object of the wish is understood, as usually happens with these verbs, as concerning the *future* of the speaker. The embedded subjunctive must, however, be a past subjunctive and cannot be a present one. This provides additional evidence in favour of the idea that the past morphology on the subjunctive does not mark any past-ness of the embedded event.

Consider now the following paradigm, which in some sense contrasts with the previous considerations:

(62)   Il testimone crede che *ieri alle 5* l'imputato fosse/*sia a casa
        The witness believes that yesterday at five the defendant was(PAST
        SUBJ)/*is(PRES SUBJ) at home

In this case the embedded verbal form must be a past subjunctive, and cannot be a present, even if the superordinate verb is a present verbal form.

Notice however that an explicit, or implicit, past time reference must be provided—i.e., in (62) the temporal locution *yesterday at five* cannot be omitted, or, if omitted, something of the same kind must be understood. If omitted, the only available form is the present subjective *sia* (is), whereas the past one, *fosse* (was), is ungrammatical. I discuss these cases in the following section.[34]

---

[34] Consider the following sentences:

i.   Gianni credeva che Maria abitasse/*abiti a Roma
      Gianni believed that Maria lived(PAST SUBJ)/* lives(PRES SUBJ) in Rome

ii.   Gianni credeva che Maria fosse/*sia incinta
      Gianni believed that Maria was(PAST SUBJ)/* is(PRES SUBJ) pregnant

To conclude this section, on one hand, it can be claimed that Sequence of Tense for the indicative verbal forms follows rules that are totally different with respect to those holding for subjunctive. On the other hand, the evidence discussed in (62) seems to show that the subjunctive can to a certain extent have an autonomous temporal status. I will consider this kind of examples again in section 2.4.3.

For the time being, note that, in spite of the fact that in most cases the subjunctive does not have an *independent* temporal interpretation of its own, it is not true that it is always immune from DAR effects. Consider the following cases:[35]

(63) Gianni ha ipotizzato che Maria fosse incinta
       Gianni hypothesized that Maria was(PAST SUBJ) pregnant

(64) Gianni ha ipotizzato che Maria sia incinta
       Gianni hypothesized that Maria is(PRES SUBJ) pregnant

The main verbal form is past in both cases, but in the complement clause the past and the present subjunctive are both available. The interpretation of the embedded clause in (64) is a DAR one. The following example is accordingly odd (the symbol '#' signals this):[36]

The embedded present subjunctive is ungrammatical. However, as far as its interpretation goes, it exhibits DAR effects. This might mean that, in order to interpret the embedded verbal form, the *wrong* C structure must be projected in the embedded clause, yielding ungrammaticality. On similar cases, which on the contrary turn out to be grammatical, see section 2.4.2.2 below.

[35] See also Giorgi (2009).

[36] Consider also the following sentence:

i.   *Gianni credeva che Maria sia incinta
     Gianni believed that Maria is(PRES SUBJ) pregnant

Even if ungrammatical, this sentence is still interpreted, and it turns out to have a DAR interpretation. This fact shows that the DAR is a property of a general syntactic configuration, given that in this case it seems independent both from the nature of the superordinate predicate and from the nature of the embedded verb—in this case a subjunctive, typically *not* exhibiting the DAR. It can be proposed in fact that ungrammaticality stems from the necessity of providing a subjunctive clause with the *wrong* Complementizer, i.e., the one containing the representation of the speaker's coordinate. See also fn. 34 above.

(65) #Due anni fa, Gianni ha ipotizzato che Maria sia incinta
      Two years ago, Gianni hypothesized that Maria is(PRES SUBJ) pregnant

This piece of evidence therefore closely parallels the phenomena discussed in section 2.2 above. Concluding the discussion of this section: on one hand, subjunctive verbal forms seem to be *inert* from the temporal point of view. On a closer look, however, the subjunctive morphology does not seem totally devoid of temporal content—even if it *looks* like that, in most cases—and the subjunctive sometimes undergoes the same SOT rules which govern the indicative, as the DAR effects just observed.

In what follows, I will try to answer the following question: What is the relation between the subjunctive and DAR? And, more generally, what triggers subjunctive morphology? The answers to these questions will not only prove relevant to a better characterization of the subjunctive in itself, but will also help clarify what exactly determines the indicative/subjunctive distinction.

2.4 The left periphery and the speaker's projection

In this section I propose a syntactic representation of embedded clauses that can contribute to explaining the temporal phenomena observed above. The starting point is constituted by the analysis of the so-called Complementizer Deletion—henceforth, CD—phenomenon. I will show, following Giorgi and Pianesi (1997, 2004b), that there is a correlation between the (im)possibility of CD and the temporal interpretation of the embedded clause, in particular DAR phenomena. These observations strongly suggests that the Complementizer—or better to say, the *C-layer*—is crucially involved in the temporal interpretation of embedded clauses. I will argue in fact that the difference between indicative and subjunctive with respect to SoT phenomena can be explained by hypothesizing a different structure of their C-layer.

More precisely, indicative and subjunctive clauses are introduced by different Complementizers, having different properties. At the interface, the indicative Complementizer is 'read' as an instruction to evaluate the embedded content with respect to the speaker's temporal coordinate. In the case of the subjunctive, the Complementizer does not provide the same information. In standard Italian, the two Complementizers are lexicalized by means of the same word, but projecting two different projections. In several Italian dialects, however, as in many other languages, the two Complementizers correspond to two different words as well.[37]

2.4.1 *Complementizer Deletion: a description*

The property I analyse in this section is the possibility of omitting the Complementizer in subjunctive clauses. Among Romance languages, this property seems to be limited to Italian, for reasons I will not investigate here. I will argue that this characteristic might shed light on the nature and the function of the Complementizer, by being systematically related to the presence of the DAR.

Italian subjunctive admits CD—as opposed to the indicative mood, which never allows it. Consider for instance the following sentences:[38]

(66) Mario ha detto *(che) ha telefonato Gianni
      Mario said that has(IND) called Gianni
      'Mario said that Gianni called'

(67) Mario credeva (che) avesse telefonato Gianni
      Mario believed (that) had(SUBJ) called Gianni
      'Mario believed that Gianni called'

---

[37] On this point, see also section 2.3.1.

[38] Descriptively, among the major Romance languages, only Italian has CD and only Romanian is a non-DAR language. I will consider the DAR/non-DAR divide in more detail in Chapters 3 and 4. Consider also that in some varieties of the Florentine dialect, the omission of the Complementizer has a wider distribution than in 'standard' Italian, being available also with verbs of saying. It is not clear, however, to what extent the omission of the Complementizer in Florentine is related to discourse factors—as for instance question-answering strategies, epistemic expressions, corrections, etc.—and to what extent it can be considered a grammatical property analogous to the one discussed here. Further dialectological investigation is required.

In sentence (66) the embedded verbal form is an indicative, whereas in sentence (67) it is a subjunctive. In example (67) the subjunctive permits CD, whereas this is impossible in (66).[39]

English as well permits the Complementizer to be omitted in some contexts. Consider for instance the following examples in English:

(68) John said (that) Mary left

(69) John believes (that) Mary was happy

(70) John hopes (that) Mary will win

In all these cases CD is allowed. One of the main differences between English and Italian lies in the fact that in Italian in the contexts created by verbs of saying the embedded verbal form is an indicative and CD is impossible. In English on the contrary there is no difference between the clauses complement of *say* and those under *believe* or *hope*, to the effect that the Complementizer can always be omitted.[40] As far as English is concerned, I endorse the traditional view according to which the empty C position is a *null* Complementizer and will not consider the issue any further.

In German the absence of the Complementizer occurs, mostly, in sentences showing embedded V2. Embedded V2 is available both with

---

[39] Notice that though permitted, CD is never *obligatory*, in that the non-CD option is always available. Another important property is constituted by the disjoint reference effect, i.e., *obviativity*, with the subjunctive, but not with the indicative, as exemplified by the following examples:

i.   Gianni$_i$ crede che pro$_{j/*i}$ parta
     Gianni believes that he leaves

ii. Gianni$_i$ ha detto che pro$_{i/j}$ partirà
     Gianni said that he will leave

A null embedded subject of a subjunctive complement clause cannot be coreferent with the main subject, whereas there is no ban if the embedded clause is an indicative one. For an analysis of these facts, as well as of some relevant exceptions to this pattern, see Costantini (2005).

[40] See also Scorretti (1994), Giorgi and Pianesi (1997, 2004b), and Poletto (1995, 2000, 2001). In German, the absence of the Complementizer might be claimed to be part of V2 phenomena. Poletto proposes that Italian CD is an instance of embedded V2, on a par with in German. On this point, Giorgi and Pianesi (1997, 2004b) disagree.

sagen (say) and *glauben* (believe), resembling with respect to this property the English pattern, and diverging from the Italian one:

(71)   Hans sagte, Marie hat das Buch gekauft
        Hans said that Marie has(IND) bought the book

(72)   Hans glaubte, Marie habe das Buch gekauft
        Hans believed that Marie has(SUBJ) bought the book

I will not consider the issue of CD in German and English, since it is not immediately relevant to the topic analysed in this book. The only point I want to stress here is the consideration that Italian CD distinguishes among verb classes in a way in which neither English nor German do.[41]

Note finally that in German the distribution of the indicative and subjunctive follows different rules, with respect to the Italian pattern, being available both with *sagen* (say) and *glauben* (believe).[42]

Giorgi and Pianesi (2004b) argued in favour of an analysis of CD that I briefly summarize here, abstracting away from the technical details. Their proposal was elaborated in the minimalist framework sketched in Chomsky (1995). Their starting point is the observation that the subjunctive Complementizer is actually part of the subjunctive morphology, even if in Italian it happens to be homophonous with the indicative one. This consideration is supported by ample evidence coming both from languages other than Italian, for instance Romanian and Greek, and from Italian dialects such as Salentinian. In these languages, the only marker signalling the presence of the

---

[41] There are some contexts in which CD is impossible both in Italian and English, such as complements of factive verbs and clauses appearing in the left or right periphery. See for instance the following examples:

i.   Gianni rimpiange *(che) Maria sia partita
     Gianni regrets *(that) Mary left(SUBJ)

ii. *(che) Maria sia partita preoccupa Gianni
     (that) Mary left(SUBJ) worries John

In these examples CD is impossible, even if the verb is a subjunctive. This means that *something* else is working in these cases to the effect of inhibiting CD. Giorgi and Pianesi (2004b) propose that these facts have to do with the peculiar syntactic structure instantiated by factive predicates.

[42] See Chapter 5 for a brief discussion of some aspects of the German subjunctive.

subjunctive is a special Complementizer, peculiar to the subjunctive form, whereas the verbal ending is usually not distinguishable—or minimally distinguishable—from the indicative one.[43]

For this reason, the Italian subjunctive is a form with a sort of discontinuous morphology, constituted by the Complementizer and the verbal ending. Simplifying, the intuitive idea that Giorgi and Pianesi aim at capturing is that the subjunctive Complementizer, being rather uninformative in Italian, can be dispensed with, in which case its position is occupied by the verbal form itself.[44]

In other words, in Italian there is some property that shows up in CD cases, distinguishing the indicative from the subjunctive. This property is not there in English, where the complement clauses are not differentiated.

I want to argue here that the study of this property of Italian complement clauses might shed light on the general characteristics of the subjunctive mood in DAR languages. In particular, I claim that in Italian the speaker's coordinates are represented in the C-layer of the embedded clause in presence of the DAR, whereas they are not there in non-DAR sentences, which explains the different behaviour in CD of indicative and subjunctive clauses.

In other words, the speaker's temporal coordinate always intervenes in DAR contexts, typically selecting the indicative. In general, the subjunctive gives rise to a representation of the embedded clause in which the speaker's coordinate is not represented.

In this section I am going to illustrate the data concerning the correlation in Italian between the absence of the Complementizer—i.e., Complementizer Deletion (CD)—and the temporal interpretation

---

[43] On Romanian, see Dobrovie Sorin (1994), d'Hulst, Coene, Avram, and Tasmowsky (2003), Farkas (1985, 1992a). On Modern Greek, see Roussou (2009), Tsoulas (1996), and Iatridou (2002). On Salentinian, see Calabrese (1984, 1993). This is obviously not intended as an exhaustive bibliography, but as possible suggestions for readers.

[44] Giorgi and Pianesi (1996, 1997, ch. 3) elaborate the theory of *syncretic categories* to explain the distribution and the properties of Italian CD. I am not going to make use of this part of their proposal and therefore I do not summarize it here. Let me simply point out that I still endorse that view and that there is no contradiction with what I am suggesting here.

of the embedded clause. The contexts I will consider are mostly the ones where the sentence is a clausal complement of the verb. In Quer's (1998) and Stowell's (1993, 1996) terminology this is the so-called *intensional* subjunctive.[45]

Interestingly, for some Italian speakers—but not for me—a verb such as *credere* (believe) can either select for a subjunctive and, usually substandardly, for an *imperfect* indicative verbal form. However, only the subjunctive admits CD. Consider for instance the following example:[46]

(73) (*)Gianni credeva *(che) aveva telefonato Maria
      Gianni believed that had(IND IMP) called Maria
      'Gianni believes that Maria called'

Modulo the marginality of the indicative, in this case CD is impossible, on a par with the verbs of *saying* such as *dire* (say), illustrated in example (66). I will consider these cases again in Chapter 5.

From this piece of evidence it follows that CD is not a property of the main verb—or at least *not only* a property of the main verb—but has to do with the indicative/subjunctive divide.

2.4.2 *The representation of the speaker's coordinate*

In this section I will briefly sketch a technical account of the phenomena just observed. The machinery needed for this purpose is minimal: I argue that in Italian the left-most position of the C-layer contains the speaker's temporal (and spatial) coordinates, which force the DAR interpretation in indicative clauses and in some subjunctive ones.[47]

---

[45] The term *Complementizer Deletion* with respect to the Italian cases was first used in generative grammar by Scorretti (1994). Here I will adopt the same term, without implying however the existence in Italian of any *deletion* operation.

[46] This phenomenon might appear especially in Central and Southern varieties. Crucially the non-imperfect of the indicative is ungrammatical for all speakers:

i. *Gianni credeva che Maria ha telefonato
    Gianni believed that Maria has(IND) called

This issue will be further discussed in Chapter 4.

[47] For a brief discussion of the relation between the position in the C-layer I hypothesize here and Rizzi's (1997, 2001, 2002) *Force*, see Chapter 3.

2.4.2.1 *In indicative clauses*   As illustrated above, the indicative Complementizer can never be deleted and always enforces the DAR. Therefore, it can be concluded that it must always be realized. This being the case, it is self-evident that unlike the subjunctive case, it is not part of the *morphology* of the verb, but a distinct lexical item with an interpretive function. Furthermore, the indicative can be characterized as a relational tense, instantiating an overlapping or preceding relation between two events. As an exemplification, analogous to the one given above in section 2.2.4 but with further details, consider a past under a past indicative clause:[48]

(74)   Gianni ha detto che Maria ha telefonato
        Gianni said that Maria has(IND) called

(75)   [.....[$_V$ detto [$_{C-\Sigma}$ ... che [$_{T-\sigma}$ ... T ... [... ha telefonato$_{\{\Sigma;\,\sigma\}}$...]]]]]

The embedded past verbal form, *called*, is a relational tense: $e\ R\ e'$, where R is *precedence*. The event e is constituted by the calling event itself. It bears a pair of features: Σ and σ. In Italian, the verb is (I-) merged with T and the feature Φ are (E-)merged with T at the next step. The feature σ must agree with the feature Φ of the bearer-of-attitude's—i.e., with the main subject's temporal coordinate. As I argued for above, in fact, the T-layer of indicative clauses contains the temporal (and spatial) coordinates of the attitude bearer in its left-most position. At this point, the embedded event is interpreted as past with respect to the temporal location of *Gianni*.[49]

Going on with the projection, the complementizer is (E-)merged and T-to-C movement takes place. In the framework developed by Chomsky and scholars in (2001) and (2005), we can say that T is

---

[48] I put aside the questions arising with the indicative imperfect, as in the following sentence:

i.   Gianni ha detto che Maria dormiva
      Gianni said that Maria slept(IMPF IND)

This question has been considered in Giorgi and Pianesi (2004b). I will not take it into account here, but see Chapter 4 below.

[49] On the reason why the notion *bearer-of-attitude* is more appropriate than the notion of superordinate *subject*, see Giorgi and Pianesi (2001a) and Giorgi (2006, 2007). See also Costantini (2005, 2006).

copied in C, but pronounced in the lower position. Analogously to what I illustrated above for T, the feature *U* is (E-)merged to C. Finally, the features Σ on T, and U in C agree. The feature Σ can be considered as a pointer to the context, interpreted at the interface as the speaker's temporal coordinate—i.e., the utterance time *now*. Its presence determines in this case that the embedded event is interpreted as past with respect to the temporal location of the speaker as well, i.e., past with respect to the utterance time.

Let's now approach the core hypothesis of this chapter. I have already illustrated two contexts in which the DAR arises with the subjunctive, i.e., with verbs of cognition working as verbs of communication, such as *ipotizzare* (hypothesize). In this case the Complementizer cannot be deleted. Moreover, the verb appears in a verbal form not predicted by the Latin-like *consecutio*, which would allow only a temporal agreeing form to be realized. In these sentences in fact a present subjunctive appears under a past verbal form, which should in principle be disallowed.

2.4.2.2 *In subjunctive clauses*

Even if *most* DAR contexts are realized by means of an indicative verbal form, *some* subjunctive embedded clauses do indeed exhibit the DAR.

The syntax of subjunctive clauses with DAR effects will be shown to parallel the syntax of embedded indicative clauses. More precisely, DAR sentences are introduced by a Complementizer projection, C, which is not realized when the complement clause does not exhibit DAR effects.

Let's consider the distribution of CD with the *ipotizzare* (hypothesize) cases. I observed in section 2.3.2 that though selecting the subjunctive, *ipotizzare* (hypothesize) exhibits the DAR. Consider the following examples:[50]

(76) Gianni ha ipotizzato (che) fosse incinta
Gianni hypothesized (that) (she) was(PAST SUBJ) pregnant

(77) Gianni ha ipotizzato *(che) sia incinta
Gianni hypothesized (that) she is(PRES SUBJ) pregnant

---

[50] For a detailed discussion of this topic, see Giorgi and Pianesi (1997, 2004b).

In sentence (76), where the embedded verbal form appears with the past subjunctive morphology—i.e., where the sequence of tenses is the *normal* one—CD is optional, as usual. In the other case, when the embedded verbal form is a present subjunctive—i.e., the sequence of tenses is anomalous with respect to the normal subjunctive distribution—CD is impossible. In sentence (77) the DAR in enforced, so that the sentence means that the pregnancy of Maria—as hypothesized by Gianni—holds both at the time of the hypothesis and at the utterance time. It clearly cannot be due to the presence of a present tense vs. a past *per se*, given that the following sentence is perfectly possible with CD:

(78)   Gianni ipotizza (che) sia incinta
       Gianni hypothesizes (that) (she) is (PRES SUBJ) pregnant

Notice also that there is a slight but systematic interpretive difference between sentence (76) and (78) on the one hand and (77) on the other. The speaker might decide to use the verb *hypothesize* to describe two different things. He might be talking about Gianni's *mental* processes—in which case, the sentence concerns a particular thought that appeared in Gianni's mind in a hypothetical form—or about Gianni's *behaviour*. In this case, the speaker is reporting a *communication* of some sort made by Gianni in a hypothetical way.[51]

In sentence (77) only the latter possibility is available, whereas in the other cases it is left unspecified. As remarked above, the verbs of communication in Italian are exactly those verbs that select the indicative. This does not seem to be a universal property, given that in many languages—French and Spanish, among others—verbs of *believing* select the indicative as well. However, this distinction is relevant in Italian.[52]

---

[51] The verb *guess* in English seems to be sensitive to the same distinction. I thank J. Higginbotham for this observation. I will consider these cases in more detail in Chapter 4.

[52] A semantic parameter might perhaps be hypothesized to account for this point: some languages might be more sensitive to the speech act/mental state distinction—e.g., Italian. Others might be more sensitive to the peculiar modal properties of the contexts, as hypothesized in Giorgi and Pianesi (1997).

Now briefly consider the distribution of indicative/subjunctive with this class of verbs. I have already shown that CD is impossible with the indicative, and therefore these sentences cannot undergo CD:

(79)   Gianni ha detto *(che) ha telefonato Maria
       Gianni said that has(IND) called Maria
       'Gianni said that Maria called'

When these verbs convey a *jussive* meaning—i.e., it represents an order or request—they select subjunctive. See also the discussion in Giorgi (2009):

(80)   Gianni ha detto *(che) partissero al più presto
       Gianni said that they leave(PAST SUBJ) as soon as possible
       'Gianni ordered that they leave as soon as possible'

(81)   Gianni ha detto *(che) partano al più presto
       Gianni said that they leave (PRES SUBJ) as soon as possible
       'Gianni ordered that they leave as soon as possible'

When conveying this meaning, *dire* (say) behaves like the verb *ordinare* (order):

(82)   Quel miliardario ha ordinato *(che) si comprasse quella villa
       That billionaire ordered that *si*-impersonal buy(PAST SUBJ) that villa
       'That billionaire ordered that they buy that villa'

(83)   Quel miliardario ha ordinato *(che) si compri quella villa
       That billionaire ordered that *si*-impersonal buy(PRES SUBJ) that villa
       'That billionaire ordered that they buy that villa'

In the embedded clauses in these cases, the verb can be realized either as a past subjunctive or as a present one and CD is always ungrammatical. The two verbal forms, however, correspond to different temporal interpretations.[53]

Let me try to explain the peculiar temporal interpretation of these sentences. In the examples given above the order concerns an event which, as naturally implied by this kind of meaning, is supposed to take place in the future with respect to its ordering. However, in sentences (80) and (82)—where the past subjunctive appears—the

---

[53] Note that both verbs can also select the infinitive.

buying of the house must be future only with respect to the issuing of the order itself. Therefore, in this sentence the buying of the house might already have taken place at utterance time and the speaker might simply be reporting the issuing of the order, without any implication concerning the time of the buying.

In the other examples—sentences (81) and (83)—where a present subjunctive is realized, the buying of the house must follow the ordering but *also* the utterance time—i.e., it must be in the future with respect to the speech event itself.

The difference between the two cases can be considered as parallel to the one just described with respect to *ipotizzare* (hypothesize). The differences between (80)–(82) and (81)–(83) can be accounted for as a DAR effect. The nature of the predicate requires that the embedded event be interpreted as the content of the order, and therefore derivatively located in the *future* with respect to it. In other words, it is possible to conceive of the *content* of the order as simultaneous with respect to the *issuing* of the order. The *carrying out* of the order, due to the semantic and pragmatic properties of ordering, must lie in the future with respect to it.

According to this view, a double evaluation applied to the content of the order predicts exactly the judgements illustrated above. In these cases, the content of the order is simultaneous both with respect to the event of issuing the order, and with respect to the utterance time; the carrying out of the order lies in the future with respect to both.

The conclusions that can be reached on the basis of the previous analysis seem to be as follows: a) a present subjunctive under a past superordinate verbal form is admitted as far as the higher verb can be interpreted as a predicate of communication; b) in this case, the DAR is enforced; c) the Complementizer cannot be omitted. Therefore, jussive verbs constitute another case in which the subjunctive shows the existence of DAR effects.[54]

---

[54] The opposite generalization however does not hold. That is, there are some contexts in which the Complementizer cannot be omitted and there is no DAR, for instance in sentences with left, or right, dislocation:

i.   *(che) Gianni fosse partito, Maria lo credeva
     That Gianni had left, Maria it-believed

At this point the question to be answered is the following: What is the relation between the Complementizer and the DAR?

Let's propose that the Complementizer introducing subjunctive clauses does not occupy the same syntactic position as the one introducing the indicative clauses.

The starting point is therefore that, even if in standard Italian the Complementizers are both realized by means of the word *che*, the indicative one and the subjunctive one fulfil different roles and occupy different positions in the syntactic tree—i.e., *che* (that) can head two different projections. Giorgi and Pianesi (1997, 2004a) addressed this question, and I will briefly summarize the issue here.

They proposed that the subjunctive verbal form is not a relational tense, in the sense indicative tenses are. As I showed above, the past or present forms of the subjunctive do not instantiate a simultaneous or a precedence relation between two events. The morphological appearance of the inflection is due to an *agreement* process between the superordinate and the embedded verbs.

As I briefly summarized in the previous section, the bulk of the hypothesis concerning the Complementizer in this case is that it is *part of* the subjunctive inflection. In other words, the Italian subjunctive exhibits a sort of *discontinuous morphology*, including both the verbal ending *and* the Complementizer. The two can either be realized together—i.e., *syncretically*, adopting Giorgi and Pianesi's terminology—or *scattered*, in which case the word *che* appears in the embedded clause.

Let's consider first the *scattered* realization. Giorgi and Pianesi claimed that the subjunctive verb carries both mood and tense-agreement features. In non-CD clauses, the features force movement of the verb at LF to the Complementizer-layer. The Complementizer in this case, as argued by Giorgi and Pianesi, lexicalizes the Mood features. Abstracting away from the distribution of embedded topic

ii.   Maria lo credeva, *(che) Gianni fosse partito
      Maria it-believed, that Gianni had left

This topic is discussed in Giorgi and Pianesi (1997, 2004a), and I will not consider it here.

and focus, the structure of the embedded clause can be represented as follows:

(84)   Gianni credeva che Maria dormisse
       Gianni believed that Maria slept(PAST SUBJ)

(85)   [.....[$_V$ credeva [$_{MOOD}$che$_{\{+mood\}}$ [$_T$ ... dormisse$_{\{+mood;\ +past\}}$...]]]]

The subjunctive verbal form *dormisse* bears two features: [+past] and [+mood]. The feature [+past] must not be confused with the bi-argumental temporal predicate discussed above. This feature only identifies a peculiar morphological ending—in this case, *-isse*—which must agree with the superordinate verbal form.

With respect to the presence of the feature [+mood], in this case the modal and temporal features of the subjunctive verb are realized on two independent projections, one headed by the verb *dormisse* and the other headed by the Complementizer *che*. Movement of the verb to Mood, triggered by the mood feature on the verb, locates the verb in the correct configuration for tense agreement with the main verb. The interpretive result is that Gianni has a belief, located in the past—given the past morphology on *credere*—concerning a call made by Maria, which *morphologically* agrees with it. Given that in this case the temporal location of the calling is not specified, the interpretation will be *simultaneity*. Recall also that, as illustrated above, temporal modifiers, either anaphoric or indexical, can variously determine the relation between the events. They can locate the embedded event in the past or in the future with respect to the main one.

The simultaneous interpretation is obtained following the proposal discussed in Giorgi and Pianesi (1997). Simplifying somewhat, Giorgi and Pianesi (2001a) propose that events can either be seen as bounded—i.e., closed—sequences of sub-events, or as unbounded ones—i.e., open sequences of sub-events. In Italian, the *marked* value is *bounded*, in the sense that the presence of a closed sequence of sub-events must be overtly signalled in the morphology of the verbal form. With respect to this property, a subjunctive form is *unbounded*—i.e., there is nothing in its morphology marking the presence of a closed sequence.[55]

---

[55] See also Franconi, Giorgi, and Pianesi (1994).

The crucial hypothesis discussed at length in Giorgi and Pianesi (2001a)—under the name of *punctuality constraint*—is that, to obtain a simultaneous interpretation of a subordinate event with a superordinate one, the subordinate one must be unbounded. Consequently, if there is no relational specification on the embedded form at all and the event is presented as an unbounded sequence, then a simultaneous interpretation obtains. This is the case with the embedded past subjunctive in example (84) above.

Let's consider now the other option—i.e., the *syncretic* one. Giorgi and Pianesi crucially suggested, in order to account for the word order properties of the embedded clause, that when the Complementizer is not realized—i.e., in CD clauses—the temporal and modal features are syncretically realized on the same verbal head. The structure obtained in this way is therefore the following one:[56]

(86)   Gianni credeva dormisse
        Gianni believed she slept(PAST SUBJ)

(87)   [.....[$_V$ credeva [$_{MOOD/T}$ dormisse$_{\{+mood; +past\}}$...]]]

In this case, there is no Complementizer in the head of the Mood projection. The verb itself occupies the MOOD/T position and verbal agreement with the superordinate verb *credeva* (believed) works as in the case illustrated above.

Therefore, in both cases, the morphology of the subjunctive form—past or present—is determined by a relation holding between the main verb and the embedded one.

The question arising in this connection is how it is possible for the present subjunctive morphology to be licensed in these configurations, where the main form is a past one. Consider again the example given above:

(88)   Gianni ha ipotizzato che Maria sia incinta
        Gianni hypothesized that Maria is(PRES SUBJ) pregnant

---

[56] The data accounted for by this hypothesis concern the impossibility of a focus phrase in CD embedded clauses, the marginality of topic ones, and the peculiar distribution of the embedded subject. See Giorgi and Pianesi (2004a).

The hypothesis discussed by Giorgi and Pianesi (1997, 2004a) is that Mood and C in this case co-occur, giving rise to the following structure:

(89) $[.....[_V$ hypothesized $[_C$ che$_\Sigma$ $[_{MOOD}$ sia$_{\{+mood; +pres\}}...]]]]$

Let's propose that the verb moves—either overtly or covertly, it does not matter for the purposes of this argument—to MOOD-P, given that it is a subjunctive form. The Complementizer *che*, occupying the head position of the C projection bears the feature Σ, which points to the speaker's temporal coordinate. As a consequence, the utterance time licenses the present form of the subjunctive. Tense agreement is instantiated exactly as in the cases given above, the only difference being that in this case the head-head configuration does not involve the main verb, but the Complementizer in C.

In other words, in this case, contrary to the indicative cases given above, since the verbal form is non-relational, the very presence of the Complementizer is enough to satisfy the requirements posed by the embedded verbal form.

Let's consider now the temporal interpretation of the clause. The embedded subjunctive is anchored to the superordinate verb—as is obligatory in all languages—and is, by default, interpreted as simultaneous with the main eventuality, even in the absence of temporal agreement. The presence of the feature Σ in C also forces the interpretation in which the embedded event is located with respect to the speaker's coordinate. Therefore, a (default) simultaneous interpretation with respect to the utterance event is assigned. The simultaneous interpretation is obtained by virtue of the same mechanism described above for example (84).

To conclude this section, a subjunctive verbal form embedded under communication verbs will give rise to the DAR by means of the same mechanism determining this reading in the indicative cases—i.e., by virtue of a double interpretation. The difference between the indicative and the subjunctive concerns the fact that the interpretation of the indicative is derived via the interpretation of a *relational* tense, locating two events one with respect to the other. The temporal interpretation of the subjunctive is always a simultaneous one, by default. However, the necessity of assigning this simultaneous interpretation twice leads to the DAR. The embedded subjunctive is interpreted once as simultaneous with respect to the subject's temporal coordinate, and once as simultaneous with respect to the speaker's temporal coordinate.

Notice finally that, as pointed out above, the somehow *exceptional* merging of C in the DAR interpretation of *ipotizzare* contexts is due to the fact that in these cases there is a communication interpretation of the verbal form—something like *explicitly communicating an hypothesis*—which in Italian requires a non-deletable C.

2.4.3 *Temporal topics and other issues*

Let's consider now the case in which the past subjunctive seems to have an independent temporal reading. I repeat the relevant example here for simplicity:[57]

(90)   Il testimone crede che ieri alle 5 l'imputato fosse/*sia a casa
       The witness believes that yesterday at five the defendant was (PAST SUBJ)/*is(PRES SUBJ) at home

In this example the main verb appears in the present tense, whereas the embedded one carries the past morphology. In order to license an embedded past subjunctive, a temporal topic is necessary. Such a topic can be provided either overtly or by the context, but it must be given, otherwise the structure is ungrammatical.

My hypothesis here is that the temporal topic can license the temporal morphology of the embedded subjunctive in a way that is analogous to the cases seen above:

(91)   [.....[$_V$ crede [$_{MOOD}$che [$_{TOP}$ ieri alle 5 [$_T$ ... fosse$_{\{+mood; +past\}}$...]]]]]

Ieri alle 5 (yesterday at five) is interpreted as a past temporal reference—by virtue of the meaning of *ieri* (yesterday)—and therefore

---

[57] Aspectual questions are put aside in this chapter, even if they are obviously relevant with respect to the final interpretation of the embedded verbal form. In the case of example (90), for instance, the interpretation of the embedded event is a continuous one, in that the being at home is supposed to have begun *before* and to be continuing *after* the temporal interval specified by the topic.

licenses the past feature on the verb. According to the proposal discussed in Rizzi (1997, 2001), left-peripheral temporal expressions are in a Topic position. The default interpretation locates the embedded event at the time specified by the topic. Further movement of the verb to Mood, required by the presence of the feature [+mood], does not modify this interpretation. Unlike the cases seen above, the speaker's coordinate is not represented in C. *Credere* (believe) is not a communication verb and, accordingly, it does not require the high C projection to be realized. Given that the past form on the embedded verb is licensed by the temporal topic, the temporal interpretation is completed, and the embedded eventuality is correctly located in the past, as specified by the time adverb.

Consider now the licensing of a past verbal form in sentence (61), repeated here:

(92)   Gianni vorrebbe che Maria partisse/*parta
        Gianni would like that Maria left(PAST SUBJ)/*leaves (PRES SUBJ)

The main verb is the present form of the so-called *conditional mood*. It is not therefore a past form and does not express a *past* meaning— i.e., Gianni's wish is located in the present, even if removed to a possible world. In the embedded clause, the subjunctive mood is licensed by virtue of being a complement of a volitional predicate, but in this case, the *modality* of the main verb, and not its tense, licenses the embedded past. Consider also that an embedded present subjunctive is ungrammatical—cf. the ungrammaticality of *parta* (leaves).[58]

The question is therefore how the past form is licensed in this context, given that no agreement process seems to be available, if we consider the feature as somehow connected to *past*. Several options come to mind. For instance, one might suggest that the feature on

---

[58] The conditional mood has a compound past form, made by an auxiliary with conditional morphology and the past participle: *avrebbe voluto* (lit: have+COND wanted). The subjunctive verbal form found in subordinate clauses is always the past one:

i.   Gianni avrebbe voluto che Maria partisse/*parta
     Gianni would like that Maria left(PAST SUBJ)/*leaves (PRES SUBJ)

the past subjunctive has to be conceived of as [−actual], instead as [+past]. Another possibility would be to encode the difference between the present subjunctive and the past subjunctive as a binary feature [±present]. In this chapter I will leave the question open. What is important to stress here is that this observation constitutes additional evidence in favour of the absence of temporal specification in the subjunctive and therefore in favour of the theory according to which the subjunctive is a non-relational form.

There is another context where the past tense is available in the absence of a visible licenser. The context in question is the so-called independent subjunctive expressing wishes by the speaker:

(93)   (Che) ti pigliasse un colpo!
        That a stroke take(PAST SUBJ) you!

In this case, however, the past form alternates with the present quite freely, without giving rise to differences in meaning:

(94)   (Che) ti pigli un colpo!
        That a stroke take(PRES SUBJ) you!

Notice also that CD is optional in this case, as in ordinary subordinate contexts. From these data, one might conclude therefore that the sentences in (93) and (94) are projections of the modal Complementizer, and not the high Complementizer C. In this respect, these examples would be analogous to the ones discussed above.[59]

---

[59] For an analysis of exclamative contexts, see Zanuttini and Portner (2000, 2003). At this point it might be relevant to say a few words on the relationship between the analysis of the C-layer proposed here and Rizzi's analysis (1997, 2001, 2002). In particular, the relation between the high C projection hypothesized here and Rizzi's *Force*.

Conceptually, they do not correspond to each other, in that Rizzi's Force is presumed to mark the *assertive force* and similar properties of the embedded clause. In the cases considered here, on the contrary, the high C projection is to be understood as a pointer to the speaker, independently of the nature of the clause—i.e., independently of its being an assertion, a question, etc. The role of C at the interface is to relate the content of the embedded clause—in particular the temporal interpretation of the event—with the speaker's *hic et nunc*. It seems to me, however, that the two approaches are certainly compatible, given that empirically this is not a counter-argument to Rizzi's work.

2.4.4 *On Sequence of Tense: the role of Agree*

Given the analysis provided above about the role of temporal topics in subjunctive clauses, it is possible now to express it in terms of Agreement.

The whole subjunctive licensing process can be viewed as a cyclic application of Agree. As an exemplification, consider the following:

(95)   Gianni credeva che Maria dormisse
       Gianni believed that Maria slept(PAST SUBJ)

The sentence can abstractly be considered as corresponding to the following schemata, where the highest verb is *credeva* (believed) and the lower one the subjunctive verbal form:

(96)   ... [... V...[... MOOD ... [... V...

The highest verb agrees with the Complementizer position, which in turn agrees with the embedded verb. As a result, only a past subjunctive can appear under a past main verb, or a past temporal topic, as in the following case:

(97)   [...TOP... [...MOOD... [...V...

In other words, one could conclude that the properties of the Complementizer constitute the obligatory bridge between the superordinate clause and the embedded one: they are determined by the superordinate verbal form—or by a temporal topic—and select the embedded verbal morphology.

One might speculate at this point why Agree happens to have such a role in Sequence of Tense phenomena. The obvious answer is that the domain of the Complementizer is a *phase*—as proposed in Chomsky (2005)—and only Agree has the power of establishing a relationship with something lying beyond this point. However, speculations of this kind are outside the scope of this book.

2.5 A remark on the morphology of the subjunctive

In this section I sketch a brief morphosyntactic analysis of the subjunctive, which should provide the grounds for an understanding of its properties with respect to the syntax of indexicality.

Summarizing, the main hypothesis of this chapter, and of this book in general, is that subjunctive verbal forms differ from indicative ones in that they do not provide reference to the context identified by means of the speaker's coordinates. In this respect, the subjunctive patterns with the infinitive even if it admits the presence of a lexical subject. However, cases such as the one of *ipotizzare* (hypothesize) show that the subjunctive can exhibit indicative-like properties when forced by lexical factors. Concluding, therefore, it can be said that the subjunctive is a sort of intermediate form, occasionally permitting fully indicative-like behaviour, but in general being compatible with contexts banning it.

This analysis differs from the one provide by Bianchi (2003, 2006), who argues that in providing a position for a lexical subject the subjunctive differs crucially from the infinitive and therefore patterns with the indicative. I think that the analysis of the DAR proposed here provides evidence in favour of my account—namely that the subjunctive, but not the indicative, is compatible with non-indexical, non-DAR, interpretation of the embedded verbal form. The possibility for a subjunctive to license a lexical subject has to do with the presence of (a certain amount of) person specification on its morphological endings. The idea of this book is that having a subject is not enough in Italian-like languages to force a DAR of the embedded event.

Moreover, a brief analysis of the subjunctive morphology seems to point to the conclusion that as far as reference of indexicality is concerned, it is not the presence of a lexical subject *per se* that matters, but the intrinsic reference to the context.

Consider the following subjunctive paradigm, reported here as can be found in traditional grammars of Italian:

(98)   1st conjugation: Che io lodi, che tu lodi, che egli lodi, che noi lodiamo, che voi lodiate, che essi lodino
That I praise (PRES SUBJ), etc.

(99)   Io lodo, tu lodi, egli loda, noi londiamo, voi lodate, essi lodano
I praise (PRES IND), etc.

(100)   2nd conjugation: Che io veda, che tu veda, che egli veda, che noi vediamo, che voi vediate, che essi vedano
That I see(PRES SUBJ), etc.

(101)   Io vedo, tu vedi, egli vede, noi vediamo, voi vedete, essi vedono
I see(PRES IND), etc.

(102)   3rd conjugation: che io parta, che tu parta, che egli parta, che noi partiamo, che voi partiate, che essi partano
That I leave (PRES SUBJ), etc.

(103)   Io parto, tu parti, egli parte, noi partiamo, voi partite, essi partono
I leave(PRES IND), etc.

These remarks should not be viewed as a full morphological account of the subjunctive and do not incorporate any etymological analysis. Here I only aim at clarifying the role that the native speaker might attribute to the subjunctive in her own (synchronic) linguistic competence.

From the paradigm given above, it can be seen that in the singular the subjunctive has no person distinction and that in the plural the first person is always identical to the indicative one. The third person plural is formed by adding to the singular verbal form the ending *–no* and the second plural has a peculiar ending of its own. Consider now the past paradigm:

(104)   1st conjugation: Che io lodassi, che tu lodassi, che egli lodasse, che noi lodassimo, che voi lodaste, che essi lodassero
That I praised (PAST SUBJ), etc.
Io lodai, tu lodasti, egli lodò, noi lodammo, voi lodaste, essi lodarono
I praised (PAST IND), etc.

(105)   2nd conjugation: Che io vedessi, che tu vedessi, che egli vedesse, che noi vedessimo, che voi vedeste, che essi vedessero
That I saw(PAST SUBJ), etc.
Io vidi, tu vedesti, egli vide, noi vedemmo, voi vedeste, essi videro
I saw (PAST IND), etc.

(106)   3rd conjugation: che io partissi, che tu partissi, che egli partisse, che noi
partissimo, che voi partiste, che essi partissero
That I left (PAST SUBJ), etc.
Io partii, tu partisti, egli partì, noi partimmo, voi partiste, essi partirono
I left (PAST IND), etc.

In the past paradigm, the first and second person singular are not
distinguished.[60]

In both cases, therefore, but especially in the present form, the
contrast with the indicative is striking, in that first and second person
singular—speaker and hearer—are not specifically marked and in
the present form are not even distinguished from the third person. In
general, it can be said that subjunctive morphology tends to be more
syncretic than indicative morphology and this property had already
been observed long ago by typologists—cf. for instance Greenberg
(1966).

The analysis provided in this chapter might shed some light on
this characteristic, in that the Italian subjunctive is supposed to lack
reference to indexicality, as opposed to the indicative, which always
marks it in its verbal morphology. Therefore, under this approach, it
might be expected that its morphological endings do not formally
encode reference to the speaker and the hearer.

2.6 Conclusion

In this chapter I proposed that the obligatoriness of the Double
Access Reading in certain embedded clauses has to be accounted for
by means of the representation in the C-layer of the speaker's
temporal coordinate. The speaker's temporal coordinate must be
represented in the case of an indicative subordinate clause, and is
usually not represented in the case of a subjunctive clause. Moreover,
in Italian the presence of the indicative in a subordinate clause seems

---

[60] The simple past of the indicative in Northern, and to a certain extent Central, Italy
is however very rarely used in everyday speech. See also fn. 27 above. Note that I am
abstracting away from the detailed analysis of the indicative past formation and the
relevance of the verbal theme.

to be tied to the presence of a lexical meaning of *communication* of the main verb.

On a closer look, however, I showed that it is not the indicative *per se* that is required by communication verbs, but the presence of the speaker's coordinate. This makes the difference between the DAR and non-DAR interpretation of *ipotizzare* (hypothesize). Interestingly, non-DAR contexts are also those contexts that permit omission of the Complementizer—i.e., CD contexts. Therefore, I proposed to identify the position of the non-deletable Complementizer with the position where the speaker's coordinate is represented.

In conclusion, analysis of communication contexts (typically selecting the indicative, but not necessarily) vs. non-communication ones (typically selecting the subjunctive) provides an important argument in favour of an analysis of the highest position of the C-layer as the syntactic position devoted to *indexicality*.

3

Can We Ever *See* the Speaker's Coordinates in the C-layer?

3.1 Introduction

So far, it might seem that the high position in the C-layer that I am hypothesizing has some relevance only for SoT phenomena. Therefore, one might be tempted to say that it is not an 'actual' syntactic position, but only an interface epi-phenomenon, showing up in the process of interpreting temporal relations. In other words, in Chapter 2 I argued that the C-layer includes a position for the speaker's temporal (and spatial) coordinates. Two questions arise at this point: Do we ever *see* such a position? That is, is it ever overtly realized with something recognizable as a first person marked item? The second question is: Where exactly does this position lie in the C-layer? The C-layer includes several distinct heads, hierarchically organized, that Rizzi (1997, 2001) and other scholars argue are the syntactic realization of different features. How is this indexical head ranked with respect to the others?

In this chapter I provide an answer to these questions. I show that the position in the C-layer projected by the speaker's coordinates is *visible* in some peculiar structures and that it can be occupied by a verbal form overtly marked with first person features—and *only* first person ones—expressing an epistemic meaning. I will also argue that the position in question is the left-most one in the C-layer. The argument comes from analysis of the distribution of verbal items such as *credo* (I believe/I think), *penso* (I think), *immagino* (I imagine) and the like. In particular I will consider here the properties of *credo*.[1]

---

[1] See also the unpublished analysis provided in Giorgi and Pianesi (2004c).

The main point is the following: *credo* (I believe/I think) is the subjectless first person present tense verbal form of the epistemic verb *credere* (to believe/to think). In Complementizer Deletion structures, the (apparently) embedded clause exhibits several properties typical of main clauses, which are incompatible with the syntax of subordinate sentences. The idea I will develop in this chapter is that when the Complementizer is not lexically realized, the sequence *credo* (I think) + *clause* must be analysed as a mono-clausal structure and not a bi-clausal one. Several arguments can be provided to this effect, which I will discuss in the following sections.

The hypothesis I discuss here is that *credo* (I think) in these cases must be analysed as a head expressing an epistemic value. It moves from a lower modifier position in the C-layer (see Rizzi 1997, 2002) to a higher one that I argue is the highest, left-most one in the layer. The reason it can move so high is because of its first person features, which are the only ones compatible with the projection containing the speaker's coordinates.[2]

3.2 Epistemic heads in Italian

As illustrated in Chapter 2, in Italian the Complementizer can be omitted in subjunctive contexts and can never be dispensed with if the embedded verb is in the indicative mood. The sentence complement to a *believe* predicate in Italian—*credere*—selects for subjunctive and, accordingly, admits Complementizer Deletion:[3]

(1)   Gianni ha detto *(che) è partita
       Gianni said that she left(IND)

---

[2] Jacqueline Guéron (p.c.) proposes an alternative view: *credo* (I believe) could be considered a modal particle, following the proposal developed in Beninca' and Poletto (1994) and Guéron (2000, 2006b) for impersonal modal forms, such as *bisogna* (it is needed), hence not an item originating in a lower modifier position. However, I prefer the modifier hypothesis, in that it can unify this item with the others expressing an epistemic value.

[3] The observation that other Romance languages do not select a subjunctive in this embedded context, though important in other respects, is not relevant with respect to the present discussion.

(2)   Gianni crede (che) sia partita
      Gianni believes that she left(SUBJ)

What is relevant for the present discussion is the distribution of the embedded subject in these sentences. Italian speakers divide in two groups: for some speakers (group (a)) CD is compatible with a preverbal lexical subject, for others (group (b)), it is not. This property is not related to the regional/ dialectal background of the speaker and is not a case of *optionality* either, given that the speakers consistently pattern in one way or the other.[4]

Consider the following sentences (the symbol '#' signals that the sentence is not acceptable for a group of speakers):

(3)   #Mario crede Luisa sia partita
      Mario believes Luisa left(SUBJ)

(4)   Mario crede sia partita Luisa
      Mario believes left(SUBJ) Luisa
      'Mario believes Luisa left'

(5)   Mario crede sia partita
      Mario believes (she) left(SUBJ)

For the (b) group of speakers sentence (3) is ungrammatical— namely, when the Complementizer is omitted, a preverbal lexical subject is impossible. For these speakers the subject must be either postverbal, as in (4), or omitted *tout court*, as in (5).[5] For group (a) all the sentences in (3)–(5) are grammatical.

For the analysis of the first piece of evidence, which I am going to discuss here, only the judgements of group (b) are relevant.

---

[4] This gives rise therefore to a case that might be dubbed as *intra-linguistic micro-variation*. In other words, the Italian language can be viewed as the conjunction of two minimally different grammars: in one of them a preverbal lexical subject is permitted with CD; in the other it is not.

[5] The distribution of pronouns follows the same pattern:

i.   #Mario crede lei sia partita
     Mario believes she left(SUBJ)

ii. Mario crede tu sia partita
     Mario believes you left(SUBJ)

Only the weak pronoun *tu* is acceptable in prenominal position for all speakers; the third person singular pronoun *lei* is acceptable only for the first group.

The important point in this respect is the existence of a contrast between 'ordinary' sentences with CD and those with *credo* and a preverbal subject. Let's now consider the following contrast:

(6)   #Gianni crede Luisa abbia telefonato
       Gianni believes that Luisa called(SUBJ)

(7)   Credo Luisa abbia telefonato
       (I) believe Luisa called(SUBJ)

Crucially, for group (b) of Italian speakers the sentence in (6) is ungrammatical, whereas for group (a) it is perfect. The difference in grammaticality judgement between the two groups disappears in example (7), however. This sentence is grammatical for all speakers, even for those rejecting the preverbal subject given in example (6).

The only observable difference between the two sentences is that the one in (6) has a third person subject, whereas that in (7) has an (empty) first person subject. My point here is that exactly this difference provides the explanation for the lack of contrast between group (a) and group (b) in the judging of sentence (7). The hypothesis I develop in this chapter, therefore, is that the subjunctive complement clause *Luisa abbia telefonato* (Luisa called) in (7) has a different status with respect to the corresponding embedded clause in example (6).

A consideration that might prove relevant in this respect is that the interpretation of sentence (6) is not quite the same as the interpretation of sentence (7).

By means of sentence (6), the speaker is telling us something about Gianni's beliefs, in particular that *Gianni has the belief that Luisa called*. In other words, the speaker is attributing to Gianni—on the basis of whatever evidence the speaker might judge appropriate and sufficient—an epistemic state concerning the calling of Luisa.

The meaning associated with sentence (7) is not of the same sort, and indeed it would be rather odd if it were. By means of this sentence the speaker is not telling us that he is attributing to himself a certain epistemic state concerning the calling of Luisa—i.e., something like *I have the belief that Luisa called*—but, rather, something like '*perhaps*'

Luisa called (I am not 100% certain about it). In other words, informally speaking, in sentence (7) the calling of Luisa is asserted, and
the assertion is qualified by means of the presence of *credo* (I think)
as something less than a certainty.[6]

This observation fits well with the previous one: the embedded
clause exhibits neither the syntax nor the semantics of a 'real'
embedded clause. The properties just listed—the availability of a
preverbal subject both for group (a) and group (b), and its assertive
nature—seem to suggest that the embedded clause is in fact more
similar to a main one, in spite of the fact that it appears with the
subjunctive mood.

The hypothesis can therefore be rephrased in the following way: in
sentence (6), the verbal form *crede* (he believes) is a 'real' verb, taking
a complement clause; the resulting structure is therefore a bi-clausal
sentence. In sentence (7) *credo* (I believe) only specifies the epistemic
status of the speaker with respect to the proposition that follows. In
these cases *credo* (I believe) must be treated as an epistemic head,
'disguised' as a verb. The sentence in (7) therefore has to be analysed
as a mono-clausal structure—analogously to *probabilmente Luisa ha
telefonato* (probably Luisa called)—and not as a sentence constituted
by two clauses.[7]

3.2.1 *The distribution of* credo *with topic and focus*

Another piece of evidence in favour of the idea that the clause
following *credo* (I think) is not an embedded one, but is the main
one, comes from the distribution of focus in topic.

---

[6] Note however that nothing prevents the meaning in (6) being attributed to (7). In
some sense, it is the other way round: it is the meaning of sentence (7) that is not available for (6).

[7] Giorgi and Pianesi (2004b) also show that this property is unique to first person
indicative present tense subjectless verbal forms followed by a clause without the
Complementizer. Namely, the behaviour of forms such as: *io credo* (I believe), *io ho
creduto* (I have believed), *io credo che* (I believe that), *tu credi* (you believe), etc. parallel
third person forms like *Gianni crede* (Gianni believes) given in (6) and differ in the
crucial points with respect to sentence (7).

Rizzi (1997) argued that in embedded clauses focus and topic projections are available in post-complementizer position and not in the pre-complementizer one. Consider the following sentences.[8]

(8)   Mario crede che A PARIGI sia andata (non a Londra)
       Mario believes that TO PARIS she went (not to London)

(9)   Mario crede che a Parigi, ci sia andata il mese scorso
       Mario believes that in Paris, (she) there-went last month
       'Mario believes that in Paris she went last month'

(10)   *Mario crede A PARIGI che sia andata (non a Londra)
       Mario believes TO PARIS that she went (not to London)

(11)   *Mario crede a Parigi, che ci sia andata il mese scorso
       Mario believes to Paris, that (she) there-went last month
       'Mario believes that to Paris she went last month'

Recall also that in main clauses, focus and topic are available in the left periphery of the sentence:

(12)   A PARIGI Maria è andata (non a Londra)
       TO PARIS Maria went (not to London)

(13)   A Parigi Maria c'è andata il mese scorso
       To Paris Maria there-went last month
       'To Paris Maria went last month'

Giorgi and Pianesi (2004b) pointed out that, when CD occurs, the acceptability of focus and topic decreases:

(14)   *Mario crede A PARIGI sia andata (non a Londra)
       Mario believes TO PARIS (she) went (not to London)

(15)   ??-*Mario crede a Parigi ci sia andata il mese scorso
       Mario believes to Paris (she) there-went last month
       'Mario believes to Paris she went last month'

The presence of a focus in a complementizer-less structure gives rise to a very degraded sentence, and the presence of a topic to a less-than-acceptable one. Giorgi and Pianesi (2004b) amply discuss this point and provide an explanation both for the contrast between (10)–(11) on one side and (12)–(13) on the other, and for the difference

---

[8] For analyses of these positions in Italian, see among the others Cecchetto and Chierchia (1999), Poletto (2000), Benincà (2001), Beninca' and Poletto (2004).

between (14) and (15). Their explanation is not relevant here, because the point with respect to the present discussion concerns the fact that—whatever the reason might be—'normally' CD is to various degrees incompatible with embedded topic and focus.

Let's consider again the hypothesis I proposed above, namely, that the clause following *credo* is *not* an *embedded* clause, given that *credo* is not a main clause, but an epistemic head. If this reasoning is correct, we expect the clause following *credo not* to behave as an embedded clause.

In particular, given that complementizer-less embedded clauses show the pattern in (14)–(15), we can check the hypothesis by comparing *credo* + clause with (14)–(15) above. *Credo* + clause can either be compatible with topic and focus or not. If it is not, then the clause behaves as an embedded one. If it is indeed compatible, then the idea put forward here—i.e., that the whole structure is a single sentence, introduced by an epistemic head—receives independent support.

Consider the following sentences:

(16)   Credo A PARIGI sia andata (non a Londra)
       (I) believe TO PARIS (she) went (not to London)

(17)   Credo a Parigi ci sia andata il mese scorso
       (I) believe to Paris (she) there-went last month
       'I believe to Paris she went last month'

Both examples are grammatical and contrast with sentences (14)–(15) above. Therefore their syntax is not like the syntax of embedded clauses, but resembles that of main sentences.

To summarize: there are several constraints on the distribution of phrases in the left periphery of a complement clause when the Complementizer is omitted: focus and topic phrases are ungrammatical, or very marginal, and preverbal subjects are allowed only for some speakers, but are ungrammatical for other ones. These constraints cease to play a role when a first person form such as *credo* appears.

In other words, in absence of the Complementizer, the clause following a first person, present tense (epistemic) verb does not exhibit the syntactic properties that are usually observed in complement clauses. The structure therefore can be better analysed as a single clause introduced by an epistemic head.[9]

The fact that the subjunctive mood appears even in these cases makes this evidence particularly interesting, because it shows that it is possible to have a dissociation between the modal–non modal value of the subjunctive form and the syntax attributed to it. In other words, as shown in the preceding chapter, a non-dependent subjunctive can only have a modal interpretation. Consider the following example, repeated from Chapter 2:

(18)   Che ti prenda un colpo!
       That you get(SUBJ) a stroke!

Sentence (18) cannot be an assertion and can only express a wish, an exclamation, etc., whereas the *credo* sentences under discussion are (qualified) assertions. The presence of the subjunctive with *credo* therefore requires an explanation. In section 3.4 below, I will consider this issue in more detail.

3.2.2 *Further evidence in favour of a mono-clausal structure: the distribution of* francamente *(frankly)*

It is well known—see among others Jackendoff (1972) and Cinque (1999, 2004)—that speech act adverbs such as *francamente* (frankly) cannot be embedded:

(19)   Francamente, Mario si e' comportato male
       Frankly, Mario has misbehaved

(20)   *Luisa credeva che francamente si fosse comportato male
       Luisa believed that frankly he had misbehaved

The presence of these adverbs requires a long pause before the rest of sentence, usually, even if not always, marked in written language with a comma; several word orders are possible. Consider for instance the following examples (the symbol '#' here signals a long pause):

---

[9] If the Complementizer is realized, as in *credo che* (I believe that), the structure is bi-clausal.

(21) Mario, #francamente#, si è comportato male
Mario, frankly, has misbehaved

(22) (?)Mario si è, #francamente#, comportato male
Mario has, frankly, misbehaved

(23) Mario si è comportato male, #francamente!
Mario has misbehaved, frankly!

The impossibility of embedding *francamente* persists even when it appears in sentence-final position:

(24) *Luisa credeva che si fosse comportato male, francamente
Luisa believed that he had misbehaved, frankly

The only interpretation for (24) is the one where *francamente* refers to the speaker—i.e., it is speaker-oriented—and not to Luisa—i.e., it is not subject-oriented—and takes the whole sentence in its scope.

The embedding of the adverb doesn't seem to improve with CD (in the relevant reading, where the adverb is referring to Luisa's thought):

(25) *Luisa credeva, francamente, si fosse comportato male
Luisa believed, frankly, (he) had misbehaved

(26) *Luisa credeva si fosse comportato male, francamente
Luisa believed (he) had misbehaved, frankly

The unavailability of an embedded reading might easily follow from the consideration that speech act adverbs must establish a relation between the speech act and its agent. Therefore, it cannot be acceptable in clauses dependent upon a propositional attitude, such as fearing, believing, etc., as it makes no sense to attribute to somebody a frank attitude in believing, fearing, etc., something. On the contrary, this is naturally possible with an act of communication:

(27) Mario disse a tutti che francamente era stanco di ascoltare sciocchezze
Mario told everybody that frankly he was tired of hearing silly things

In sentence (27) the adverb *frankly* can be attributed to the subject *Mario* as well, given that he is the agent of a speech act. Concluding, *francamente* never appears in embedded contexts, unless they express speech acts.

Let's now compare these cases with the clauses appearing with complementizer-less *credo*. The following sentence is perfectly grammatical:

(28)   Credo, francamente, si sia comportato male
         (I) believe, frankly, (he) has misbehaved

As illustrated by the following example, the post-sentential position of the adverb is grammatical as well:

(29)   Credo si sia comportato male, francamente
         (I) believe (he) has misbehaved, frankly

These sentences all mean that the speaker judges frankly that the subject has misbehaved. There is therefore a systematic contrast between the *credo* cases in the sentences (28) and (29) and (24)–(26) with a third person main verb.

It can be immediately observed that this pattern is what one would expect given a mono-clausal analysis for the *credo* sentences under scrutiny. First, notice that the grammaticality of the sentence decreases if the Complementizer is introduced, either to the right of the adverb or to its left:

(30)   ?(?)Credo che, francamente, si sia comportato male
              (I) believe that, frankly, (he) has misbehaved

(31)   ?(?)Credo, francamente, che si sia comportato male
              (I) believe, frankly, that (he) has misbehaved

The contrast with (28) might be not very sharp, but it is still quite systematic. Consider also that as soon as the main verb is a past form, the sentence is strongly degraded:

(32)   ??Ho creduto/credetti, francamente, si fosse comportato male
              (I) believed(PR PERF/SIMPLE PAST), frankly, he had misbehaved

The meaning of (32) is that at utterance time the speaker is frank when he says that he had a belief that such and such. In other words, the sentence is grammatical only if interpreted bi-clausally, where *frankly* modifies the main verbal form and the word order is acceptable only if there is a long pause between the *creduto/credetti* (I believed) and the adverb. Notice that we find a decreased grammaticality even when the subject, *io* (I) is overt, analogously to the cases we discussed in the previous section:

(33) ??Io credo francamente si sia sbagliato
 I believe frankly (he) was wrong

These data show that if we have a true main clause propositional attitude predicate, there is no room—or, at least, less room—for an embedded *frankly*. This is not true with *credo* followed by a complementizer-less clause.

If this is the case, the hypothesis discussed in this chapter seems to be correct: the complementizer-less clause following *credo* does not exhibit the properties of embedded clauses. On the contrary, the grammar for main clauses can accommodate the phenomena just described, under the hypothesis that *credo* occupies a head position in the left, pre-subject, layer of the sentence.

3.2.3 *The structural position of epistemic heads*

Let's consider now the exact location of the epistemic item *credo* in the C-layer. In this section I will show that *credo* originates in the position typical of epistemics in Italian—Rizzi's (2002) Modifier position—and then it must move to a higher position in the C-layer. I will argue that this happens because it incorporates first person morphological features. This analysis will provide additional arguments in favour of the existence of a projection dedicated to the syntactic representation of the speaker's coordinates in the left periphery of the clause. I will also compare its distribution with the one of another verbal element used adverbially, i.e., the third person plural present form of the verb *dire* (say), *dicono* (they say), and show that it might provide further arguments in favour of the conclusion proposed here.

In the following discussion I compare *credo* with the epistemic adverb *probabilmente* (probably, possibly), trying to determine whether the two occupy the same position or not. Given that both are epistemic items, one would expect *probabilmente* and *credo* to exhibit the same distribution, modulo the fact that *probabilmente* is a phrase, whereas *credo* is a head.

Consider the following contrast, where the epistemic adverb/head is combined with a focused phrase:

(34)   ??Probabilmente A PARIGI Paolo è già stato (non a Londra)
        Probably to Paris Paolo has already been (not to London)

(35)   Credo A PARIGI Maria sia andata (non a Londra)
        (I) believe TO PARIS Maria went (not to London)

The example in (35) is actually better than the one in (34). Recall also that, as discussed in the previous section, the word order found in a sentence such as (35) does not obtain with *real* CD subordinate clauses:

(36)   *Gianni crede A PARIGI (#Maria) sia andata (non a Londra)
        Gianni believes TO PARIS (Maria) went (not to London)

I argued above that, while in a complementizer-less embedded clause a focus projection in the left periphery position is not acceptable, in sentence (35) it is possible because it is a mono-clausal structure and not a bi-clausal one.

The sentence in (34), however, is also clearly mono-clausal, therefore, if nothing else is added to the analysis, the contrast would remain unaccounted for.

In the spirit of the cartographic approach (Rizzi 1997, Cinque 1999)—which connects word order to syntactic structures, passing through Kayne's (1994) anti-symmetry—it can be said that, since *credo* is on the *left* of the focus projection, it must also occupy a higher position in the syntactic structure. On the other hand, *probabilmente* does not have this option, and must appear in a position lower than focus. But *where* exactly in the structure? Moreover, the following question would be still more relevant: *why* do we find the contrast between *credo* and *probabilmente* illustrated by sentences (34) and (35)?

Rizzi (2001, 2002) and Cinque (2004) convincingly argue that left-peripheral adverbs are located in a *Modifier* position in the left-side layer of the clause. They provide arguments in favour of the hypothesis that such a position is lower than the focus position. According to their proposal, therefore, the basic location for an adverb like *probabilmente* should be on the right—therefore, lower in the syntactic structure—of the focus phrase, as in the following case:

(37)   A PARIGI probabilmente Paolo è già stato (non a Londra)
       To PARIS probably Paolo has already been (not to London)

(38)   [[$_{FocP}$ A PARIGI] [$_{ModP}$ probabilmente] Paolo è già stato (non a Londra)]
       To PARIS probably Paolo has already been (not to London)

The structure in (38) would account for the fact that a focus phrase must precede the adverb and cannot follow it, as shown by the marginality of example (34) above. The word order in (34) would be a violation of the hierarchical ordering of functional projections in the left periphery given in (38). Hence, it is correctly predicted to be ungrammatical.

This account leaves a problem remaining, though. If *credo* behaves as an epistemic head that can appear in the same projection as *probabilmente*, e.g., ModP, then (35) should be on a par with (34), whereas it is not.

The proposal I will argue for in this section is that Rizzi's idea can be maintained, but should be supplemented with the hypothesis that *credo* in mono-clausal structures, by virtue of its inherent properties, moves to a still higher position. This idea would answer the questions above: *credo* raises to the left periphery where the speaker's coordinate is represented, because it is specified as a first person item, whereas *probabilmente* cannot do this, since it is not marked that way.

Morphologically, *credo* is a bi-morphemic verbal form. It is constituted by the verbal root *cred-* and the morphological ending -*o*—i.e., the first person singular morpheme. Hence, even when it works as an epistemic adverb, it maintains its ordinary phi-features, which must be checked. This cannot obtain, as in normal cases, in the T position, because *credo*, due to its peculiar adverbial status, is generated too high up to make it possible. The only possibility, therefore, is that *credo*'s first person singular phi-features are checked in the higher Complementizer projection where the speaker's coordinates are represented. Hence, the word order in (35) is obtained through overt movement.[10]

---

[10] In principle, an explanation should also be provided for the non-fully ungrammatical status of (34). The sentence is in fact judged from 'marginal' to 'very marginal', but not fully ungrammatical. A possible account would be to say that in sentence (34) *probabilmente*, by virtue of its being semantically related with the speaker—given that it expresses an epistemic status of the speaker—can be properly interpreted in the speaker's projection. The semantics of the sentence therefore works out properly, but the syntactic requirements are violated, given that the movement is not triggered as it should be.

3.3 *Dicono* (they say) as an evidential head

A further argument in favour of overt movement of *credo* to a speaker-dedicated projection is provided by its distribution when appearing together with the evidential item *dicono* (they say). *Dicono* (they say) can be analysed in a way analogous to *credo* as an evidential head, i.e., as a verbal form actually expressing a functional head. In this section I will consider the properties of *dicono* (they say) in this particular usage and compare it with the analysis of *credo* discussed in the previous section.[11]

3.3.1 *The distribution of* dicono

Dicono is the third person plural present tense form of the verb *dire* (say). Giorgi and Pianesi (2004c) argue that this form shares with *credo* the possibility of being analysed as an adverbial head, when it appears in a subjectless context and is followed by a complementizer-less clause. In particular, they claim that it can be considered as an *evidential* head.[12]

The analysis of *dicono* parallels the one provided for *credo*. From the interpretive point of view, analogously to the case of *credo*, this verbal form does not express the literal meaning it expresses 'normally'. Consider for instance the following cases:

(39)   Gianni e Mario dicono che Paola è partita
        Gianni and Maria say that Paola left(IND)

(40)   Dicono Paola sia partita
        (They) say Paola left(SUBJ)

Sentence (39) is the usual bi-clausal structure, where the speaker tells us about a speech act by Gianni and Mario concerning the leaving of Paola. Sentence (40), on the contrary, does not have this

[11] See, in a similar vein, the analysis of *bisogna* (lit: is needed) proposed in Beninca' and Poletto (1994) and Guéron (2000). *Bisogna* is a verb of necessity, which is taken to occupy a functional left-peripheral position.

[12] There is a very extensive and very interesting literature on the notion of evidentiality. Here I am adopting a narrow view of it, namely I only consider heads, expressing the *source* of the information. Typologically and philosophically, the issue is much broader than that, and I will not even attempt to provide an analysis of the general notion.

interpretation. By means of this sentence the speaker is not informing her audience about a speech act by a plurality of people concerning the leaving of Paola. As a matter of fact, sentence (40) does not imply the existence of any actual speech act. What this sentence means is that *there is a rumor* concerning the leaving of Paola. In other words, by means of *dicono* the speaker signals that she does not take responsibility for the following content. Notice also that in these cases, as exemplified by (40), the embedded verb appears in the subjunctive, an option not allowed in the normal usage of the verb *dire* (say):[13]

(41)   *Gianni e Mario dicono che Paola sia partita
       Gianni and Mario say that Paola left(SUBJ)

The evidential head interpretation is allowed when the subjectless form *dicono* is followed by a complementizer-less clause containing a subjunctive verbal form. If these conditions are not met, the interpretation is the bi-clausal one. Consider for instance the following contrast:

(42)   Dicono Gianni sia partito all'alba
       (They) say Gianni has(SUBJ) left at dawn

(43)   *Loro dicono Gianni sia partito all'alba
       They say Gianni has(SUBJ) left at dawn

The introduction of a lexical subject, even if pronominal, as in (43), makes the sentence ungrammatical. In (43) the embedded verbal form must in fact appear in the indicative, and CD is not available, as expected:

---

[13] I will not discuss in depth the very nature of the epistemicity and evidentiality. For the sake of this work, I will follow Giorgi and Pianesi (2004c) and use the term epistemicity as referring to the (internal) relationship between a subject and a given propositional content and the term *evidentiality* as referring to the source of the reported content, as known to the speaker. Implicitly, by means of an evidential the speaker often provides an assessment of the reliability of the information. The fact that *credo* bears first person features, and that *dicono*—or *si dice*—third person ones, might therefore be intuitively connected with the distinction between epistemicity and evidentiality: the internal state of the speaker, on one side, and the external source of information on the other one. For an analysis of evidentiality in Romance, see also Squartini (2001b).

(44)   Loro dicono *(che) Gianni è partito all'alba
       They say that Gianni has(IND) left at dawn

The complementizer cannot be omitted, as is always the case in indicative clauses. Like *credo*, *dicono* must have a head status and cannot be combined with other phrases, such as a subject, or a temporal morpheme, which might compel an analysis in which it projects as a full Verb.

Furthermore, analogously to what I illustrated above for *credo*, the interpretation of (44) is the standard one: the speaker is reporting a speech act by somebody concerning the leaving of Gianni. The same is true with respect to a past form:

(45)   *Hanno detto che Gianni sia/fosse partito all'alba
       They said that Gianni left (PRES SUBJ/PAST SUBJ) at dawn

(46)   Hanno detto *(che) Gianni è partito all'alba
       They said that Gianni left(IND) at dawn

When *dire* (say) appears in the past, the embedded verb cannot appear in the subjunctive and the Complementizer cannot be omitted. Therefore, the form that is compatible with the structure CD+subjunctive is only the subjectless present tense form.[14]

As a final argument in favour of this analysis of *dicono* as a functional head, note that the verb *dire* can take an indirect object, as in the following sentence:

(47)   Gianni ha detto a Paolo che Maria è partita
       Gianni said to Paolo that Maria has(IND) left

---

[14] The imperfect of the indicative gives much better results, even if judgements vary among speakers:

i.   Dicevano Gianni fosse partito all'alba
     They said(IMPF IND) Gianni left (PAST SUBJ) at dawn

I will consider the properties of the imperfect in Chapter 4 and suggest an explanation for its acceptability in this sentence and in similar ones.

Finally, note also that the third person singular impersonal form of *dire* (say) formed by the clitic *si* followed by the third person singular form of the verb, *si dice* (CLsi-says), has the same properties as *dicono*:

i.   Si dice Gianni sia partito all'alba
     SI-says Gianni has(PRES SUBJ) left at dawn

The presence of the dative is totally excluded in the construal under scrutiny here:

(48) *Dicono a tutti Maria sia partita
      (They) say to everybody Maria has(SUBJ) left

(49) Dicono a tutti che Maria è partita
      (They) say to everybody that Maria has(IND) left

There is a clear contrast between these examples: the sentence in (48) can only have the literal meaning as a *saying* predicate. Therefore if there is a dative, the verb must be followed by the Complementizer *che* (that) and an embedded indicative verbal form, as in sentence (49).

The main observation relevant to the present discussion is that in sentence (40), as in sentence (42), the embedded subject can appear in preverbal position. We know that for a group of Italian speakers CD clauses cannot have a preverbal subject. In this case, however, the sentence is grammatical for everybody.

All these properties can be explained in the same way as for *credo*. *Dicono* contrasts with *loro dicono* (they say), or *hanno detto* (they said), in that the former is interpreted as an evidential head—giving rise to a mono-clausal structure—whereas the latter are regular saying verbs taking a subordinate clause. Therefore, when *dicono* is a functional head there is no constraint concerning the appearance of a preverbal subject, as there is none in regular main clauses.

3.3.2 *The structural position of evidential heads*

Let's consider now what is the position occupied by *dicono* when it must be analysed as an evidential head. Recall that I showed above that *credo* moves from its base modifier position to the speaker projection in C. Analogously to what is illustrated above for *credo*, *dicono* in these cases can be followed by a topic:

(50) Credo a Parigi ci sia andata il mese scorso
      (I) believe to Paris she there-went last month

(51) Dicono a Parigi ci sia andata il mese scorso
      (They) say to Paris she there-went(SUBJ) last month

A Parigi (in Paris) appears in between the verbal form *dicono* and the complementizer-less clause. I showed above that this is not a possible option for structures to be analysed as instances of CD. Consider again example (15), which I repeat here for simplicity:

(52)   ??-*Mario crede a Parigi ci sia andata il mese scorso
           Mario believes to Paris (she) there-went last month
           'Mario believes to Paris she went last month'

The contrast cannot be made minimal, because *dire* (say) in normal cases selects for an indicative, which never admits CD. However, what is relevant here is that sentence (51) patterns with sentence (50) and not with (52).

   Consider however the following data:

(53)   Credo A PARIGI sia andata (non a Londra)
           (I) believe TO PARIS she went(SUBJ) (not to London)

(54)   ?*Dicono A PARIGI sia andata (non a Londra)
           They say TO PARIS she went(SUBJ) (not to London)

I illustrated above that intervening focus and topic behave alike with respect to *credo*. This is not the case with *dicono*. A focused constituent following *dicono* does not give rise to an acceptable sentence. In this case there is a contrast with *credo*.

   A natural way to look at (54) is to say that *dicono* cannot move past the focus projection contained in the C-layer. Recall also that in Italian there is only one such projection, therefore, there is no other way to obtain the word order in example (54).

   A plausible explanation for this contrast immediately comes to mind: this phenomenon can be traced back to the different feature specification of the two verbal forms. *Credo*, being marked with first-person features, can move overtly to the speaker's projection in the C-layer, whereas *dicono*, being third person plural and not referring to the speaker, but to an external source, cannot. Therefore *dicono* cannot appear on the left of the focus projection.

   On the other hand, as pointed out by Rizzi (2001, 2002), topic phrases can appear much more liberally in the tree, so that the issue does not arise in connection with the reciprocal order with respect to a topic. In this case, in fact, it is possible to hypothesize the existence of a topic lower than the Modifier projection.

As expected under this hypothesis, the following example is a considerable improvement on the one given above:

(55)   A PARIGI dicono sia andata (non a Londra)
       TO PARIS they say she went (not to London)

Let us consider now the reciprocal distribution of epistemics and evidentials. Cinque (1999) investigated the distribution of adverbs appearing in the upper part of the clause. He convincingly showed that the evidential projection intervenes between the evaluative and the epistemic projection, as exemplified by the relative orders of adverbs (cf. Cinque 1999, ch. 4):

(56)   Fortunately$_{evaluative}$ > allegedly$_{evidential}$ > probably$_{epistemic}$

Leaving aside the evaluative projection, on which I have nothing to say here, evidential items occupy a position on the left of the epistemic ones. *Dicono* complies with this generalization, as shown by the following example:[15]

(57)   Dicono probabilmente Gianni sia partito
       (They) say probably Gianni has(SUBJ) left

Word order in (57) is as predicted by Cinque's hierarchy, given that the evidential head *dicono* precedes the epistemic adverb *probabilmente*.[16]

Consider now the following examples including the epistemic head *credo*, instead of an adverb like *probabilmente*:

(58)   *Dicono creda Maria sia partita
       (They) say (I) believe Maria left(SUBJ)

(59)   Credo dicano Maria sia partita
       (I) believe (they) say Maria left(SUBJ)

These sentences contrast with the examples given above. As I just illustrated, the grammatical word order according to Cinque's

---

[15] I thank G. Cinque for pointing out this important piece of evidence to me.
[16] The reverse word order is also possible:
i.   Probabilmente dicono sia partito
     Probably (they) say (he) left

hierarchy should be the one in (58), and not the one in (59), contrary to facts.

This contrast however is predicted by the hypothesis proposed above: *credo* must move to a higher position to check its first person, speaker-oriented features, whereas *dicono* does not. The meaning obtained in this way is accordingly the following: 'according to the epistemic state of the speaker—i.e., less than absolute certainty—there is evidence—coming from an external unspecified source—that P'.

To conclude this section, therefore, it is possible to claim that there is a syntactic position in the left periphery of the clause explicitly marked as speaker-related to which items overtly move under the appropriate conditions.

Where exactly is this position located? According to the analysis given above, it is the left-most one in the C-layer. Putting together these observations with Rizzi's (2001, 2002) and Cinque's (1999), it is possible to hypothesize the following structure for the left-peripheral structure. The evidential head *dicono* is located in the Evidential position in the Modifier layer, higher than epistemics. Differently from *credo*, however, it cannot raise out of it:

(60) $dicono_{evidential} > credo_{epistemic}$

(61) $[_{C\text{-Speaker}} \text{ credo } \dots [_{INT} [_{FOC} [_{MODIFIER} \cdots$

(62)   MODIFIER has to be expanded as: $\dots [_{evaluative} [_{evidential} [_{epistemic} \cdots$

Dicono is therefore originally higher than *credo*. The latter however can appear in the left-periphery, whereas *dicono* cannot. The distribution of a focus projection follows from this view.[17]

The interpretation is, however, totally different, in that, as expected, *dicono* ceases to be an evidential. Therefore the sentence means something like: 'probably there are people who say that Gianni left'. Importantly, epistemicity does not concern the leaving of Gianni, but the saying by the people. As a consequence, the example is not relevant to the present analysis.

[17] Rizzi (2002) considers the position in Spec,MOD(ifier) as recursive, in order to permit multiple adverbs to appear. However, this layer must be internally structured in a fixed hierarchical fashion, in order to cope with Cinque's (1999) observations. If the present analysis is correct, presumably Rizzi's suggestion cannot be maintained, given that multiple heads positions are also needed, beside the specifiers. I will not consider this point any further in this book, because it is not central to the argument developed here.

3.4 A brief remark on parentheticals

Credo, together with other similar verbal forms such as *suppongo* (I suppose), *temo* (I fear), *spero* (I hope), can be used as a parenthetical, occurring in various positions inside the clause. The literature on parentheticals is huge and very complex, also because this kind of structure comes in many varieties. Exhaustive analysis and unification of their typology is not my goal here. The parentheticals relevant to my topic are those constituted in Italian by a single subjectless verb—as opposed to a whole sentence. I will consider e.g. *credo* (I believe), but not the *as* parenthetical *come Maria sostiene* (as Maria claims). I dub these *mono-verbal parentheticals*.[18]

Consider the following example:

(63)   Maria (credo)₁ è (credo)₂ andata (credo)₃ a Parigi (credo)₄
        Maria ((I) believe) has(IND) ((I) believe) gone ((I) believe) to Paris ((I) believe)

In example (63) an indicative verbal form appears; I will come back to this point in a while. The single verb parenthetical can appear in many positions inside the clause. These positions are also available for left-peripheral adverbs in general, such as *probabilmente* (probably), *forse* (perhaps), *sicuramente* (surely), *fortunatamente* (fortunately), *presumibilmente* (presumably), etc.[19]

---

[18] Rooryck (2001a, 2001b) proposes a unification of parentheticals with evidentiality and treats evaluative and epistemic modals on a par with evidentials.

[19] Consider also that as soon as the head analysis is not available any more, grammaticality decreases. This is the case if the first person *credo* (I believe) is substituted by the third person one *crede* (believes) with the subject *Gianni*:

i.   ??Maria, Gianni crede, è andata a Parigi
     Maria, Gianni believes, has gone to Paris

ii. ?*Maria è, Gianni crede, andata a Parigi
     Maria has, Gianni believes, gone to Paris

iii. ?*Maria è andata, Gianni crede, a Parigi
     Maria has gone, Gianni believes, to Paris

iv. ??Maria è andata a Parigi, Gianni crede
     Maria has gone to Paris, Gianni believes

(64)   Maria (forse)$_1$ è (forse)$_2$ andata (forse)$_3$ a Parigi (forse)$_4$
      Maria (perhaps) has(IND) (perhaps) gone (perhaps) to Paris (perhaps)

As I remarked above, the main difference between the parenthetical *credo* and the left-periphery one is that the latter triggers the subjunctive mood, whereas all the positions in (63) do not:

(65)   *Maria (credo)$_1$ sia (credo)$_2$ andata (credo)$_3$ a Parigi (credo)$_4$
      Maria ((I) believe) has(SUBJ) ((I) believe) gone ((I) believe) to Paris ((I) believe)

A possible hypothesis unifying the left-most *credo* structures we saw above, with the parenthetical construals like (64), would be to say that *credo* can occupy various head positions inside the clause, and that they are related through movement.

The triggering of the subjunctive only takes place when *credo* lands in the left-most position in the C-layer. This is a most natural assumption, given that the presence of a subjunctive according to the present hypothesis is triggered exclusively under a C-T relation. If this relation fails to be established, no subjunctive can appear—modulo the *modal* meanings discussed in Chapter 2 section 3 above.[20]

According to Rizzi (2001, 2002), the basic position for adverbs is the one marked in sentences (63) and (64) by subscript 2, namely, the position inside the main VP, higher than the participle projection. The position marked with the subscript 3 is inside the participial projection and is basically given as well. *Credo*$_1$ might be taken to appear in Rizzi's left-periphery position *Modifier*—the Modifier position discussed in the previous section—with topicalization of the subject. Therefore, this case would be obtained by means of movement of *credo* to Mod(ifier). As far as position 4 is concerned, various analyses seem possible. It might be obtained via movement of the participial projection, followed by movement of the rest of the

With respect to these cases, there is a minimal contrast with *as* parentheticals:
v.   Maria (come Gianni crede) è (come Gianni crede) andata (come Gianni crede) a Parigi (come Gianni crede)
     Maria (as Gianni believes) has (as Gianni believes) gone (as Gianni believes) to Paris (as Gianni believes)

   [20] For further discussion of this point, see section 3.5 below.

clause to its left. Conversely, it might also be thought that the right-most position is a basic position as well, conveying a peculiar after-thought meaning. In this perspective, therefore, the parenthetical *credo* would be no parenthetical at all. It is always a functional head allowed to occupy several positions inside the clause.

Consider finally that both parenthetical *credo* and left-periphery *credo* cannot be embedded:

(66)   *Paolo ha detto che Maria, credo, è andata a Parigi
      Paolo said that Maria, (I) believe, went(IND) to Paris

(67)   #Paolo ha detto che credo Maria sia andata a Parigi
      Paolo said that (I) believe Maria went(SUBJ) to Paris

Sentence (67) is grammatical only for the speakers who accept a preverbal subject with CD, showing therefore that the mono-clausal analysis triggered by epistemic *credo* is not available, analogously to what illustrated in section 3.2.3.

Note that *dicono* exhibits similar properties:

(68)   Maria (dicono)$_1$ è (dicono)$_2$ andata (dicono)$_3$ a Parigi (dicono)$_4$
      Maria ((they) say) has(IND) ((they) say) gone ((they) say) to Paris
      ((they) say)

Analogously to parenthetical *credo*, *dicono* can only trigger the indicative and not the subjunctive, as shown by the following example:

(69)   *Maria (dicono)$_1$ sia (dicono)$_2$ andata (dicono)$_3$ a Parigi (dicono)$_4$
      Maria ((they) say) has(SUBJ) ((they) say) gone ((they) say) to Paris
      ((they) say)

The same explanation as above can be taken to hold here as well: only under a C-T relation can the subjunctive appear, given that it is not a main assertive verbal form. Other expressions, such as the already mentioned *si dice* (SI-says), *raccontano/si racconta* (they tell/SI-tell), etc., pattern like *dicono*.

Naturally enough, the verbs listed above with *credo*—i.e., *suppongo* (I suppose), *temo* (I fear), *spero* (I hope)—are all intuitively amenable to an epistemic analysis, expressing different degrees of certainty. Analogously, the verbs patterning with *dicono* are all interpretable as evidentials. Interestingly, other verbs which cannot be analysed in this way are not acceptable as verbal parentheticals. Consider for instance the following examples:[21]

(70) *Maria (rimpiango)₁ è (rimpiango)₂ andata (rimpiango)₃ a Parigi (rimpiango)₄
       Maria ((I) regret) has(IND) ((I) regret) gone ((I) regret) to Paris ((I) regret)

(71) *Maria (so)₁ è (so)₂ andata (so)₃ a Parigi (so)₄
       Maria ((I) know) has(IND) ((I) know) gone ((I) know) to Paris ((I) know)

(72) *Maria (telefonano)₁ è (telefonano)₂ andata (telefonano)₃ a Parigi (telefonano)₄
       Maria ((they) call) has(IND) ((they) call) gone ((they) call) to Paris ((they) call)

The reason for this incompatibility might follow from the analysis of the mono-verbal parentheticals I proposed above. Only the verbs which are compatible with an epistemic or evidential analysis can be generated as epistemic and evidential adverbs, and consequently occupy the Modifier position licensing them as mono-verbal parentheticals. Other first person or third person verbal forms, even if looking superficially identical, cannot.[22]

---

[21] Notice that the English translation might be misleading. The English *I regret*, which is certainly acceptable, at least in position 4:

i.   Mary left, I regret

is not in this case really corresponding to *rimpiango*, which would be its literal translation, but rather to the Italian *temo* (lit: I fear), which is acceptable as well:

ii.   Maria è partita, temo
      Mary left, I regret (lit: I fear)

Consider also that *so* (I know) gives unacceptable results, but the locution *per quel che ne so* (as far as I know) is on the contrary acceptable in both languages:

iii. Maria (per quel che ne so)₁ è (per quel che ne so)₂ andata (per quel che ne so)₃ a Parigi (per quel che ne so)₄
      Maria (as far as I know) has(IND) (as far as I know) gone (as far as I know) to Paris (as far as I know)

[22] Following the analysis provided by Cinque (1999), evaluative adverbs are structurally very close to evidential and epistemic ones. So far, however, I have not been able to identify a verbal evaluative item similar to *credo* and *dicono*. Further investigation is required.

3.5 Further issues: interrogatives and embedded contexts

In this section I consider some issues closely connected with the investigation of the position occupied by *credo* in the sentence and therefore with the syntactic properties of the speaker's projection. I show that, due to its first person feature specification, epistemic *credo* is incompatible with questions, behaving differently in this respect from other epistemic adverbs. For the same reason, I show that it cannot appear in embedded clauses. I briefly analyse the distribution of items that might linearly and hierarchically precede the speaker's projection in the left periphery.

As briefly discussed in section 3.4, according to Rizzi (2002), the pre-sentential position of an adverb is derived via movement from a sentence internal one. The MOD(ifier) position is lower than that of wh-items and interrogative phrases such as *perché* (why). Rizzi (2002) does not consider epistemic and evaluative adverbs in particular, but they seem to follow the same generalization, in that they cannot precede the interrogative position:

(73) *Fortunatamente, chi ha vinto la gara?
      Luckily, who won the race?

(74) *Fortunatamente, perché Gianni ha vinto la gara?
      Luckily, why did Gianni win the race?

(75) Chi fortunatamente ha vinto la gara?
      Who luckily won the race?

(76) Perché fortunatamente Gianni ha vinto la gara?
      Why did luckily Gianni win the race?

(77) *Sicuramente, chi ha vinto la gara?
      Surely, who won the race?

(78) *Sicuramente, perché Gianni ha vinto la gara?
      Surely, why did Gianni win the race?

(79) Chi sicuramente ha vinto la gara?
      Who surely won the race?

(80) Perché sicuramente Gianni ha vinto la gara?
      Why did surely Gianni win the race?

Both *fortunatamente* (fortunately) and *sicuramente* (surely) can only follow the interrogative phrase, as expected if its position is higher than the Modifier one. *Credo* does not pattern in this way, given that it does not exhibit any contrast between a pre-interrogative position and a post-interrogative one:

(81)   *Chi credo abbia vinto la gara?
        Who do (I) believe won the race?

(82)   *Perché credo Gianni abbia vinto la gara?
        Why do (I) believe Gianni won the race?

(83)   *Credo chi abbia vinto la gara?
        (I) believe who won the race?

(84)   *Credo perché Gianni abbia vinto la gara?
        (I) believe why Gianni won the race?

A sentence such as (81) can only be accepted as a pseudo-echo, rhetorical, question when endowed with an appropriate intonation. The non-echo reading, in which I ask myself about the person I believe has won the race, is syntactically available but semantically nonsense. As to (82), it can be used again as a pseudo-echo question, on a par with (81), or as a way to ask the reason why I (the speaker) have that specific belief, a nonsense again. Excluding the pseudo-echo question case, therefore, the only possibility for these sentences to be grammatical consists in assigning them a bi-clausal analysis. Even this possibility, however, is ruled out in examples (83) and (84), because of the impossibility of assigning them the correct syntactic structure. Therefore, there is no way in which epistemic *credo* can be compatible with interrogative phrases.

The analysis discussed here provides an explanation for these observations. In examples (81) and (82) *credo*, if interpreted as an epistemic head, must be taken to appear in the basic Modifier position. Since it bears first person singular features it is *speaker-oriented*. Questions, however, are typically hearer-oriented: it is the point of view of the addressee that they ask about. Hence, there is no way of making the two compatible and the only possible reading is the bi-clausal one.

In examples (83) and (84) on the other hand, *credo* has moved to the high speaker position in the C-layer. The mono-clausal analysis is impossible for the reasons just given and the bi-clausal one is also ruled out, due to the syntactic position of *credo*. Consequently, in this case even the pseudo-echo interpretation is not available. *Dicono*, on the contrary, is predicted to be compatible with questions:

(85) Chi dicono abbia vinto la gara?
      Who do (they) say won the race?

(86) *Dicono chi abbia vinto la gara?
      They say who won the race?

As expected, *dicono* can only follow and not precede the Interrogative position because it is not forced out of its Modifier position.

This analysis also predicts that *credo* is incompatible with embedded contexts. To illustrate this point, let's consider more closely the meaning associated with epistemic adverbs:

(87) Probabilmente Gianni è partito
      Probably Gianni left

(88) Maria ha detto che probabilmente Gianni è partito
      Maria said that probably Gianni left(IND)

(89) Maria crede che probabilmente Gianni sia partito
      Maria believes that probably Gianni left(SUBJ)

The adverb *probabilmente* (probably) in sentence (87) expresses the opinion of the *speaker* concerning the embedded event. Namely, according to the speaker, the (past) leaving of Gianni is probable. The adverb in the embedded clause in example (88) does not express the point of view of the speaker, but of the referent of the grammatical subject—that is, *Maria*. The same holds of (89): the bearer of the attitude with respect to the content expressed by the embedded clause, Maria, is the person whose epistemic point of view is reported by means of the epistemic adverb. On the other hand, the epistemic adverbs in examples (88) and (89) cannot be used to express the point of view of the speaker. In other words, they are interpreted *locally*, and, to the extent the metaphor goes, they cannot be interpreted *de-re*.

It is possible to express these properties by saying that the epistemic adverb is *anchored* at the interface to the bearer of the attitude. The anchoring has the purpose and the effect of linking the epistemic state to a subject: the speaker in the case of main clauses, and the bearer of the attitude in the case of embedded ones. In a way, this process is analogous to what happens with the temporal interpretation—see Giorgi and Pianesi (2001a, 2003, 2004b)—and with the binding of long distance anaphors—see Giorgi (2006, 2007).

With these remarks in mind, consider what happens in the case of an interrogative sentence:

(90)   Chi probabilmente è andato a Parigi?
       Who probably went to Paris?

The adverb *probably* in this case does not refer to the epistemic state of the speaker. It can have the *objective* meaning—i.e., the speaker might be enquiring about the people having an objective probability of having left for Paris. The speaker might also be asking about the person who *probably* left *according to the hearer's opinion*. Namely, in this case the interpretation is epistemic again and the bearer of the epistemic state is the addressee. Even in this case, therefore, the anchoring of the epistemic adverb is shifted, in the sense that it is not referred to the speaker, but to another discourse participant.

Consider now epistemic *credo* in embedded clauses. Recall that a preverbal subject in CD structures is acceptable only for a group of speakers, call it group (a). For group (b), i.e., the speakers who do not admit a preverbal lexical subject with CD sentences, its presence gives rise to ungrammaticality:

(91)   Maria ha detto che credo Gianni si sia sbagliato ("*"for group (b))
       Maria said that (I) believe (Gianni) was wrong

(92)   Maria ha detto a tutti che io credo che Gianni si sia sbagliato
       Maria told everybody that I believe that Gianni was wrong

For group (b) speakers, therefore, the presence of subject *Gianni* in sentence (91) is a test for mono-clausality, i.e., can only be possible with the epistemic interpretation of *credo*. Interestingly, for these speakers the sentence in (91) is ungrammatical. This piece of evidence can be readily explained on the basis of the hypothesis proposed here: the anchoring of epistemics must be local, but *credo* can only refer to the speaker, because of its feature specifications.

The sentence in (92), on the other hand, is a normal sentence, in which *credo* heads a verbal projection and takes a C projection as a complement—no CD—and is therefore grammatical for everybody.

One might wonder why in a sentence such as (92), which is a Double Access Reading one, the embedded C-speaker position is not available for valuing the features of the epistemic *credo*.

My proposal is that actually the intermediate speaker's coordinates are available for valuing *credo*, from the syntactic point of view. The interpretive component, however, gives a deviant result. Note in fact that by means of a communication verb such as *dire* (say), the speaker reports the content of a speech act by the subject, so that it is impossible to assign *credo* an epistemic interpretation obligatorily referring to the actual speaker, while being embedded under a communication predicate. In other words, *credo* must have been part of the original speech act, but if so, it cannot be reported by means of an item marked with unvalued first person features. The appropriate report would therefore be something like the following one:

(93)   Maria ha detto che *secondo lei* Gianni si era sbagliato
       Maria said that *according to her* Gianni was wrong

Or, conversely, something like the following:

(94)   Maria ha detto che *secondo me* Gianni si era sbagliato
       Maria said that *according to me* Gianni was wrong

It depends on the owner of the reported epistemic opinion. Note also that, as expected under this hypothesis, the epistemic reading of *credo* is much more acceptable if the main clause features the first person:

(95)   Ho scritto a Luisa che credo Gianni si sia sbagliato
       I wrote to Luisa that I believe Gianni was wrong

According to my judgement, and that of other speakers as well, in this case, it is possible to understand the sentence in the following way: the content I wrote is '*Gianni was wrong*', but in reporting it I am further qualifying it as less than a certainty—i.e., I am attributing to it my own epistemic evaluation. Notice that for group (b) speakers, rejecting the preverbal subject with CD, this is the only possible interpretation. Speakers who accept a preverbal subject might also have a second reading, according to which *credo* is part of the content of my writing—i.e., *I wrote that I think*, etc.

Finally, compare epistemic adverbs with speech act ones. A speech act adverb like *francamente* cannot be embedded, analogously to what happens for *credo*:

(96)   Francamente, Gianni si è sbagliato
        Frankly, Gianni was wrong

(97)   *Maria credeva che, francamente, si fosse sbagliato
        Maria believed that, frankly, he was wrong

However, it can appear in interrogative clauses:

(98)   Francamente, chi si è sbagliato?
        Frankly, who was wrong?

Interestingly, this sentence is ambiguous. It can have a rhetorical meaning, to convey, e.g., that I, the speaker, do not think that anybody was wrong: *Francamente, chi si e' sbagliato? Nessuno!* (Frankly, who was wrong? Nobody!) But if interpreted as a real question, *frankly* necessarily refers to the hearer—namely, the speaker is asking for the hearer's frank opinion: you, the hearer, be frank, and tell me who was wrong. This adverb can therefore shift from the speaker to the hearer, though it cannot shift to the bearer of an attitude. As it seems, the shifting is licensed in (98) because the hearer is supposed to be the performer of the speech act that follows.

To conclude, it is possible to hypothesize the presence of three different groups of adverbs. *Probably* can freely shift, as required by the context. *Credo* never shifts and can only refer to the speaker—as expected, given its first person features. *Frankly* can shift, but only as far as a communicative act is involved.

Speculatively, these facts might be accounted for by claiming that there is a very high left position including the *situation* coordinates where *frankly* ends up.

For completeness, notice that *francamente* (frankly) can precede *credo*, though the latter occupies the left-most position in the C-layer:

(99)   Francamente, credo dicano Maria sia andata a Parigi
        Frankly, I believe they say Maria went to Paris

The presence of *dicono* makes sure that *credo* actually moved past it in C-speaker. This piece of evidence might point to the conclusion that there is a root layer connecting the sentence to the actual discourse. Though this consideration is certainly intriguing, I will not pursue this topic any further in this book, because it would lead me too far way from the main topics under discussion.

3.6 Conclusions

Summarizing so far, the presence of a subjunctive in the sentences headed by *credo* and *dicono* is due to a syntactic relation among the main verb, the C-layer, and the embedded verbal form. The superordinate verb selects for a peculiar configuration of the C-layer, which in turn selects the subjunctive form. Therefore, the subjunctive is locally due to a peculiar relation between the C-layer and the projections of the verb. The items in question however are not verbal forms, realizing a syntactic clause, but functional heads, expressing epistemicity—*credo*—and evidentiality—*dicono*.

The properties of the epistemic head *credo* (I believe) and of the evidential one *dicono* provide an argument in favour of the existence of a position dedicated to the representation of the speaker's coordinates. The contrast between the two items can be traced back to the impossibility for *dicono*—a third person plural form—to move to this left-periphery head. *Credo*, by contrast, being first-person, can be hosted there, giving rise to the variety of phenomena just discussed.

Therefore, even if in Italian there is no specific lexical realization of the C-speaker position, it can be concluded that under special conditions a lexical item with first person features can appear there.

This piece of evidence is important because it shows that the Complementizer position hypothesized in this book is relevant both for interpretive purposes, as exemplified in the previous chapter, and also for purely syntactic ones—i.e., for mere word order considerations. In the minimalist perspective, this would be to say that the position is both spelled out when necessary and interpreted when required.

4

Is the Speaker There? An Analysis of Some Anomalous Contexts

4.1 Introduction

In this chapter I am going to analyse two cases in Italian in which the embedded verbal form does not give rise to the Double Access Reading, even if it is not a subjunctive: the imperfect of the indicative and the future-in-the-past.

The issue is relevant with respect to the syntax of the Complementizer, because in both cases—with a special *proviso* for the future-in-the-past—the Complementizer is the same one appearing in the usual indicative contexts and therefore providing the speaker's coordinates. As a consequence, a DAR interpretation is in principle expected, contrary to the facts. These cases therefore constitute a *prima facie* problem for the thesis discussed in this book: if the interface between the sentence and the context is provided by the presence of a certain projection in the C-layer, a uniform behaviour is predicted, but this prediction is apparently not borne out.

I will show that in both cases the theoretical proposal argued for in this book can be maintained and, more interestingly, it contributes to clarifying some facts with respect to these verbal forms, which would remain otherwise unexplained.

In particular, the imperfect will be characterized as an *anti-speaker* form, formally marked as [−speaker]. This specification will be shown to account not only for its lack of DAR, but also for a set of other properties, such as the obligatoriness of a temporal topic— the so-called *anaphoricity* of the imperfect—its availability in fictional contexts, and its (substandard) acceptability in subjunctive environments. In this light, I will also consider the properties of the English past, given that in many cases, in particular in modal and fictional contexts, it plays the same role as the Italian imperfect of the indicative.

I will also consider the future-in-the-past in Italian, comparing it with the English one. I will show that it is compatible both with the Complementizer endowed with the speaker's coordinates and with the subjunctive Complementizer. Temporally, it expresses a present tense value, combined with a resultant state—similarly to the English present perfect. Its peculiar interpretive properties, as a future-in-the-past, are obtained by means of an empty modal expressing futurity. Its apparent lack of DAR in indicative contexts is actually due to the fact that the item which is located with respect to the subject's and speaker's coordinates is the (empty) modal expressing futurity.

4.2 The imperfect

4.2.1 *The issue*

The analysis of the imperfect I provide here is exclusively focused on the topic of this book, i.e., the presence of the speaker's coordinates in the C-layer. Therefore, I will not consider its properties exhaustively, given that such a discussion would not be pertinent to the issue addressed here.[1]

The imperfect verbal form is usually considered a form of the indicative, often characterized as an *anaphoric* past form. This characterization stems from the fact that its usage is infelicitous in out-of-the-blue sentences—i.e., those sentences that are not connected to the previous discourse. It requires a temporal topic locating it in the past:[2]

---

[1] See, among others, Delfitto (2004), Delfitto and Bertinetto (2000), Bertinetto and Delfitto (2000), Ippolito (2001, 2004). For a general view concerning the very complex relationships between verb classes and aspect, see among others, Ramchand (1997).

[2] In example (3) the star is in brackets. In some cases, the imperfect is compatible with a future temporal expression, as I will discuss in a while.

(1)   #Gianni mangiava un panino
       Gianni was eating a sandwich

(2)   Ieri alle tre Gianni mangiava un panino
       Yesterday at three Gianni was eating a sandwich

(3)   (*)Domani alle tre Gianni mangiava un panino
       Tomorrow at three Gianni was eating a sandwich

Sentence (1) is acceptable only if the context provides a suitable temporal topic. Example (2) is acceptable even without a preceding context and contrasts with example (3), where the temporal reference is not past but future. On the compatibility of the imperfect with the future, there is however more to be said and I will return to this topic below. For the time being, if suffices to note that in absence of any further specification the 'natural' usage of the imperfect is as given in example (2).

It also important to point out that the imperfect encodes a peculiar aspectual value. Note for instance that the English glosses of (1)–(3) are given by means of the English progressive. Even if in Italian there is a *real* progressive form, the translation in English of a sentence such as (2) is best given as a past progressive. The Italian progressive periphrasis is given in example (4):

(4)   Ieri alle tre Gianni **stava mangiando** una mela
       Yesterday at three Gianni was eating a sandwich

The progressive periphrasis is constituted by the auxiliary *stare* (stay) plus the gerund of the verb.

Giorgi and Pianesi (2001b and 2004a) pointed out that the English progressive is actually closer to the Italian progressive periphrasis than to the imperfect. In many contexts, however, the two are functionally equivalent. The aspectual value of the imperfect has been described as opposed to the perfective one—see for instance Delfitto (2004). The imperfect allows a perspective on the event *from the inside*, cf. Bertinetto (1986, 1997), permitting overlap between different events, as in the following case:

(5)   Mentre Gianni suonava il piano, Maria lavava i piatti
       While Gianni was playing(IMPF) the piano, Maria was washing(IMPF) the dishes

In a sentence such as (5) the two events are seen as simultaneous. The playing of the piano provides the temporal reference for the washing of the dishes and vice versa. Although the aspectual considerations play an important role in the analysis of the imperfect, in this work I will try to abstract away from them. The focus of this work lies in the relationships between the various verbal forms and the C-layer and not in the perspective they allow on the events. I will only occasionally mention the aspectual properties of the imperfect when necessary; for a more thorough discussion, I refer the reader to the cited references.[3]

4.2.2 *The imperfect as an indicative verbal form*

There are several arguments that assimilate the imperfect to the indicative forms. For instance, it can appear in main clauses and give rise to an assertion like an ordinary indicative and as opposed to a subjunctive verbal form:

(6)   Ieri alle tre Gianni ha mangiato un panino
      Yesterday at three Gianni ate (PAST) a sandwich

(7)   *Ieri alle tre Gianni mangiasse un panino
       Yesterday at three Gianni ate (PAST SUBJ) a sandwich

(8)   Ieri alle tre Gianni mangiava un panino
      Yesterday at three Gianni ate (IMPF) a sandwich

Example (7) is not an assertion, contrasting with the sentence containing an indicative past verb in example (6). The imperfect in (8) patterns with the indicative and not with the subjunctive.

   The other important property the imperfect shares with the indicative concerns the embedded contexts in which it is allowed. Again it patterns with the indicative forms and not with the subjunctive, as in the following cases:

(9)   Gianni ha detto che Maria è partita
      Gianni said that Maria left (lit: has(PRES IND) left)

---

[3] See among others Smith (1997) for an analysis of the imperfect as a form that does not identify event boundaries. A discussion of this issue is however outside the scope of the present work.

(10)   Gianni ha detto che Maria era partita
       Gianni said that Maria had(IMPF) left

(11)   Gianni desiderava che Maria partisse
       Gianni wished that Maria left(PAST SUBJ)

(12)   *Gianni desiderava che Maria è partita
       Gianni wished that Maria left (lit: has (PRES IND) left)

(13)   *Gianni desiderava che Maria partiva
       Gianni wished that Maria left(IMPF)

The imperfect is compatible only with those environments allowing the indicative, whereas it is not compatible as a subordinate form under a verb like *desiderare* (wish), which in Italian strongly requires a subjunctive—cf. examples (12) and (13).

Etymologically, the modern Italian imperfect is derived from the Latin imperfect. The morphological derivation is rather transparent; for instance, in *laud-a-ba-nt* (they praised) the morphemes are ordered as follows: verbal root (praise) + thematic vowel + temporal morpheme + inflection. The Italian *lod-a-va-no* has exactly the same sequence, with only minor phonological changes: verbal root + thematic vowel + temporal morpheme + inflection. The Latin form had the temporal value of a past, in a very similar way to the Italian. Giorgi and Pianesi (1991) remarked that even if the Latin indicative temporal system is different from the Italian one, the relation of the imperfect form *laudabam* (I praised-IMPF) with the perfect *laudavi* (I praised-PERF) closely resembles the opposition between the contemporary Italian present perfect *ho lodato* (I have praised) and the imperfect *lodavo*. The imperfect is fully inflected for person and number, with no syncretism, and the inflectional endings are exactly the ones used in the present tense:[4]

(14)   Io lodav**o** (I praised)
       Tu lodav**i** (you praised)
       Egli lodav**a** (etc.)

---

[4] Notice also that it is fully regular, as opposed to the present tense and the simple past. Namely, when the verb exhibits suppletive forms in the present or in the simple past, the imperfect never does, being derived fully regularly from the stem of the infinitive. *Io vado* (I go) vs *io andavo* (I went-IMPF) and *io vidi* (I saw-SIMPLE PAST) vs *io vedevo* (I saw-IMPF).

> Noi loda**va**mo
> Voi loda**va**te
> Essi loda**va**no

(15) Io lod**o** (I praise)
Tu lod**i** (You praise)
Egli lod**a** (etc.)
Noi lod**iamo**
Voi lod**ate**
Essi loda**no**

Assuming that the function of the inflectional morpheme is self-evident, one might ask what is the role of the intermediate morpheme *-va-* that characterizes the imperfect, as opposed to the present. The first answer one can think of is that somehow it expresses a *past* value, and as a matter of fact sentences such as (3) above are deviant. Apparently, the reason is that in sentence (3) there is a future time reference, contrasting with the verbal morphology. There is however an important consideration: it is not always the case that the future time reference with the imperfect gives rise to a deviant result. With a suitable background, it is possible to combine a future reference with an imperfect verbal form, whereas this is never possible with other past forms, such as a simple past or a present perfect. Consider the following discourse:

(16) A: Verrà anche Gianni alla festa di domani?
A: Will Gianni come as well to tomorrow's party?

(17) B: Non so. Domani usciva con Maria
B: I do not know. Tomorrow he *went*(IMPF) out with Maria

The answer given by speaker B is perfectly appropriate. It has a *modal* flavor, meaning something like *he is supposed to leave with Maria*.
Compare example (17) with the following ones:

(18) B: Non so. Domani esce con Maria
B: I do not know. Tomorrow he goes(PRES) out with Maria

(19) B: Non so. Domani uscirà con Maria
B: I do not know. Tomorrow he will go(FUT) out with Maria

What is the difference between the imperfect and the other two forms? I will not extensively discuss here the value of the present *pro* future in (18) with respect to the future. Simplifying, the usage of the present tense with future time reference is appropriate when at utterance time the conditions already hold for a future event. In this sense, the Italian present pro future resembles the English one, with the only difference that in English this effect is even stronger and actually requires the existence of a real *agenda*, or schedule, to be appropriate. Consider for instance the following sentence:

(20)   John leaves tomorrow at three

This sentence is acceptable only in the context in according to which the person speaking is talking about the *already scheduled* activities by John.

Conversely, a past form other than the imperfect is never compatible with future time reference:

(21)   B: *Non so. Domani è uscito con Maria
       B: I do not know. Tomorrow he went(PRES PERF) out with Maria

(22)   B: *Non so. Domani uscì con Maria
       B: I do not know. Tomorrow he went(SIMPLE PAST) out with Maria

Therefore, though behaving as an indicative, the imperfect does not share the distributional properties of the other past forms.

Coherently with its characterization as an indicative, it disallows Complementizer Deletion:

(23)   Gianni ha detto *(che) era partita
       Gianni said (that) she had(IMPF) left

As was illustrated in the preceding chapter, this is different from the subjunctive verbal forms:

(24)   Gianni credeva (che) fosse partita
       Gianni believed that she had(SUBJ) left

Unlike the indicative, however, the imperfect does not give rise to any Double Access Reading effect. In the previous chapter, I characterized the DAR as a double interpretation of the tense, once with respect to the subject's coordinate, and once with respect to the speaker's coordinate. Therefore, in the case of a past under past, the embedded verbal form is interpreted as past both with respect to the temporal location of the superordinate subject and with respect to the temporal location of the utterer, both in Italian and English:

(25) Gianni ha detto che Maria ha mangiato/mangiò un panino
      Gianni said that Maria ate(PRES PERF/SIMPLE PAST) a sandwich

In this case, the only available interpretation is that the eating precedes both the saying and *now*.

In Italian, however, if the present perfect/simple past is substituted by an imperfect, the interpretation is not the same any more:

(26) Gianni ha detto che Maria mangiava un panino
      Gianni said that Maria ate(IMPF) a sandwich
      'Gianni said that Maria was eating a sandwich'

In this case, the interpretation is that the eating is simultaneous to the superordinate event—namely, the eating takes place during the saying. Since the saying precedes the utterance time, the embedded event is taken to precede it as well.

The imperfect by itself however does not need to be interpreted as past with respect to *now*. Consider for instance the following example:

(27) Sono sicura che domani Gianni e Maria litigheranno. Ma fra due giorni Gianni dirà che Maria aveva ragione
      I'm certain that tomorrow Gianni and Maria will quarrel. But in two days Gianni will say that Maria was(IMPF) right

In example (27) the scene is explicitly set in the future by means of the first sentence. In the second sentence there is an embedded imperfect, clearly referring to a state following the utterance time. The dependencies from the future verbal forms will be analysed in Chapter 5, but for the time being it might be relevant to consider how the imperfect does not necessarily refers to events or states located in the speaker's past. Notice also that in example (27) there is no *modal* flavor at all associated with the embedded imperfect, contrary to what was argued with respect to sentence (17) above.

Consider finally the following sentence:

(28) Gianni ha detto che Maria partiva ieri/oggi/domani
      Gianni said that Maria left(IMPF) yesterday/today/tomorrow

The imperfect in the embedded clause in this case is totally undetermined with respect to the utterance time, to the effect that any indexical time reference whatsoever is compatible with it.[5]

To conclude, the imperfect is not a *past* verbal form. For one thing, it is not necessarily interpreted as a past with respect to *now*, and secondly, it is not always interpreted as a past with respect to a main verbal form.

Consider finally another important property of the imperfect. As discussed by Giorgi and Pianesi (2001b), it appears in many languages in the contexts created by fictional predicates, as for instance *dream*:

(29)   Gianni ha sognato che Maria partiva
       Gianni dreamed that Maria left(IMPF)

In this case, the imperfect is totally atemporal. It is not a *past*, either with respect to the utterance time or with respect to the main predicate. It simply contributes to expressing the *content* of the dream. Consider also that in these contexts, the subjunctive is not acceptable:

(30)   *Gianni ha sognato che Maria partisse
       Gianni dreamed that Maria left(PAST SUBJ)

This observation shows again that the imperfect does not pattern with the subjunctive.

4.2.3 *The interpretation of the imperfect -va- morpheme*

What is the interpretive value that has to be assigned to the imperfect morphology? Summarizing the results of the previous section: the imperfect is an indicative verbal form; it appears in main assertions; it is *not* a past—though it is *compatible* with a past interpretation, which is very frequently assigned to it. My proposal in this book is that the morpheme *-va-* is the lexicalization of the feature [−speaker].[6]

---

[5] The dependencies from a main future will be discussed in Chapter 5.

[6] Following a remark by a reviewer, let me point out that the feature [± speaker] exclusively concerns verbal morphology, and is not associated with DP, even with first or second person pronouns. The fact that there might be verbal properties as opposed to nominal

Iatridou (2000), von Fintel and Iatridou (2006), and Iatridou and von Fintel (2007) account for the fact that in many languages the past morphology can be used with a *modal* meaning—i.e., a meaning not involving a past *temporal* value—suggesting that such a morphology can realize an *exclusion* feature. In the temporal domain such a feature implies that the topic time excludes the utterance time—hence, as a (necessary) default it gives rise to a past temporal interpretation. In the modal domain, their proposal amounts to saying—simplifying somehow—that the topic worlds exclude the actual world, whence the *modal* meaning.

The hypothesis I argue for in this chapter is much in the same vein, with the difference that according to my suggestion the feature specification of the imperfect is not only relevant at the interface, but is part of the syntactic process itself.

Iatridou (2000), von Fintel and Iatridou (2006), and Iatridou and von Fintel (2007)'s proposal would in fact be too general for Italian. The main empirical problem with it is that only the imperfect morphology seems to have this ambivalent status (i.e., modal and temporal) whereas the (other) past tenses (both the present perfect and the simple past) and the future do not exhibit this bivalent behaviour. Moreover, the important property I try to account for is that the imperfect, when temporally interpreted, obligatorily requires a temporal topic. I am going to propose that by means of the feature [−speaker], it is possible on one hand immediately to connect the imperfect to the characteristics of the C-layer I am discussing here—without postponing the outcome to an interpretive level—and on the other, to account for its temporal/modal value alternation.

This proposal shares some preliminary considerations with the one discussed in Giorgi and Pianesi (2004b).[7] Giorgi and Pianesi argued that the imperfect is not a relational, two-place predicate verbal form, such as the 'normal' past and future tenses of the

property is a not an *ad hoc* hypothesis, given that this is the case with many inflectional morphemes, which may occur with nouns, but not with verbs and vice versa.

[7] On the semantic value of the Italian imperfect in *if* clauses, see also Ippolito (2004).

indicative, but is a one-place predicate, hence, not *a priori* specified as a tense. They claimed that its peculiar behaviour and distribution were due to its additional feature specifications, to the effect of requiring it to be a *present in the past* of some sort.

In this chapter I am crucially *not* assuming that the imperfect is a present in the past, but I will assume that it is a non-relational verbal form—i.e., not in the form of a two-place predicate, but with a single position—obligatorily anchored like all other verbal forms, and specified as being an anti-speaker—i.e., [-speaker]—tense.

4.2.3.1 *The temporal value of the imperfect in main clauses* Let's consider as a first case the interpretation of the imperfect as a main clause past. As illustrated in examples (1)–(3) it obligatorily requires a temporal topic, either in the previous discourse or in the sentence. Consider examples (1) and (2) again:

(31)   #Gianni mangiava un panino
        Gianni was eating a sandwich

(32)   Ieri alle tre Gianni mangiava un panino
        Yesterday at three Gianni was eating a sandwich

Once Tense is merged with vP, the feature on the phase edge accessible to the probe-goal relation is the uninterpretable feature [−speaker], corresponding to the imperfect morphology. Recall also that events are obligatorily anchored, as discussed in Chapter 2. The anchoring is provided through the interpretable feature τ in C-speaker, i.e., the speaker's coordinate. But the probe in C cannot value the uninterpretable feature of v^*, which therefore cannot be deleted. Hence, the derivation crashes.

The temporal topic *ieri alle tre* (yesterday at three), by contrast, bears the interpretable feature [−speaker], given that its contribution to the meaning is to locate the event somewhere *else*—and precisely *yesterday at three*—with respect to the speaker's temporal location. It probes the goal and deletes the feature carried by the imperfect. The event of eating, located *yesterday at three*, is then anchored to C-speaker. The final interpretation is therefore that there is an event of eating taking place *not* at the speaker's temporal location, but in her past, and precisely *yesterday at three*.

The derivation of a sentence with a future temporal topic is identical. Consider for instance the following example (see also example (17) above):

(33)   Domani Gianni usciva con Maria
        Tomorrow Gianni went(IMPF) out with Maria

The only difference is that the leaving event in this case is located in the future of the speaker, by means of *tomorrow*, and not in her past.

If this is the case, where does the modal flavour of (33) come from? My proposal is that this kind of interpretation is nothing else than a specialization of the imperfect with respect to the other types of futures—i.e., the present-*pro*-future and the future. The other types of future require an explicit location of the event with respect to the speaker's coordinate. As illustrated in Chapters 2 and 3, present, past, and future verbal forms are directly connect to the C-layer, which triggers the interpretation of the verbal form as past, present, or future with respect to the speaker's temporal coordinate. The idea I want to develop in this chapter is that the imperfect is *not* anchored to the speaker and therefore cannot assert the existence of a future event, but only of a *simultaneous* one, demoted in the future by means of temporal specification, such as for instance *domani* (tomorrow). In a way, therefore, the final result is a present-time *expectation* of an event projected in the future.[8]

The event, in other words, when appearing with imperfect morphology, must be interpreted as simultaneous with the temporal specification, which is obligatorily realized—at least in main clauses. Therefore, when the temporal specification is in the future, it does not have the flavour of a *prediction*, as in *Gianni partirà domani*, but of a sort of assertion concerning a future time.[9]

---

[8] I thank a reviewer for this observation.

[9] Some scholars—cf. among others Ippolito (2004)—point out that when in the future, the imperfect loses its aspectual properties and cannot be interpreted as a real imperfective. I would rather adopt Giorgi and Pianesi's (2004a) characterization of the imperfect as a *continuous* verbal form, rather than as an *imperfective* one. I agree that in a sentence such as (33) the verb *usciva* (went out-IMPF) cannot be interpreted as a continuous form. On the other hand, I do not agree with the conclusion usually drawn

The imperfect has a specialized meaning even in the past interpretation. The peculiarity of the imperfect with respect to the other past forms resides in its aspectual properties. Giorgi and Pianesi (2004b) argue that both the simple past and the present perfect are perfective, whereas the imperfect is aspectually neutral, permitting an imperfective interpretation with predicates admitting it.[10] In the future cases, the perfective/imperfective interpretation disappears— given that future events tend to be regarded in general as potentially perfective, hence the modal flavour. In other words: I consider the modal-like interpretation of the future imperfect as an epiphenom- enon and not as a substantial property.

In the following discussion this point will emerge more clearly. For the time being let me only point out that the following sentence might constitute additional evidence in favour of this view:

(34)   Domani Gianni doveva partire
        Tomorrow Gianni was supposed(IMPF) to leave

by the authors—i.e., that this is a typical effect of *modality*. It seems to me that this is part of a more general phenomenon connecting future interpretations with perfectivity. In languages such as Russian, overtly marking perfectivity on the verb, a present perfec- tive must be interpreted as a future. The discussion of aspectual properties however lies beyond the scope of this monograph and I leave the question open for further research.

[10] The main argument provided by Giorgi and Pianesi (2004b) is constituted by the discussion of achievement predicates, such as *raggiungere la vetta* (reach the top). These predicates, which are always telic, are still compatible with the imperfective morphology. Contrary to what happens with the progressive periphrasis, the reaching of the *telos* is not blocked, but the whole event is seen as a perfective continuous one. Consider for instance the following contrast:

i.   Mentre Gianni raggiungeva la vetta, sua madre pregava
      While Gianni reached (IMPF) the top, his mother was praying

ii.   #Mentre Gianni raggiungeva la vetta, un fulmine lo colpì e lui non arrivò mai in cima
      While Gianni reached(IMPF) the top, he was struck by lightning and he never got on top

iii. Mentre Gianni stava raggiungendo la vetta, un fulmine lo colpì, e lui non arrivò mai in cima
      While Gianni was reaching(PROGR) the top, he was struck by lightning and he never got on top

Again, it is impossible to discuss the aspectual properties in this work, and I refer the reader to the quoted references.

In this case the modal meaning is rendered explicit by the presence of the modal *doveva*. The imperfect morphology is however still there and the result in this case is an epistemic interpretation. The sentence in (34) contrasts with the following examples:

(35)   Domani Gianni dovrà partire
       Tomorrow Gianni must(FUT) leave
       'Tomorrow Gianni will have to leave'

(36)   Ieri Gianni è dovuto/dovette partire
       Yesterday Gianni must(PRES PERF/SIMPLE PAST) leave
       'Yesterday Gianni had to leave'

In these cases the modal is interpreted as a root modal, and cannot be an epistemic.[11]

Apparently, the only difference between (34) on one side, and (35)–(36), on the other, is that in the former an imperfect—hence, non-relational—verbal form appears, whereas in the other cases a normal relational tense is realized on the modal.

My proposal provides a simple explanation for this fact. In example (34) the presence of the imperfect prevents the modal from being valued with respect to the speaker's temporal location, thus inhibiting the root reading. The only available reading is the epistemic one, in which the modal does not occupy the verbal head, but a higher epistemic position.[12]

---

[11] On various perspectives concerning the relation between tense and modality see Guéron and Lecarme (2008). In particular for an analysis of the interactions between tense and epistemic/root modals, see Demirdache and Uribe-Extebarria (2006), Guéron (2007), Zagona (2008). See also Zagona (2007).

[12] See Cinque (1999). A reviewer questions this point on the basis that the epistemic reading is a function of the speaker, whereas the temporal root interpretation of the modal is not. This point is certainly correct, and my discussion will not be exhaustive. Let me point out, however, that here I am talking about a syntactic formal relation between the verbal morpheme and the C-layer. This relation is in terms of feature valuing, i.e., of formal anchoring of the predicate/morpheme. This anchoring, as pointed out in general in the literature on the topic, and in particular in Chapter 2 above, is *obligatory*. The epistemic interpretation, being modal, undergoes different requirements, and can be exempted from a formal T-to-C relation. But, if the modal is combined with a regular tense, this is not possible any more, hence, the modal reading is inhibited. The epistemic value comes not from a syntactic anchoring, but as an interpretation assigned to the particular *head* in which the modal is inserted.

Concluding this brief analysis, the presence of the imperfect turns the root modal into an epistemic modal, given that it makes the anchoring of the event to the speaker impossible. When the imperfect co-occurs with a future temporal reference, again the event cannot be (directly) anchored to the utterance event, but it can do so only through the intervention of the temporal specification. Given that a future-located event must be perfective, the particular flavour associated with an imperfect future emphasizes not its aspectual properties but the non-relational nature of the verbal form, which distinguishes it from the normal future. Further arguments in favour of this conclusion will come from the analysis of embedded contexts.

4.2.3.2 *The imperfect in embedded clauses*   Let's consider now the interpretation of the imperfect in embedded contexts:

(37)   Gianni ha detto che Maria mangiava un panino
       Gianni said that Maria ate(IMPF) a sandwich
       'Gianni said that Maria was eating a sandwich'

(38)   Gianni ha detto che Maria era felice
       Gianni said that Maria was happy

The embedded verbal forms—an eventive predicate in (37) and a stative one in (38)—are interpreted as simultaneous with the main predicate—i.e., the *saying*. Both the [−speaker] constraint of the imperfect and the anchoring requirement are therefore met, since the uninterpretable feature of the imperfect is valued by the main past verbal form, which also anchors it. Crucially, the temporal topic can be missing in these cases, precisely because the main verb is a present tense. Consider in this light the following example:[13]

---

[13] A reviewer points out that the judgement in (39) only holds if the eventuality is not a generic one, as for instance, in:

i.   Gianni dice che Maria correva la maratona
     Gianni says that Maria run (IMPF) marathons

I adopt here the analysis provided for these contexts in Giorgi and Pianesi (2001b). They hypothesize, following Chierchia (1995), the presence of a generic operator assigning generic reference to the embedded predicate. Under this assumption, the generic cases should be considered separately, and their properties would not bear on the argument developed here.

(39) #Gianni dice che Maria mangiava un panino
      Gianni says that Maria ate(IMPF) a sandwich
      'Gianni says that Maria was eating a sandwich'

In this case the main verb is a present tense. The embedded imperfect requires a temporal topic, which must either be provided by the discourse or by the sentence:

(40) Gianni dice che ieri alle tre Maria mangiava un panino
      Gianni says that yesterday at three Maria ate(IMPF) a sandwich
      'Gianni says that yesterday at three Maria was eating a sandwich'

In this respect, an embedded imperfect contrasts with an embedded past, which has no need of an explicit or implicit temporal topic:

(41) Gianni dice che Maria ha mangiato un panino
      Gianni says that Maria ate(PRES PERF) a sandwich

The hypothesis I just discussed explains this contrast: the uninterpretable feature of the imperfect cannot be valued by a main present, given that a present does refer to, or at least includes, the utterance time. A non-present temporal topic is therefore needed. No such requirement exists for an embedded relational verbal form like a present perfect/past.

(42) Gianni ha detto che ieri Maria mangiava un panino
      Gianni said that yesterday Maria ate(IMPF) a sandwich

(43) Gianni ha detto che domani Maria mangiava un panino
      Gianni said that tomorrow Maria ate(IMPF) a sandwich

4.3 The imperfect and the subjunctive

It has been often observed that the subjunctive belongs to a higher register and that in normal speech it is often substituted by the indicative. These considerations might deserve a quantitative analysis, both with respect to written and spoken language, but such research would lie outside the domain of this book. On the other hand, however, there are a few observations that might follow from the analysis provided so far with respect to this point.

When asked, Italian speakers usually reject the possibility of substituting an indicative for a subjunctive with verbs belonging to the *wish* class:

(44)   Gianni desiderava che Maria vincesse la gara
        Gianni wished that Maria win(PAST SUBJ) the race

(45)   *Gianni desiderava che Maria ha vinto/vinse la gara
        Gianni wished that Maria has won/won (PRES PERF/SIMPLE PAST) the race

(46)   *?Gianni desiderava che Maria vinceva la gara
        Gianni wished that Maria won(IMPF IND) the race

Between the two ungrammatical options, however, Italian speakers point to (46) as the best one. With *believe* predicates the judgements are, on average, the following:[14]

(47)   Gianni credeva che Maria abitasse a Parigi
        Gianni believed that Maria lived(PAST SUBJ) in Paris

(48)   ?*Gianni credeva che Maria ha abitato/abitò a Parigi
        Gianni believed that Maria lived (PRES PERF/SIMPLE PAST) in Paris

(49)   ?(?)Gianni credeva che Maria abitava a Parigi
        Gianni believed that Maria lived (IMPF) in Paris

Notice that *believe* predicates are the ones that among Romance languages often require the indicative and not the subjunctive, with the exception of Italian and Portuguese.

Here I will not discuss linguistic variation among languages, but will try to explain why the imperfect ranks second after the subjunctive in these contexts.

According to the theory I am proposing here, the subjunctive and the imperfect share certain properties. The subjunctive *does not require* anchoring to the speaker's temporal coordinate and the imperfect *cannot* be anchored to the speaker's temporal coordinate. Recall also, as I discussed above, that the Complementizer preceding the imperfect verbal form cannot be deleted, so that the following sentence is ungrammatical:[15]

---

[14] Notice that in example (48) the interpretation of the embedded past is as a *real* past—i.e., past with respect to the believing—whereas the interpretation given in (47) is a simultaneous one.

[15] Recall also that for some speakers the preverbal subject is incompatible with CD. For this reason, I put the subject *Maria* in brackets.

(50)   *Gianni credeva (Maria) abitava a Parigi
Gianni believed (Maria) lived (IMPF) in Paris

It can be concluded from this evidence that the predicates selecting the subjunctive do so to avoid anchoring the verb in the embedded clause to the speaker's temporal coordinate. Both the subjunctive and the imperfect serve this purpose and therefore some speakers can substitute the one for the other. This possibility follows immediately from the consideration that the imperfect, like the subjunctive, does not give rise to the DAR, so that the interpretative requirements of the main verb are met.[16]

4.4 Is there an imperfect in English?

In the discussion of the DAR in Chapter 2, I pointed out that in non-DAR languages an embedded present tense form would be interpreted like an Italian imperfect, or like an English past tense with stative predicates. Consider the following sentences:

(51)   Gianni ha detto che Maria era malata
Gianni said that Maria was(IMPF) sick

(52)   John said that Mary was sick

As discussed in Chapter 2, sentence (51) does not exhibit any DAR effect. According to the hypothesis just developed, the imperfect is not a relational form, so the presence of the speaker's temporal coordinate in C does not give rise to an interpretation in which the embedded event is evaluated with respect to it. The interpretation of example (51) is that the embedded eventuality holds at the time Gianni said it. The state might persist up to the present moment— i.e., might still hold at utterance time, as discussed in Chapter 2, section 2.2.2—but it *does not have to*. The English sentence has the same meaning, with the interesting addition that, at least for some speakers, it is possible to interpret the temporal location of the

---

[16] Recall, again, that in English there is no detectable difference between the properties of the Complementizer under *say* and under *believe*, given that it can be omitted in both cases.

embedded state as *preceding* the main event of saying. As I have just discussed, this is not possible in Italian, unless a temporal topic is provided—or *understood*, thanks to the previous contexts—in the embedded clause.

The main difference between Italian and English, however, concerns the behaviour of eventive predicates. In Italian they can appear with imperfect morphology and be interpreted in the same way as a stative predicate. Consider for instance the following examples:

(53)   Gianni ha detto che Maria mangiava un panino
Gianni said that Maria eat(IMP) a sandwich
'Gianni said that Maria *was eating* a sandwich'

Here the embedded imperfect is interpreted as a continuous event, simultaneous with the main one. But this meaning cannot be expressed by the English simple past and the embedded verbal form must be translated with a progressive, as shown by the glosses above. If a past tense is used, the reading of the sentence is that the eating event *precedes* the saying event—namely, it is located in the past with respect to it, as in the following example:

(54)   Gianni said that Maria ate a sandwich

Notice also that the equivalent in English of sentence (53)—i.e., the one with the progressive form *was eating*—is actually ambiguous, contrary to the Italian cases with an imperfect, in that many speakers can also interpret it analogously to sentence (54), namely, as a past also with respect to the main verb. In this case, the eventuality is taken to hold at a time preceding the saying. Importantly, this interpretation is not available for the Italian sentence (53), unless a suitable temporal topic is provided. In other words, even in this case it is possible to observe the ambiguity found in the interpretation of sentence (52).

The issue at this point is to verify the nature of the past tense when combined with stative predicates in English and to check whether my proposal can make coherent predictions in this case as well.

Let me now summarize some aspects of the discussion in Giorgi and Pianesi (1997, 2001a) about the role of aspect in the anchoring process. They discussed the aspectual properties of the English and Italian verbal forms and proposed that English eventive verbs are always bounded—i.e., they must be represented as closed sequences of sub-events, hence they always are aspectually *perfective*. Statives, by contrast, are unbounded. Due to the *punctuality constraint*, a bounded sequence cannot coincide with the utterance time, whereas an unbounded one can. The past tense morpheme does not contribute anything in terms of aspectuality—the aspectual value of the English verb being already encoded in the verbal root, contrary to Italian—but only in terms of temporal specifications. It follows, therefore, that an eventive past form is always perfective, hence bounded, whereas a stative verbal form starts as unbounded and will continue to be so, even when combined with a past tense morpheme.

In other words, the basic difference between the Italian past—for instance, Italian *mangiai* (I ate) and English past *I ate*—is that the past morpheme in Italian crucially contributes an aspectual value, i.e., perfectivity, whereas the English past morphology does not, even if in both cases the resulting past form is perfective.[17] In one case—Italian—this is due to past morphology; in the other case—English—it is due to the intrinsic nature of the verbal root itself. The fact that both *mangiai* and *I ate* turn out as perfective is due to the fact that in English an eventive verb is *always* perfective and does not need a special morphology to be interpreted that way.[18]

---

[17] Giorgi and Pianesi (1997, 2001b) consider various phenomena as arguments to this end. An important one is the interpretation of bare VPs in perception contexts. For instance, in English there is a contrast between the following two cases:

i. I saw John play two games

ii. I saw John playing two games

In the first case the meaning of the sentence is that I saw John play the games in a sequence. In the second case, the sentence means that I saw him playing them simultaneously. In the first sentence, the verbal form identifies a closed—bounded, hence perfective—sequence. In the second one it is an open—i.e., unbounded, imperfective—sequence. Given that the only difference between the two cases lies in the verbal morphology, this must be the source of the different interpretation. In particular, since the predicate in (i) is taken to be a bare VP, then it must be concluded that a bare V is perfective in English, contrasting in this respect with other languages, such as for instance Italian. The-*ing* morpheme in (ii) modifies the perfective status of the verb, rendering it an imperfective one.

[18] Recall that in many Italian variants the simple past *mangiai* (I ate) would be substituted with the present perfect *ho mangiato* (lit: I have eaten). The Italian present perfect in these varieties does not have the same value as the English one.

This idea provides an answer to the issue concerning the possibility for an English stative past form to be interpreted as simultaneous with a superordinate saying verb. Still, it does not explain the lack of the DAR in these cases. According to the hypothesis developed here, the embedded verbal form should be evaluated with respect to the matrix predicate *and* with respect to the speaker's temporal coordinate. Therefore, it should be interpreted basically as a present tense, analogously to a sentence such as *John said that Mary is sick.*

Let's pursue the hypothesis discussed above for the Italian imperfect. I will hypothesize here that the English past form is basically ambiguous between a relational form and a non-relational one.

The relational form is *e precedes e'*, where *e'* must be identified both with the utterance event—i.e., the speaker's coordinate—and with the superordinate event. If this is the case, the interpretation of (54) is the usual one—namely, Gianni said that in his past (and in the speaker's past, *a fortiori*) there is an event of Maria eating a sandwich. The interpretation of (52) is the one according to which the state of sickness is taken to precede the event of saying—i.e., to have been originated prior to it.

If the past morpheme is not relational, then one might take into account the possibility that its past flavour is due to the presence of a feature *past*. Even in this case, an embedded verbal form must be anchored to the superordinate one, because anchoring is obligatory. In the absence of any predicate specifying an ordering between events—as for instance, *precede* in the case of a past—the embedded event must be anchored with the *default* interpretation, that is, simultaneity with respect to the anchoring event.

As I discussed above, however, in the case of eventive predicates such an interpretation cannot be provided, since the sequence is bounded and the punctuality constraint prevents the anchoring of a closed sequence with the utterance event.

If the predicate is a stative one, such an anchoring is possible and the interpretation is, coherently, simultaneity. Analogously to the Italian imperfect, when T agrees with C nothing happens, given that it is not a relational tense and the only requirement to be satisfied is the obligatory anchoring to the superordinate attitude predicate.

To conclude, the idea I propose here is that the past form in English is ambiguous between a *real* past and an imperfect-like, in the sense of non-relational, past. This ambiguity shows up only in the case of stative predicates, because, due to aspectual properties, eventive predicates cannot be anchored in the same way as statives, unless they appear in the progressive form.[19]

One might ask at this point if there is any context that selects for one form or the other. In what follows I provide an example of the distribution of past forms in British English in the context created by *believe*. Consider the following paradigm (BE stands for British English, AE for American English):[20]

(55)   John believed Mary is pregnant (*BE; AE)

(56)   John believed Mary was pregnant (BE; AE)

(57)   John believed Mary has been sick (*BE; AE)

(58)   John believed Mary had been sick (BE; AE)

(59)   John believed Mary will be sick (*BE; AE)

(60)   John believed Mary would be sick (BE; AE)

From these examples a pattern emerges showing that British and American English allow a different distribution of the past tense in this context. Note that all the embedded predicates are stative ones, so the differences cannot be traced back to aspectual properties.

However, putting together these observations with the ones above concerning the double specification of the past tense in English, it is possible to account for these differences.

---

[19] See Giorgi and Pianesi (1997, 2004a) for a comparison between the Italian progressive periphrasis and the English progressive form. See also Higginbotham (2004) for a discussion of the properties of the progressive in English. Also Zucchi (1999).

[20] These data are also discussed in a somewhat different perspective in Giorgi and Pianesi (1997). Let me point out that Giorgi and Pianesi first observed it by discussing Abusch's (1997) paper with a British native speaker of English. Then they systematically investigated the pattern and found, as remarked in their work (1997, ch. 4), that British speakers and many American English native speakers do not share the judgement discussed in Abusch (1997). Interestingly, sentence (59) is ungrammatical even for some AE speakers.

Let's hypothesize that for British English speakers—and for some American English speakers as well—*believe* selects for the imperfect-like verbal forms, i.e., for a non-relational verbal form characterized by the feature *past*. Or, as a mirror image of the morphological properties, one might propose that *believe* has an interpretive condition disfavouring the DAR.

This condition would resemble the Italian distribution of indicative and subjunctive: the indicative is selected by communication predicates, whereas *believe* predicates require the subjunctive. That is, in Italian communication predicates such as *dire* require the embedded eventuality to be evaluated also with respect to the speaker's coordinate, hence the DAR. *Credere* (believe) does not have this requirement, in that, being a verb expressing a cognitive state of the subject with respect to a certain content, it does not require the speaker to 'share' responsibility with respect to that content.

The difference between English and Italian is twofold, however: on the one hand, in Italian there are (at least) two possible options with respect to the morphosyntactic structure of the C-layer, in that the high Complementizer C can either be selected or not. In English there is only one possible projection, which I take to correspond to the Italian high C. On the other hand, the form of the verb varies accordingly, indicative vs. subjunctive, whereas this is not the case in English.[21]

This is also exemplified, as pointed out above, by the fact that in some Italian varieties it is possible to have a substandard complement clause, featuring the imperfect instead of the subjunctive, as illustrated above in Chapter 2, section 2.4.1.

Going back to the paradigm (55)–(60), it is possible to see that AE requires the DAR in this context. This is not the case for British English. Let's consider the examples in turn. In example (55) an embedded present tense appears. According to the discussion so far, therefore, the embedded eventuality must be interpreted as overlapping both the superordinate one *and* the speaker's temporal

---

[21] I put aside here the so-called subjunctive in English. For a discussion, see Portner (1997).

coordinate—i.e., the utterance event. The sentence is grammatical in AE, but is ungrammatical in BE. Under the hypothesis that in (British and American) English the high (indicative-like) Complementizer appears, it must be concluded that what differs in this case between the two varieties of English is the nature of the embedded verb.

In British English, *believe* can only appear followed by a non-relational verbal form, so the verbal form *was* must be selected. Its interpretation will be *simultaneity*—i.e., overlapping—with respect to the main event. The present tense cannot appear in this context in BE, given its relational nature. The present tense, when moved in C, would necessarily be interpreted with respect to the utterance time as well, giving rise to the DAR.

In the pair (57)–(58), again in BE the tense morpheme attached to the verb—in this case an auxiliary—must be a non-relational one. Therefore the present perfect is ruled out and the past perfect must be used, since the past form in English has the option of realizing the non-relational *past*. The past interpretation, like in the Italian compound subjunctive, is obtained by means of the past participle.

In the third pair—examples (59)–(60)—the embedded eventuality must be interpreted as a future with respect to the main one. In BE the *will* future is ruled out, since it gives rise to the DAR, and the *would* future is selected.

In the next section, I will provide a brief discussion of the future-in-the-past. For the time being, let me only point out that, according to the reasoning developed so far, the past tense morpheme on the modal must be taken to be the non-relational one. It is possible to conclude, therefore, that the complex modal+past is interpreted as simultaneous with the main eventuality. Since the modal expresses futurity, then the interpretation is the one corresponding to a future with respect to the *believing*.

Let me summarize this brief discussion. In English there is a form functionally equivalent to the Italian imperfect, which is a non-relational past form. In the examples given above, it turns out that this form is compatible only with stative predicates. I explained this property following the analysis provided in Giorgi and Pianesi (1997, 2001a), who argue that it is due to the peculiar aspectual properties of the English verb. As I briefly discussed above, in English an eventive verb is always perfective, unless explicitly marked as a progressive. Therefore, in a context where aspectuality is relevant—in that the embedded form cannot be perfective—this phenomenon can only be observed with stative predicates and not with eventive ones. To illustrate, consider the following example:

(61)   John believed Mary ate a sandwich

Sentence (61) cannot be interpreted as if the event of eating were simultaneous to the believing, but only as a past-under-past, where the eating is in the past with respect to the believing.

In the next section I will consider some cases concerning the non-relational interpretation of eventive predicates.

4.5 Inside a dream

In this section I analyse fictional predicates and in particular the anchoring conditions under a verb such as *sognare* in Italian and *dream* in English. This discussion is not directly relevant with respect to the main hypothesis advanced in this book—i.e., the presence of the speaker's coordinate in C—but only indirectly so, providing strong evidence in favour of the analysis of the imperfect in Italian and of the past tense in English as given above.

Giorgi and Pianesi (2001b) discussed the properties of fictional predicates such as *dream* with respect to Sequence of Tense. Here I will provide a discussion of these contexts in the light of the proposal I am arguing for here.[22]

Giorgi and Pianesi's proposal is that *dream* contexts, both in Italian and English, do not enforce temporal anchoring. The reason for this is that they are not attitude predicates—i.e., they do not entail an attitude by the subject with respect to their propositional content.

---

[22] In this my analysis differs from the one provided by Ippolito (2001) who considers the distribution of the Italian imperfect under *sognare* (dream) as a simple case of *modal imperfect*.

The authors discuss many arguments to this effect; here I will reproduce two.

The first argument concerns the distribution of anaphoric temporal locutions in the context created by *sognare* (dream). These temporal locutions require an antecedent to be provided, either in the sentence or in the previous discourse. Consider for instance the following:

(62) A: Cosa è accaduto ieri alle cinque?
        What happened yesterday at five?

      B: Non so. In quel momento dormivo
        I don't know. At that moment I was sleeping

In this case, the anaphoric temporal locution picks up its reference from the discourse and precisely from *yesterday at five*. The same is true of other locutions such as *il giorno prima* (the day before), *il giorno dopo* (the day after), etc.[23]

In the next chapter I will discuss in more detail how the temporal locution can relate the event with a certain temporal reference—cf. Chapter 5 below. For the time being let me simply propose that whenever the anchoring conditions are not enforced, as in *dream* contexts, reference to the anchor is not possible, hence the anaphoric temporal locution is infelicitous.

If we compare in fact a predicate such as *sognare* (dream) with others such as *dire* (say) and *credere* (believe), we can observe that *credere* and *dire* introduce a temporal referent, which can be picked up by any temporal locution embedded in the subordinate clause. Consider for instance the following examples:

(63) Gianni credeva che in quel momento Maria dormisse
      Gianni believed that in that moment Maria sleep(PAST SUBJ)
      'Gianni believed that in that moment Maria was sleeping'

(64) Gianni ha detto che in quel momento Maria dormiva
      Gianni said that in that moment Maria sleep(IMPF)
      'Gianni said that in that moment Maria was sleeping'

---

[23] For an analysis of temporal locutions in this framework, see Giorgi and Pianesi (2003).

In these examples, the anaphoric temporal locution embedded in the subordinate clause picks up the main eventuality as its reference—namely, the *moment* in question is identified with the time of the saying and the time of the believing respectively. The result emphasizes the simultaneous interpretation, which is normally assigned to these clauses—cf. the discussion above. Importantly, both examples are well formed even in absence of any previous context, i.e., even when used out of the blue.

If the main verb is *sognare* (dream), judgements are different. Consider the following example:

(65)   #Gianni ha sognato che in quel momento Maria dormiva
       Gianni dreamed that in that moment Maria sleep(IMPF)
       'Gianni dreamed that in that moment Maria was sleeping'

This sentence, if uttered out of the blue, is infelicitous, in that it is not possible for the anaphoric temporal locution *in that moment* to refer to the matrix eventuality. The grammatical status of this sentence is similar, to some extent, to that of the following example, used in the absence of any previous context:

(66)   #In quel momento Maria dormiva
       In that moment Maria sleep(IMPF)
       'In that moment Maria was sleeping'

The same results would obtain with other anaphoric temporal locutions, such as *il giorno prima* (the day before):

(67)   #Gianni ha sognato che Maria partiva il giorno prima
       Gianni dreamed that Maria left(IMPF) the day before

It is not possible in this case to assign a correct interpretation to the temporal locution. The sentence in fact should, but cannot, mean that 'Gianni dreamed that Maria left the day before his dream'. In other words, reference to the dreaming event cannot obtain from within the dream itself.

The idea developed by Giorgi and Pianesi is that in these cases the dreamer is not an attitude bearer and therefore the dreaming event itself cannot be part of the embedded content. This reasoning is in line with the proposal put forward by Higginbotham (1995) in his article on tensed thought, and in a way represents its mirror image. Higginbotham (1995) in fact proposed that the clause embedded under an attitude predicate—such as *think*, *fear*, and the like—must include reference to the attitude episode itself. Giorgi and Pianesi strengthened this view by claiming that if something is *not* an attitude predicate it *cannot* be represented in its complement clause, as part of its propositional content.[24]

In this way, a *fearer*, a *believer*, a *wisher*, etc., is conceived of as somebody having an attitude towards a certain content, such as desire, fear, etc. A *dreamer*, on the contrary, does not have any attitude towards the dreamed content, the dream being something that *happens*. A dreamer does not fear, wish, believe, etc., the content of her dream.[25]

The example I provided in (66) contrasts with the following one:

(68)   Ieri alle 5 Gianni ha vinto la gara. Stanotte Paolo ha sognato che in quel momento Mario partiva

Yesterday at 5 Gianni won the race. Last night Paolo dreamed that in that moment Mario leave(IMPF)

'Yesterday at 5 Gianni won the race. Last night Paolo dreamed that in that moment Mario was leaving'

---

[24] For further discussion, see also Higginbotham (2003).

[25] One might fear, believe, wish the content of her dream *after* the dream itself, i.e., when the dream is remembered. This is not relevant to the present discussion. Also a reviewer points out that it might seem that in certain contexts there is actually an ordering between the dreaming event and the content of the event. Consider for instance the following example:

i. Maria ha sognato che Gianni sposava Luisa
    Maria dreamed that Gianni married Luisa

ii. Maria ha sognato che Gianni aveva sposato Luisa
    Maria dreamed that Gianni had married Luisa

It might seem at first sight that sentence (ii) actually means that Maria dreamed of an event past with respect to the dream. I do not think that this is the correct way of describing the meaning of this sentence. The example in (ii) does not mean that Gianni married and *then* Maria dreamed of his marriage. Coherently with what I said in the text, sentence (ii) means that Maria dreamed of an event that, with respect to herself located in certain temporal point *in her dream*, was past with respect *to it*. If we know that Gianni in the real world has married somebody else, this sentence might have a counterfactual flavour, which might perhaps account for the misleading judgement with respect to the temporal ordering.

In (68) *in quel momento* (in that moment) can refer to the event of winning the race. Such an event is provided *outside* the dream context. The ungrammaticality of (65), or of (67), therefore, is not due to the fact that, for some reason, the phrase *in quel momento* (in that moment) cannot find an antecedent when embedded under *dream*, but to a specific property of these contexts, namely, the fact that they are *not* attitude predicates.

According to the discussion above and to the proposal put forth in the preceding chapters, if the attitude bearer is not represented in the embedded clause—i.e., in T, as proposed above—then the embedded verbal form cannot be anchored.

The second argument comes from the observation than in Italian the verb *dream* does not select for a subjunctive, but for an indicative. Actually this is the case quite consistently across languages. Namely, in the languages exhibiting an indicative/subjunctive alternation, the mood appearing in *dream* contexts is always the indicative.

Consider for instance the following examples:

(69)   *Gianni ha sognato che Maria partisse
         Gianni dreamed that Maria leave(PAST SUBJ)

(70)   Gianni ha sognato che Maria partiva
         Gianni dreamed that Maria left(IMPF)

The example in (69) contrasts with the one in (70) precisely for this reason, because in (69) the subjunctive appears, whereas in (70) the verbal bears the imperfect indicative morphology.

The explanation is quite straightforward. The subjunctive *must* be anchored to the superordinate attitude, or otherwise have a modal interpretation, as discussed in the previous chapters. The reason is that the subjunctive must be selected, and selection is the mirror-image of anchoring, namely, a verbal form, if selected, is also necessarily anchored to the item selecting it.[26]

As briefly discussed above, the imperfect is usually anchored. However it is not *selected*, being an indicative, and can therefore

---

[26] Anchoring is implicit in the notion of *selection*. Note that this hypothesis is at odds with Schlenker's (2005) proposal concerning the appearance of the subjunctive, which according to his view is a sort of *default* option.

yield grammatical results even in contexts that do not permit anchoring.

Crucially for the present discussion, the imperfect is also a non-relational verbal form, so it satisfies both requirements imposed by these contexts: there is no mood selection and no anchoring. A non-relational indicative form satisfies both conditions.

The Italian imperfect, as illustrated above, is the only verbal form in the Italian system that is endowed with these properties. In English, I argued above that the past forms are ambiguously specified as both relational and non-relational. In what follows, I discuss the distribution of the English past forms according to the hypotheses illustrated so far.

I proposed in the previous section of this chapter that in an embedded clause a stative predicate can appear without giving rise to the DAR. Consider again the following example:

(71)   John said that Mary was pregnant

In sentence (71) anchoring is enforced, but the possibility for a past tense in English to be non-relational permits anchoring to take place and yield a simultaneous interpretation, as discussed above. However, an eventive predicate is still ungrammatical in the same contexts, due to the *punctuality constraint* holding on temporal anchoring:

(72)   John said that Mary ate an apple

Sentence (72) can only mean that the eating took place *before* the saying, and cannot be simultaneous with it. Therefore, according to the hypothesis, the difference in the interpretation of (71) and (72) stems from the interplay between aspect, temporal morphemes, and anchoring.

As I discussed above, however, *dream* contexts do not require anchoring. Consequently, no contrast should be expected between stative and eventive verbs. Consider the following example:

(73)   John dreamed that Mary was sick

(74)   John dreamed that Mary ate an apple

Sentences (73) and (74) do not contrast, whereas (72) and (74) clearly do. In sentences (73) and (74) there is no *ordering* of the events, namely, the embedded clause only describes the content of the dream. The embedded event is not temporally located in any way with respect to the matrix one. In other words, neither the state of sickness, nor the eating of the apple, are taken to follow, precede, or be simultaneous with the event of dreaming. For (72) to be true, for instance, it must be the case that when John said 'Mary ate an apple', the event had already taken place. By contrast, it is not the case that (74) conveys the meaning that John dreamed of an eating event that took place before his dream. The eating of the apple is simply a *description* of the content of the dream. The past tense therefore is not relational, and the fact that it is admissible even with eventive predicates shows that there is no anchoring at all.

As a further argument in favour of the idea that there is no representation of the dreamer in the embedded clause, consider the following piece of evidence:[27]

(75)   Gianni gli disse che Maria era là
        Gianni told him that Maria was there

(76)   Gianni credeva che Maria fosse là
        Gianni believed that Maria was there

(77)   #Gianni ha sognato che Maria era là
        Gianni dreamed that Maria was there

Indexical reference to the subject's, i.e., Gianni's, spatial location is possible with both *say* and *believe*, whereas it is not available with *dream*. These data parallel the pattern discussed so far with respect to the temporal location and support the idea that, whereas normal attitude contexts (including matrix assertions) incorporate (or provide access to) the coordinate of the attitude bearer, dreams do not. This property shows up both in temporal and in spatial locations.

The remaining question concerns the status of the speaker's projection in these contexts. The proposal I develop here is that the high Complementizer C appears in clauses embedded under *dream*, as shown by the fact that the indicative is selected and that, according to

---

[27] For further arguments and discussion, see Giorgi and Pianesi (2001b).

the main hypothesis, the Complementizer cannot be omitted, as illustrated by the following example:

(78)   Gianni ha sognato *(che) Maria partiva
       Gianni dreamed (that) Maria was leaving (IMPF)

However, given that the imperfect is a non-relational verbal form, the presence of the speaker's coordinate does not have any consequence in terms of DAR. The situation is different when a relational verbal form—i.e., a non-imperfect indicative—appears in the embedded clause. Consider the following cases:

(79)   Gianni ha sognato che c'**è stato** un terremoto
       Gianni dreamed that there has been (PAST IND) an earthquake

(80)   Gianni ha sognato che c'**era** un terremoto
       Gianni dreamed that there was (IMPF) an earthquake

In sentence (79) a non-imperfect indicative appears. The interpretation, contrasting with the one given in (80), is that the dream was in some sense a *prophetic* one, i.e., Gianni dreamed something, which was going to happen (or maybe had already happened). This is dubbed by Giorgi and Pianesi (2001b) *evidential dream*. This effect is absent in (80), where an imperfect appears. The explanation follows precisely from the fact that in (80) an attitude interpretation of the dream is required—namely, the dreamer in this case must have an attitude towards the dream content—and consequently, an ordinary anchoring procedure is needed, as with attitude predicates such as *believe* or *say*. This requirement can only be satisfied by a *real* relational verbal form such as a past form, which must be located with respect to the *dreamer's* coordinates and with respect to the speaker's, as in normal DAR sentences.

4.6 What about languages with no *tense*?

In this section I will briefly address an important issue concerning differences among languages. Besides languages like Italian, showing complex verbal morphology incorporating both temporal and aspectual distinctions, there are languages in which no tense morphemes

show up and the temporal interpretation seems to be totally derivative from aspectual considerations. Languages that have been argued
to exhibit this property are, for instance, Chinese (cf. Lin (2003,
2006), Smith (1997, 2007)), Navajo (cf. Smith (2007)), and Haitian
Creole (cf. DeGraff (2005)).

The obvious question is therefore the following: how do these
languages relate to the context? Are they radically different from
languages showing morphologized temporal distinctions, or is the
absence of temporal morphemes simply an accident with no consequences for the theory proposed here?

In this section I am going to show that the presence of a projection
related to the speaker shows up in environments that are not immediately related to Sequence of Tense issues. Namely, the presence of
the speaker's coordinate gives rise to effects which are detectable in
domains other than the distribution of verbal forms, such as long
distance binding. Here I will briefly discuss evidence from Chinese—
cf. Giorgi (2007, 2006).

4.6.1 *The speaker's projection and long distance anaphors*

As I briefly said above, Italian and Chinese are very different from a
morphological point of view. Italian is a language rich in verbal and
nominal morphology and with a quite complex system of tenses and
moods marked on the verb. Chinese, by contrast, is a language with
almost no morphology and with no tense and mood distinctions
detectable on the verb. One might think therefore that, since there
would not be any use for it, the speaker's representation in embedded
clauses is superfluous and presumably not there at all.

In this section I will show that the presence of a syntactic representation of the speaker's coordinate is necessary in Chinese as well, and
that in this way it is possible to account for (many of) the properties
of the anaphor *ziji* (self), a long distance anaphor.

Long distance anaphors—henceforth LDAs—can be bound
outside the minimal clause containing them and can cross an overt
subject, which is what makes them *long distance* as opposed to *clause
bound*. On the other hand, however, the domain in which they are

allowed to find an antecedent is not unlimited: it does not necessarily extend to include the whole sentence.

The anaphors that I will consider here are the Italian *proprio* (self's)—a third person singular and plural possessive anaphor—and Chinese *ziji* (self)—an anaphor which is neither marked for person nor for number and which can even work as a possessive. These anaphoric items can either be clause bound or long distance bound. Here I will consider their occurrence as LDAs.[28]

The important point for the present investigation concerns the properties delimiting the binding domain for these anaphors in the two languages. Apparently, the conditions forcing the anaphor to find an antecedent inside a certain domain are very different in the two languages—as one might expect, given the great typological distance between them. The conditions delimiting the domain in Italian—and Italian-like languages—have been dubbed in the literature *verbal blocking effect*. The conditions delimiting the binding domain in Chinese—and Chinese-like languages—have been called *nominal blocking effect*. Let me consider first Italian and the verbal blocking effect.[29]

LDAs in Italian show sensitivity to the distinction subjunctive/ infinitive vs. indicative. This property shows up in languages with long distance anaphors having a mood distinction, such as Italian and Icelandic. In these languages, the binding domain of an LDA is usually defined by an indicative mood, whereas a subjunctive/infinitive can be crossed over. Consider for instance the following examples:

(81)   Quel dittatore$_i$ spera che i notiziari televisivi parlino a lungo delle proprie$_i$
gesta
That dictator hopes that TV news programmes will talk (SUBJ) for a long time about self's deeds

(82)   Quel dittatore$_i$ ha detto che il primo ministro$_j$ era convinto che i notiziari
televisi avessero parlato a lungo delle proprie$_{j/*i}$ gesta
That dictator said that the prime minister was(IND) convinced that the TV news programme had(SUBJ) talked a lot about self's deeds

---

[28]   For further details, I refer the reader to Giorgi (2006) and Huang and Liu (2001).

[29]   See Giorgi (2007), and Cole, Hermon, and Huang (2001, and papers published there).

(83)   *Quel dittatore$_i$ ha detto che i notiziari televisivi hanno parlato a lungo
delle proprie$_i$ gesta
That dictator said that the TV news programmes talked(IND) for a long
time about self's deeds

(84)   *Quel dittatore$_i$ ha detto che i notiziari televisivi parleranno a lungo delle
proprie$_i$ gesta
That dictator said that the TV news programmes will(IND) talk a lot
about self's deeds

This paradigm shows that the main verb of the embedded clause
must be a subjunctive. In particular, the ungrammaticality of (83)
and (84) shows that an indicative prevents the anaphor from looking
any further for an antecedent, whereas the grammaticality of (81)
and (82) shows that a subjunctive is *transparent* to his purpose.[30]

Other languages, however, like Chinese, have LDAs without
having any indicative/subjunctive distinction in their verbal system.
However, even in these cases, the domain is limited by intervening
items, which do not have a *verbal* nature but a *nominal* one, as
mentioned above.

In Chinese intervening first or second person nominal items
prevent the anaphor from being bound in a clause superordinate to
the one containing the first or second person pronoun.

As pointed out by Huang and Liu (2001), however, in Chinese the
blocking effect is asymmetrical and even non-potential binders may
act as blockers. Consider the following example (Huang and Liu
2001, example 11a):[31]

(85)   Zhangsan$_i$ danxin wo/ni$_j$ hui piping ziji$_{*i/j}$
Zhangsan is worried that I/you might criticize myself/yourself/*him

This example illustrates that intervening first or second person
pronouns prevent the anaphor *ziji* from referring to the higher third
person Noun Phrase *Zhangsan*. Interestingly, they also show that an

---

[30] The actual pattern is more complex than that, in ways that however are not relevant to the present discussion. See Giorgi (2006, 2007) and references cited there.

[31] For an analysis, see Huang (1984), Pollard and Xue (1998, 2001), and Huang and Liu
(2001). See also the discussion of English and Chinese examples in Pollard and Sag
(1992).

intervening third person Noun Phrase does not have the same effect (Huang and Liu 2001, example 11b):[32]

(86) Wo$_i$ danxin Zhangsan$_j$ hui piping ziji$_{i/j}$
      I am worried that Zhangsan will criticize me/himself

The fact that an example such as (86) is grammatical shows that in order to act as a blocker, the intervening Noun Phrase must belong to a special class, in this case the class of first and second person pronouns. Huang and Liu (2001) show that this is true even if the blocking NP does not occur in a position where it may count as a potential antecedent. Consider now the following example (Huang and Liu 2001, example 8a):

(87) Zhangsan$_i$ gaosu wo$_j$ Lisi$_k$ hen ziji$_{*i/*j/k}$
      Zhangsan told me that Lisi hated self

In this example *wo*—the first person pronoun—is not a potential antecedent, given that it does not appear in subject position, and as we know LDAs are subject-oriented. Even so, however, the binding domain of the LDA is limited to the embedded clause.

Notice moreover that in some cases a third person NP can act as a blocker, when it is deictically identified—for instance, by means of an ostensive gesture—as illustrated by the following example (Huang and Liu 2001, example 12):

(88) Zhangsan$_i$ shuo DEICTIC-ta$_k$ qipian-le ziji$_{*i/k}$
      Zhangsan said that she/he cheated himself/herself

The word DEICTIC in this example stands for the pointing at a person present in the contextual setting. In this case, the superordinate

---

[32] Huang and Liu (2001) notice that some sentences with an intervening third person antecedent might be controversial. Namely, some speakers might find it hard to pass over a third person intervening subject. Their own judgement, however, is that the sentences with an intervening third person are fully acceptable. Here, for consistency, I assume their range of data. Notice, however, that some of the problems with these judgements might be due to the complex effects arising in Chinese with plural antecedents (see Huang and Liu 2001, sect. 3.2.4), if plurals are used in the relevant contexts. Furthermore, if the third person is deictically identified it can also act as a blocker, as I discuss below. On the effects caused by an intervening third person, see also Tang (1989, fnn.11 and 15).

subject *Zhangsan* is not available as an antecedent, and the anaphor must necessarily find its antecedent inside the embedded domain. In this particular case, the antecedent is the indexically identified item.

Finally, explicit time expressions can be used to indicate the sequence of events—namely, the ordering of the events of the complement and superordinate clause with respect to each other. Recall that Chinese does not have temporal morphemes, but only aspectual ones.

As pointed out by Huang and Liu (2001: 181), these temporal expressions interact in an interesting way with LD binding. Consider the following examples (Huang and Liu 2001, examples 107 and 109):

(89)   ?Zhangsan$_i$ kuanjiang-guo houlai sha si ziji$_i$ de naxie ren
       Zhangsan has praised those persons who **later** killed him

(90)   *Zhangsan$_i$ shang xingqi zanmei-le jin zao piping ziji$_i$ de nei-ge ren
       Zhangsan praised last week the person who criticized self **this morning**

Later is an anaphoric temporal expression, given that it must refer back to a time already given in the sentence. The expression *this morning*, on the contrary, is an indexical expression, and as such its location depends solely on the temporal coordinate of the speaker. Interestingly, the indexical temporal expression seems to act as a blocker for the LDA, so that the superordinate subject *Zhangsan* in (90) is not available as an antecedent. By contrast, in (89) the anaphor can refer back to it.[33]

In the literature, the different patterns for LDA binding found in Italian and Chinese are often considered two different sets of phenomena. According to this perspective, on one side there are languages with tense and mood distinctions, and on the other there are languages in which such distinctions do not exist. In the two language groups the properties relevant to identify the binding domain for an LDA are different, so that a general theory for LD binding must incorporate all the various conditions.

---

[33] Huang and Liu (2001) actually mark this example as '?'. The reason is not clear, but it nevertheless seems to me that the examples significantly contrast with each other.

However, my claim is that in light of the hypothesis discussed in this book, it is possible to propose a better account. The crucial question is the following: what do the verbal blocking effect on one side and the nominal blocking effect on the other have in common? What property do they share? The answer seems clear: the indicative—the mood with *blocking* properties—has an indexical component, as argued in the preceding chapters. Analogously, from the data given above it turns out that in Chinese all the nominal expressions exhibiting blocking effects are indexically related items: first and second person pronouns, deixis, and indexical temporal expressions.

On the basis of the theory proposed here, it is possible to conclude that in all the unacceptable cases of LD binding reported above, the utterance context—i.e., the speaker's coordinate—appears in the embedded clause, both in Italian and in Chinese, giving rise to a blocking effect.

The presence of the speaker's coordinate shows up in different ways, due to the fact that the two languages differ with respect to their morphosyntactic properties. The main difference between Italian and Chinese is that the latter lacks verbal morphology. Therefore in such a language, the speaker's coordinate does not correlate with the existence of DAR phenomena—as is the case in languages with rich verbal morphology such as Italian. However, the effects detectable on the binding domani of the LDA are exactly the same.

Following Giorgi (2006), it is possible to hypothesize that the principle for the interpretation of LDAs prescribes that the domain in which the antecedent has to be found cannot extend beyond the clause where the speaker's coordinate appears. The principle stated in Giorgi (2006) is the following:

(91)   **Blocking condition:** an event located with respect to the speaker's coordinate must be *fully saturated*

Fully saturated—as argued in Giorgi (2006, 2007)—means that a syntactic domain cannot contain LDAs. In other words, looking at the phenomena from a syntactic point of view, an LDA must have its antecedent in the domain defined by the position in the C-layer projected by the speaker's coordinate.[34] Therefore, in Italian the domain is defined on the basis of the presence of an indicative, or in any case, in all the contexts which enforce the DAR. In Chinese even if there is no indicative/subjunctive distinction, the domain is identified by means of the speaker's coordinates, which are projected whenever an indexically related item appears. In both cases, the event has to be located with respect to the indexical context and cannot contain LDAs.[35]

As a final remark, notice that from the proposal sketched above, it follows that the verbal blocking effect is not uniquely connected to the presence of an indicative verbal form, since it is a consequence of the presence of the speaker's coordinate. In Chapter 2 I showed that the speaker's coordinate is also projected in some subjunctive contexts which give rise to the DAR, for instance the *ipotizzare* (hypothesize) cases. The prediction is therefore that in these cases long distance binding should be blocked, on a par with the indicative cases given above. Consider the following examples:

(92)   Quel dittatore$_i$ ha ipotizzato che il primo ministro venda illegalmente i propri$_{?*i}$ tesori
That dictator hypothesized that the prime minister illegally sells(PRES SUBJ) self's treasures

(93)   Quel dittatore$_i$ ha ipotizzato che il primo ministro vendesse illegalmente i propri$_i$ tesori
That dictator hypothesized that the prime minister illegally sold(PAST SUBJ) self's treasures

The contrast between the examples in (92)–(93), though subtle, certainly goes in the same direction as the one in examples (81)–(84) discussed above.

In sentence (92) the DAR is enforced, so in order to reach *quel dittatore* (that dictator) the anaphor has to cross a projection endowed with the speaker's coordinate. This is not permitted, as proposed above. Therefore, the sentence is not acceptable. In the example (93),

---

[34] Giorgi (2006, 2007, 2009) argues that such a domain is an *interpretive phase*, and for this reason long distance anaphors cannot look for an antecedent outside it.

[35] On the relation between *saturation* and *binding*, see Giorgi (2007).

on the contrary, no DAR is enforced, as is the case in the *normal* subjunctive dependencies analysed in Chapter 2. Consequently, the crossing is possible and the anaphor *propri* can take the superordinate subject as an antecedent.[36]

Therefore, it can be concluded that even if the embedded verbal form is a subjunctive in both cases, the condition on LD binding concerns the presence of the speaker's coordinate, thus strengthening the argument in favour of a general explanation, which might also account for the Chinese cases discussed above.

Finally, the imperfect is not transparent to long distance binding— i.e., it does not admit a long distance anaphor to be bound outside its domain. Consider the following cases:

(94)   Quel dittatore$_i$ ha detto che i libri di storia parlavano spesso delle proprie$_{*i}$ gesta
That dictator said that the books of history often spoke (IMPF) about self's deeds

(95)   Quel dittatore$_i$ ha detto che i libri di storia hanno parlato spesso delle proprie$_{*i}$ gesta
That dictator said that the books of history often spoke (PAST IND) about self's deeds

(96)   Quel dittatore$_i$ sperava che i libri di storia parlassero spesso delle proprie$_i$ gesta
That dictator hoped that the books of history often spoke (SUBJ) about self's deeds

In sentence (94) the LDA is embedded inside a clause containing an imperfect, whereas in (95) there is an indicative past. The two sentences have the same status, namely, they are both unacceptable with the LDA referring back to the matrix subject. In example (96), finally, the LDA is embedded inside a subjunctive clause and the matrix subject is accessible as an antecedent, as discussed in Chapter 2.

From all these arguments, it follows that the imperfect is actually a well-behaved indicative verbal form. As expected, in other

---

[36] Irrelevantly, the intermediate subject, *il primo ministro* (the prime minister) is available as an antecedent in both cases.

words, even if it does not show DAR effects, the imperfect does encode reference to indexicality in the C-layer. The effect on the temporal interpretation is not detectable, but the effects on LD binding still are.

An important issue remains open here, namely, is the position where the speaker's coordinate is represented the same in Chinese and Italian? Tentatively, I would propose the strongest hypothesis compatible with the data so far, that is, that the position in question is the same in both languages, and lies at the left periphery of the C-layer. However, as far as Italian is concerned, I discussed some data to this extent, showing that the speaker's features are represented—and sometimes even lexicalized—in a high C position. I do not have equally strong arguments here for Chinese and the issue remains open for future research. Let me only consider an interesting piece of evidence—already analysed in Giorgi (2006)—showing that the evidence of Chinese and Italian are much more similar than previously thought. Consider the following examples:

(97)   Gianni$_i$ pensa che **tutti** siano innamorati della propria$_i$ moglie
         Gianni believes that everybody is in love with self's wife

(98)   Gianni$_i$ crede che **Mario** sia innamorato della propria$_i$ moglie
         Gianni believes that Mario is in love with self's wife

(99)   ?*Gianni$_i$ crede che **tu** sia innamorato della propria$_i$ moglie
         Gianni believes that you are in love with self's wife

(100)   ?*Gianni$_i$ crede che **io** sia innamorato della propria$_i$ moglie
         Gianni believes that I am in love with self's wife

The contrast between (97)–(98) on one side, and (99)–(100) on the other, looks very similar to the nominal blocking effect discussed for the Chinese cases above. The only difference between the grammatical pair and the ungrammatical one lies in the nature of the intervening subject: third person, either singular or plural, vs. first and second person. The ungrammaticality effect of (99) and (100) is, according to native speakers, milder than the effect due to the intervening indicative verbal form, as in examples (83)–(84) above, but is still systematic. The explanation, informally, can be in the same vein: though the canonical way in Italian for instantiating the (temporal) speaker's coordinate in the syntax is by means of the verbal morph-ology, still, the presence of a strong indexical form, such as first and second person pronouns, has a blocking effect on the LDA. I will not discuss this issue here any further, and I refer the reader for more details on pattern to Giorgi (2006).[37]

4.7 The future-in-the-past

In the previous sections, I discussed the characteristics of the imper-fect with respect to the DAR. I concluded that the speaker's coordi-nate is represented in the Complementizer in the C-layer, but that it does not have any detectable effect, due to the intrinsic nature of the imperfect. The imperfect is a non-relational verbal form, specified as [-speaker], and the speaker's temporal coordinate present in the C-layer is therefore inert. Its presence however, is still detectable when considering long distance binding.

The future-in-the-past exhibits very similar properties, in that it appears to be compatible both with well-behaved indicative contexts and with subjunctive ones and, analogously to the English *would* future, it does not imply that the event has to take place in the future with respect to the temporal location of the speaker, but only in the future with respect to the subject. In Italian it is expressed by means of the perfect conditional—i.e., of a past participle preceded by the conditional form of the auxiliary. In the next section I discuss the status of this verbal form with respect to the DAR.[38]

---

[37] I thank a reviewer for having brought this issue up.

[38] On the future-in-the-past in a non-DAR language, see Coene, D'Hulst, and Avram (2004). The authors argue that in Romanian there is no morphological form expressing something similar to the Italian future-in-the-past. Note that this is actually expected, given that the future-in-the-past and the 'normal' future, when appearing in subordi-nate clauses, differ only with respect to the availability of the speaker's temporal coordi-nate. As argued above, in non-DAR languages the speaker's coordinate of the embedded clause is not relevant for the location of the embedded event. Moreover, again as expected, in Bulgarian as well—another non-DAR language—there is only the 'normal' future. I thank Vesselina Laskova for discussion on this point.

4.7.1 *The issue*

The issue concerning the future-in-the-past is very similar to the one discussed above for the imperfect. This form can in fact appear in contexts in which normally the DAR is found—i.e., contexts normally selecting for an indicative—without giving rise to it. Let me illustrate its distribution precisely in these contexts. Consider the following example:

(101)   Gianni ha detto che Maria sarebbe partita
         Gianni said that Maria would leave

The meaning of this sentence corresponds quite literally to the English glosses. As discussed in Chapter 2, the leaving of Maria must be located in the future with respect to the saying, and is not necessarily located in the future with respect to the utterance event, i.e., the speaker's coordinate. This observation emerges very clearly from the following examples, with overt temporal specifications:[39]

(102)   Oggi è il 26 dicembre. Il 22 dicembre Gianni ha detto che Maria
         sarebbe partita il 25/ieri
         Today is 26 December. On 22 December Gianni said that Maria would
         leave on the 25th/yesterday

(103)   Gianni ha detto che Maria sarebbe partita domani
         Gianni said that Maria would leave tomorrow

Again, even in these cases the Italian sentence and the English one have the same meaning: the embedded event can, but need not, lie in the future with respect to the speech event, as shown by the lack of contrast between the sentence with *ieri* (yesterday)—cf. (102)—and the one with *domani* (tomorrow)—cf. (103). Note however that the embedded event must be in the future with respect to the main one and cannot be past with respect to it:

(104)   #Il 22 dicembre Gianni ha detto che Maria sarebbe partita il 20/il giorno
         prima
         #On 22 December Gianni said that Maria would leave on the 20th/the
         day before

---

[39] For a discussion of temporal locutions, see Giorgi and Pianesi (2003). For an analysis of the relations between future and conditional in Italian, see Squartini (2004). See also Squartini (2001a).

Both in Italian and English, the temporal locution in the embedded clause is inappropriate, given that it would locate the embedded event in the past with respect to the superordinate one, and not in its future.

As also discussed in Chapter 2, it can be concluded that this verbal form must be anchored to the superordinate one—as is *always* the case, cf. Giorgi and Pianesi (2001a)—but it is not temporally located with respect to the speaker's coordinate.

The interesting observation is that this form can also appear in subjunctive contexts—i.e., in the contexts that normally require the subjunctive:

(105) Gianni credeva che Maria sarebbe partita il giorno dopo/domani
       Gianni believed that Maria would leave the next day/tomorrow

(106) Gianni sperava che Maria sarebbe partita il giorno dopo/domani
       Gianni hoped that Maria would leave the next day/tomorrow

(107) #Gianni credeva che Maria sarebbe partita il giorno prima
       Gianni believed that Maria would leave the day before

(108) #Gianni sperava che Maria sarebbe partita il giorno prima
       Gianni hoped that Maria would leave the day before

The future-in-the-past is acceptable both in the context created by *credere* (believe) and in the context created by *sperare* (hope) and it locates the embedded event in the future with respect to it. Sentences (107) and (108) are deviant because the temporal locution does not comply with this requirement.

On the one hand, therefore, the future-in-the-past resembles the imperfect, in that it does not locate the event with respect to the speaker's coordinate. On the other, it cannot be considered its mirror image in the future, given that, contrary to the imperfect, it can even appear in subjunctive environments—with no 'substandard' flavour.

For the imperfect the proposal I argued for is that it is an indicative form, and that therefore the high Complementizer C endowed with the speaker's coordinate is always represented in the sentence in which it appears. This also makes it possible for the imperfect to appear in main clauses, yielding assertions, once the necessary temporal topic is provided. The same proposal could not apply to the future-in-the-past because it would rule out sentences (105) and (106), which depend on a verb selecting the subjunctive.

4.7.2 *Complementizer Deletion and long distance anaphors*

In this section I will consider the syntax of the Complementizer layer and the properties of the clauses containing a future-in-the-past with respect to the distribution of long distance anaphors. The omission of the Complementizer with the indicative contexts gives intermediate results. On the one hand, as discussed in Chapter 2, it can be omitted under *credere* (believe) and cannot be omitted under *dire* (say). On the other, its omission with the future-in-the-past gives rise to intermediate judgements:

(109)   Gianni ha detto *(che) è partita/partirà
        Gianni said that (she) left/will leave

(110)   Gianni crede (che) sia partita
        Gianni believes (she) left

(111)   ?(?)Gianni ha detto sarebbe partita
        Gianni said she would leave

For most speakers, Complementizer Deletion in sentence (111) is not as ungrammatical as in sentence (109), even if it is not perfect. As expected, when the future-in-the-past depends on *credere* (believe)— a verb that selects the subjunctive—CD is perfectly grammatical:

(112)   Gianni credeva (che) sarebbe partita
        Gianni believed (that) she would leave

There is evidence therefore to conclude that CD in (111) produces a (mild) violation. Let me propose the following explanation. In sentence (109)—i.e., in sentences with an indicative—the omission of the Complementizer violates on one side the selection properties of the superordinate verb *dire*, and on the other, the requirement of the embedded verbal form that must value its features in C. In other words, the clause embedded under *dire* (say) must be introduced by a non-deletable Complementizer *and* the embedded verbal form must be valued with respect to speaker's coordinate.

The intermediate status of (111) can therefore be explained by means of the hypothesis that in this case only the first requirement is violated—i.e., the one prescribing that the superordinate *dire* requires a non-omittable C. The embedded verbal form does not have to value its feature in C, as shown by its compatibility with subjunctive environments, as in (112). Therefore, the violation in (111) turns out to be *milder* than the violation in (109). Consider now the distribution of long distance anaphors in these contexts:

(113) ?(?)Quel dittatore ha detto che i libri di storia avrebbero parlato a lungo
di sé e delle proprie gesta
That dictator said that the book of history would talk for a long time
about self and self's deeds

(114) Quel dittatore credeva che i libri di storia avrebbero parlato a lungo di
sé e delle proprie gesta
That dictator believed that the book of history would talk for a long time
about self and self's deeds

(115) *Quel dittatore ha detto che i libri di storia hanno parlato a lungo di sé e
delle proprie gesta
That dictator said that the book of history talked for a long time about
self and self's deeds

Sentence (113) again occupies an intermediate position between the grammatical (114) and the ungrammatical (115). This is so because the speaker's coordinate is there, and therefore intervenes in the interpretation—giving rise to a partial *blocking* effect. On the other hand, it does not formally require the embedded event to be located with respect to it. As discussed in Giorgi (2006, 2007) and summarized above, there is independent evidence to claim that in Italian what determines strong ungrammaticality is the fact that the event is located with respect to the speaker's coordinate, which in this case does not happen, hence the violation is *milder* in (113) than in (115).

The status of (113) in this respect is more or less the same as in the following example:

(116) ?(?)Quel dittatore credeva che nei tuoi libri *tu* avessi parlato a lungo di
sé e delle proprie gesta
That dictator believed that in your books you talked for a long time
about self and self's deeds.

In example (116) the intervention of a second person—i.e., of an indexically related item—seems to create an environment where a long distance anaphor cannot appear, similarly to the Chinese cases analysed above, but, interestingly, the violation is milder than the one in (115), where an indicative appears. The reason for the milder status of the violation in (116) is similar to the one proposed above for (113). Consider that in subjunctive sentences the C-projection containing the speaker's coordinates is not required (with the exception of some cases, such as *ipotizzare* (hypothesize) examples). Hence, the embedded event is not temporally located with respect to the speaker's temporal coordinate.

In other words, the presence of the indexical item at the *interpretive* level creates an environment in which a long distance anaphor should be interpreted—i.e., the LD anaphor is blocked in the minimal domain containing the indexical item. But, as far the Italian *syntactic* requirements are concerned, the anaphor is still allowed to look for an antecedent beyond the embedded clause, given that no blocking C is projected and therefore the embedded event is not temporally evaluated with respect to the speaker's coordinate. In a certain sense, in this case there is a discrepancy between the requirements imposed by syntax—no blocking—and those imposed by the presence of an indexical—i.e., blocking. The result is a slightly ungrammatical sentence.

From this analysis it can therefore be concluded that, when the future-in-the-past depends on *dire* (say)—that is, from verbs selecting an embedded indicative—its clause is introduced by the high Complementizer C. When it depends on *credere* (believe)—that is, from verbs selecting the subjunctive—it is introduced by the subjunctive Complementizer MOOD. The formal requirements of this verbal form are met in both cases.

4.7.3 *A proposal*

In this section I will propose a morphosyntactic structure for the future-in-the-past that will also shed light on its properties with respect to the DAR. As a matter of fact, it is quite surprising that this temporal relation is expressed by means of this morphological form. Why the *perfect conditional*? What properties of this form make it the form of choice to express future-in-the-past? Let me consider first the properties of the conditional mood in Italian.

The conditional mood can appear as a main clause verbal form, provided that is *licensed* by something creating a modal environment—i.e., it must be associated with a modal meaning. Consider the following examples:

(117)   #Gianni telefonerebbe
        Gianni would call(PRES COND)

(118)   Gianni telefonerebbe, se arrivasse in tempo
        Gianni would call(PRES COND), if he arrived(PAST SUBJ) on time

(119)   Gianni vorrebbe/potrebbe/dovrebbe telefonare
        Gianni would/could/should(PRES COND) call

A sentence such as (117), uttered out of the blue, is not acceptable, much like the imperfect described above. In (118) the event of *calling*, appearing in the present conditional mood, is associated to an *if-clause*, where a past subjunctive appears. In (119) it is associated with an explicit modal verb. Both the *if*-clause and the explicit modal verb can license the conditional verbal form.

In these pages I will not consider the semantics of these clauses in detail, but will only highlight their temporal interpretation as far as the issues considered in this book are concerned. The temporal interpretation in both cases, either with the conditional or the modal, is a present one, in that in (118) the condition holds *now*, and analogously in (119) the modality is understood as holding *now*. Therefore, it can be concluded that the event associated with the conditional morphology has the same *temporal* properties as a present tense of the indicative, once the licensing requirements are met.

Let's now consider what happens when the present conditional appears in an embedded context, for instance under a verb of saying. Being temporally a present tense, the expectation is that, once licensed as a conditional mood, it exhibits the same properties as an indicative present tense:[40]

---

[40] The *if*-clause can be omitted, but it must be retrievable from the context. Notice that the conditional licensed by a modal tends to have an adversative interpretation:

i. Gianni avrebbe voluto partire, ma non lo ha fatto
   Lit: Gianni had(COND) wanted to leave, but he didn't do it
   'Gianni wanted to leave, but he didn't do it'

(120)   Mario ha detto che Gianni telefonerebbe, se arrivasse in tempo
Mario said that Gianni would call(PRES COND), if he arrived(PAST SUBJ)
on time

(121)   Mario ha detto che Gianni vorrebbe/potrebbe/dovrebbe telefonare
Mario said that Gianni would/could/should(PRES COND) call

In sentence (120) the embedded *if-then* conditional holds at utterance time and at the time of the saying, i.e., the DAR is enforced, as
expected.

Analogously, sentence (121) means that the state of affairs expressed
in the embedded clause held *then* and holds *now*, as happens in DAR
sentences.[41]

Consider now the perfect conditional, formed by the auxiliary
followed by the conditional morpheme (*-ebbe*), followed by the past
participle: *avrebbe mangiato* (have-*ebbe* PP).[42]

Analogously to what I illustrated above, if appearing in main
clauses this form must be licensed by an item creating a modal context,
for instance an *if*-clause, or a modal verb:

(122)   #Gianni avrebbe telefonato
Gianni have-*ebbe* called
'Gianni would have called'

(123)   Gianni avrebbe telefonato, se fosse arrivato in tempo
Gianni have-*ebbe* called, if he had(PAST SUBJ) arrived on time
'Gianni would have called, if he had arrived on time'

(124)   Gianni avrebbe voluto/potuto/dovuto telefonare
Gianni have-*ebbe* want-PP/can-PP/must-PP call(INF)
'Gianni could (want/must) have called'

The conditional verbal form in sentence (122) is not licensed and
consequently the sentence is infelicitous, analogously to what is

---

[41] The difference between the indicative and the subjunctive conditionals has been
extensively investigated by many scholars, and I do not have anything to add to the
discussion of this aspect. Therefore I will simply ignore this issue in this work. See,
among many others, Iatridou (2000), Iatridou and von Fintel (2007).

[42] This is the whole paradigm for a present conditional: *io mangerei, tu mangeresti,
egli mangerebbe, noi mangeremmo, voi mangereste, essi mangerebbero* (I would eat, you
would eat, etc.). The part in bold is the morpheme expressing the conditional mood for
the different persons. In the text I am using only the third person singular form, hence
I am talking about the *-ebbe* morpheme as the present conditional one.

illustrated above by example (117). The licensing is possible exactly as in the case of the simple form, i.e., by means of an *if*-clause or a modal, as shown in examples (123) and (124). The difference between the simple and the perfect conditional is a temporal one, derived on the basis of the usual aspectual difference. In the simple form, as I said above, the temporal interpretation is simultaneity with the utterance time. In sentence (123), the whole conditional is taken to hold in the past, because the resultant state, expressed by the past participle, must hold *now*. Hence, derivatively, the event, or better to say the *if-then* construction, is understood as being past. The same holds with respect to (124): the obligation, the will, etc., is expressed as a present resultant state, hence derivatively interpreted as past. Note that the *calling* event is understood as future with respect to the modality expressed by *can*, *want*, *must*, etc., as part of the necessary meaning of these modals.

Let's consider now what happens if the clause containing the conditional is embedded:

(125)   Mario ha detto che Gianni avrebbe telefonato, se fosse arrivato in tempo
        'Mario said that Gianni have-*ebbe* called, if he had(PAST SUBJ) on time'
        Mario said that Gianni would have called, if he had arrived on time

The temporal interpretation of the embedded *if-then* clause is ambiguous. Under one interpretation, the *if-then* conditional can be taken to hold in the past with respect to the saying, and consequently in the past with respect to *now*. In other words, (125) can be the report of the following discourse:[43]

(126)   Mario ha detto: 'Se Gianni (ieri) fosse arrivato in tempo, avrebbe telefonato'
        Mario said: 'If Gianni (yesterday) had arrived on time, he would have called (PERF COND)'

On the other hand, it could also express a future conditional, reporting the following discourse:

(127)   Mario ha detto: 'Se Gianni (domani) arrivasse in tempo, telefonerebbe'
        Mario said: 'If John (tomorrow) arrived on time, he would call(PRES COND)'

---

[43] I will not consider here special cases under which the *if* part can precede the saying and the *-ebbe* part can follow it.

Recall also that the future-in-the-past can appear in whatever environment—i.e., it is *neutral* with respect to the kind of Complementizer introducing its clause, in that it can appear both in environments requiring the indicative and in environments requiring the subjunctive.

Consider the following examples:

(128) Mario ha detto che Gianni avrebbe voluto/potuto/dovuto telefonare
       Mario said that Gianni would/could/should have called

(129) Mario ha detto che Gianni avrebbe telefonato
       Mario said that Gianni would have called

My proposal is that in (128) the explicit modal—want, must, etc.—licenses the conditional and that in (129) the licenser is empty. The modal form intrinsically expresses futurity, as happens in the simple cases. For instance in *John wants to eat*, both in Italian and English, the eating must necessarily be located in a hypothetical future, and certainly not in the speaker's past.

Notice that sentence (125), containing an *if*-clause, clearly contrasts with sentence (129), where there is no *if*-clause. In (130), the perfect conditional can only be interpreted as a future with respect to the saying, and not as a past with respect to it.

With respect to this point, recall that the past participle should not be considered on a par with the past form, but as the expression of the *resultant state*—see among others Parsons (1990), Higginbotham (1995)—equivalent therefore to the past participle appearing in the absolute constructions:

(130) Arrivata Maria, tutti lasciarono la stanza
       Lit: arrived (past part) Maria, everybody left the room
       'Maria having arrived, everybody left the room'

To conclude, my proposal for the future-in-the-past is the following: in Italian the future-in-the-past is expressed by means of a perfect conditional because in this way it is possible to express that there is a (modal) future time—future with respect to the saying—where a resultant state X is taken to hold.

In English the *would* future works in a very similar way. The modal in English is not empty, but is expressed as a free morpheme and is marked as past, resulting in the form *would*.

Finally, the future-in-the-past is a non-relational tense and therefore the presence of the speaker's temporal coordinate in C does not give rise to the DAR, as was the case with an embedded imperfect of the indicative.[44]

Concluding this section, it is possible to say that from the morphosyntactic point of view, the conditional mood, which is also used in the future-in-the-past, must be *licensed*. By 'licensed' I mean that something must create the right environment in which this particular modal form can appear. Usually, the licensing is operated by an *if*-clause. I illustrated above that if the conditional modal form is in the present tense, then the only way of licensing it is by means of an *if*-clause with a past subjunctive. In this case, if in dependence from a past tense, the whole *if-then* construction undergoes the DAR.

If the conditional verbal form is in the perfect form—i.e., auxiliary + past participle—and the licensing takes place through an *if*-clause, then the event expressed by the conditional can either be located in the past or in the future with respect to the main verbal form.

When no *if*-clause is around—as is the case with the future-in-the-past—I proposed that an empty modal is licensing the conditional mood.

4.8 Summary and conclusion

In this chapter I examined the properties of the imperfect, the conditional, and the perfect conditional with respect to the speaker's projection. The (non-perfect) conditional is not used in Italian to express a peculiar temporal relation, but a modal one, hence I considered it only marginally relevant to the issue in question.

---

[44] In Spanish the future-in-the-past is constituted by the simple form of the conditional, contrasting with Italian, where the perfect form is used. This difference could be due to the fact that in Iberic languages, but not in Italian, the conditional verbal ending might still be (cognitively) interpretable as an incorporated auxiliary form. This way, Spanish can realize synthetically what must be realized analytically in Italian. This might be a reasonable hypothesis, given the residual existence in Portuguese of meso-cliticization phenomena. For an in-depth comparative discussion, however, further study would be needed.

The main idea I developed here is that there are relational and non-relational verbal forms, and that the prototypical cases are respectively represented by the indicative present, past, and future vs. the subjunctive forms. There are however some *intermediate* cases, which can appear both in indicative and subjunctive contexts, such as the imperfect—sub-standard in subjunctive contexts—and the future-in-the-past.

My proposal with respect to the imperfect is that it is endowed with a feature [−speaker] and that this can account both for its distribution with respect to the DAR, CD, and LDAs, and for its anaphoric-like properties. I also argued that the English past, in spite of appearances, has the option of appearing in the same contexts as the Italian imperfect, as shown by the similar distribution in *dream* contexts and in the lack of DAR with stative predicates. The remaining differences, primarily concerning the interpretation of the past with eventive predicates, are due to peculiar aspectual properties of the English verb, as is argued in Giorgi and Pianesi (1997).

The future-in-the-past is also a non-relational verbal form, as shown by the fact that it can also appear in subjunctive contexts. I propose here that the simple and perfect conditional must always be licensed by a modal item. Such a modal item can be an *if*-clause—and in this case the sentence is a hypothetical period—or a modal verb. In this way, therefore, the conditional mood appearing in *if*-clauses and the one expressing the future-in-the-past turn out to be the same verbal form, subject to exactly the same constraints—a result not achieved before. The different interpretation is due to the syntactic contexts and to the specific licenser. I propose that in the particular case of the future-in-the-past in Italian, the verbal form is licensed by an empty modal; the modal can also in some cases be explicitly expressed, as in sentences (124) and (128). In English the *would* future is exactly parallel to the Italian one, the only difference being that the modal is overt.

To conclude, the result achieved in this chapter is that certain verbal forms, whose behaviour has previously had to be considered *deviant*, or *special*, have been accounted for by means of exactly the same mechanisms adopted for the other cases. In particular, the idea is that these verbal forms are non-relational like the subjunctive forms, but can also appear in contexts requiring the indicative, hence are endowed with the high speaker-related C-position. Note also that this intermediate case is expected under the present proposal, because there is no principled reason excluding it, once the basic requirement—i.e., anchoring—is satisfied.[45]

---

[45] A reviewer asks about the presence of the speaker's projection in impersonal sentences. I do not analyse these structures in this monograph. It seems to me however that the present proposal might easily be maintained on the assumption that what is anchored to the speaker's coordinate is the implicit modal present in the sentences. Consider for instance a sentence such as the following one:

i. Two plus two is four

The implicit gnomic modal is anchored and holds *now*. The universal and atemporal flavour of the sentence is due to exactly this process, in that the verbal form itself is not anchored.

5

Depending on the Future: The Speaker Changes her Perspective

5.1 Introduction

In this chapter I consider a challenging set of data: the dependencies from a future verbal form. So far, I have proposed that in Italian and English, both DAR languages, an embedded context requires that the subject's coordinate be syntactically represented. Recall that, as discussed in Chapter 2, anchoring to the subject temporal coordinate is obligatory in all languages when depending on an attitude predicates.

In certain cases—in indicative-like contexts—the speaker's coordinates are represented as well and the DAR arises. Some verbal forms, such as the (Italian and English) present perfect/simple past, future and present, require that the embedded eventuality with which they are associated be located with respect to both sets of coordinates, as opposed to the Italian subjunctive, as discussed in chapters 2 and 3.[1]

Other verbal forms, such as the Italian imperfect of the indicative, to some extent the English past, and the future-in-the-past, are not to be located with respect to both sets of coordinates, given that they do not have to be valued with respect to the speaker's coordinate, being non-relational verbal forms. Consequently, as proposed in Chapter 4, they do not give rise to a DAR interpretation, even if the embedded contexts are in every respect identical to the DAR ones.

In all the examples discussed in the preceding chapters, however, the main verbal form is a present or a past tense one. In particular,

---

[1] For an analysis of the future in Romance, both in synchrony and in diachrony, see Fleischmann (2009).

I have not considered superordinate sentences with a future. The reason is that the contexts created by a future constitute a systematic exception to all the generalizations proposed so far. For instance, a present tense sentence embedded under a future—such as *Mary is pregnant*—discussed as a prototypical case of DAR in Italian and English in Chapter 2, is no longer interpreted with the DAR.

The aim of this chapter, however, is to show that simply claiming that there is no DAR in dependence on a future is not the correct way of looking at the facts. As soon as we enlarge the empirical basis, considering for instance the compatibility of the embedded verbal form with temporal locutions of various kinds, the picture changes and does not turn out to be *exceptional* any longer.

5.2 Dependencies from a future tense

One might expect the properties of the verbal forms embedded under a main future to be the mirror image of what is observed under a main past. This is not what happens, though.

Consider first the case of an embedded present tense:

(1) (Domani, quando gli porterai il caffè,) Gianni dirà che c'è poco zucchero
     (Tomorrow, when you will take him the coffee,) Gianni will say that there is too little sugar

The obvious interpretation, by far the most natural, is that the embedded state only holds at the time of the saying—namely, in the future with respect to the utterance time. For this sentence to be felicitous there is no need for the sugar to be *already* in the coffee, when the speaker utters the sentence. In other words, the embedded state does not hold at utterance time, but only at the time of the saying. Consequently, there is no DAR, which typically requires the embedded eventuality to hold at both times. Sentence (1) contrasts with sentence (2):

(2) (Ieri) Gianni ha detto che c'è poco zucchero nel caffè
     (Yesterday) Gianni said that there is too little sugar in the coffee

Sentence (2) has a DAR interpretation: the speaker is reporting about the situation of the sugar in the coffee both at the time Gianni said the sentence and at the time the speaker is uttering it. In other words, sentence (2) implies that the sugar was put in the coffee yesterday and that we are still talking about the same coffee, still with too little sugar in it.[2]

Consider now an embedded past verbal form:

(3)   (Domani, quando gli porterai il caffè,) Gianni dirà che ci hai messo poco zucchero
      (Tomorrow, when you will take him the coffee,) Gianni will say that you put(PRES PERF) in it too little sugar

In this case, as in sentence (1), the most natural interpretation is that the sugar is *not* in the coffee at the time of the utterance, but that it will be by the time the coffee is given to Gianni. That is, the embedded event is interpreted as past only with respect to Gianni's saying, but not with respect to the utterance event; therefore there is no DAR interpretation.

Prima facie, therefore, as far as the DAR is concerned, the verbal forms depending on a future exhibit the same properties as an imperfect, in that they are only located with respect to the speaker's coordinate.[3]

For completeness, consider now an example featuring an embedded future:

(4)   Gianni dirà che Maria partirà presto
      Gianni will say that Maria will(FUT) leave soon

---

[2] Consider also the following contrast in English, suggested to me by J. Guéron:

i.   In two years, John will say/claim that Mary is pregnant

This sentence clearly contrasts with the following one.

ii.   *Two years ago, John said/claimed that Mary is pregnant

It is clear that in the first case, Mary is not pregnant *now*.

[3] They differ from a subjunctive, in that the latter agrees with the main verb, whereas no agreement is detectable in this case. Note also that the subjunctive is ungrammatical in these contexts, as expected:

i.   *Gianni dirà che Maria parta/partisse
     Gianni will say that Maria leave(PRES SUBJ/PAST SUBJ)

This is relevant for an account of the dependencies from a future. It cannot be said that they give rise to an *irrealis* context—whatever this might mean—given that they do not admit the verbal form that is usually taken to express *irrealis* modality. As discussed by Giorgi and Pianesi (1997) and Giorgi (2009), I do share this view about the subjunctive and I also do no think it might be relevant for future dependencies, also given the very clear judgement in (i).

In this case, the leaving of Maria is located in the future with respect to Gianni's saying and therefore, *a fortiori*, after the utterance event. Notice that it is not possible to locate the embedded event in the future *only* with respect to the utterance time—i.e., in between the utterance event and the main event of saying. I will come back to this point in section 5.3 below.

Interestingly, an embedded imperfect can appear under a future, as well:

(5) (Domani, quando gli porterai il caffè,) Gianni dirà che ci avevi messo poco zucchero
(Tomorrow, when you will take him the coffee,) Gianni will say that you had (IMPF) put in it too little sugar.

Notice also that I observed above—cf. Chapter 4—that the imperfect has the role of *neutralizing* the DAR. That is, by means of the imperfect morphology, the embedded event is located only with respect to the subject's coordinate and not with respect to the speaker's, being specified as an *anti-speaker* form. Given the discussion above, about the absence of DAR effects, one might wonder, then, what the role of the imperfect might be in cases such as (5), which so far seem totally redundant with respect to those such as (3). I will consider the issue again in section 5.4.

Concluding these observations, it is possible to say that the context created by a main future has different properties with respect to the one created by a main past. The embedded eventuality has to be located only with respect to the main event and not with respect to the utterance event, even in the case of an embedded present tense. In other words, apparently, in these cases there is no DAR.

Note that as far as the syntactic properties are concerned, the future-depending contexts pattern with indicative contexts and not with subjunctive ones. As shown above, in chapters 2 and 3, we can use Complementizer Deletion as a test. In Italian, in some cases it is possible to omit the Complementizer introducing subjunctive clauses, but not the one introducing indicative ones. Consider the following examples:

(6) Gianni credeva (che) tu fossi partito ieri
Gianni believed (that) you had(SUBJ) left yesterday

(7) Gianni ha detto *(che) tu sei partito ieri
Gianni said (that) you left yesterday

The Complementizer cannot be omitted in example (7), contrasting with (6). In the contexts depending from a future it cannot be omitted either:

(8)   Gianni dirà *(che) sei partito ieri
       Gianni will say that you left yesterday

These contexts therefore exhibit the standard syntactic properties of the indicative ones.

Concluding these preliminary remarks, the problem is constituted by the fact that the DAR, in the account I am arguing for in this book, is due to two factors. First, a verb of saying, as opposed for instance to a verb of wishing, selects for the subordinate clause an undeletable Complementizer endowed with the speaker's coordinate. Second, conversely, an embedded indicative, such as an Italian present perfect, a simple past, or a present tense, necessarily requires such a Complementizer. The verbal form must therefore obligatorily be evaluated with respect to the speaker's coordinate. Given that the main verb selects an undeletable Complementizer and that the embedded verbal form is an ordinary indicative, as shown in examples (2) and (3), the DAR is expected to arise, but apparently it does not.

In what follows I will show that as soon as other properties are considered, even the contexts created by a main future turn out to pattern with DAR ones—i.e., the speaker's coordinate is represented in the C-layer. Therefore the problem will be reduced to the following: given that the speaker's temporal coordinate is there, how come that in sentences such as (2) and (3) the embedded event seems not to be located with respect to *now*, but only with respect to the saying?

5.3 The distribution of temporal locutions

An interesting piece of evidence that will be shown to clarify the issue comes from the distribution of temporal adverbs in these contexts. The distribution and interpretation of such locutions point to the conclusion that the contexts created by a past tense and the one created by a future are not symmetrical.

Roughly speaking, it is possible to distinguish three kinds of temporal locutions. The referential ones—such as *il 23 maggio* 1997 (May 23rd 1997), *ottobre 2004* (October 2004), etc.—the indexical ones—such as *ieri* (yesterday), *domani* (tomorrow), *questa mattina* (this morning), *tre ore fa* (three hours ago), etc.—and the anaphoric ones—*il giorno prima/dopo* (the day before/after), *tre ore prima/dopo* (three hours before/after), etc.[4]

In the first group, the temporal reference is *built into* the expression itself. For the second group it is supplied by the indexical context—i.e., the context surrounding the utterance event. For the third group it is supplied by the linguistic context—i.e., the information provided by the sentence or the discourse.

5.3.1 *Referential locutions*

The locutions of the first group are compatible with all tenses and moods. Consider the following examples:[5]

---

[4] There is also a fourth type of expression, which I dub *incomplete* temporal locutions: *il 23 maggio* (23 May), *giovedì alle 7* (Thursday at 7). The reference to a specific month or day is not *complete* in the sense that in order to be uniquely identified more information must be supplied by the context. For instance in the case of a locution such as *il 23 maggio*, the year should be supplied; in the case of *giovedì alle 7* (Thursday at 7), the week of the year. It seems to me however that this case is no different from that of a proper name. To exemplify, the proper name *Alessandra Giorgi* does not uniquely identify a referent in the world, being quite a frequent one. The information, however, is pragmatically supplied. The readers of this work, for instance, will have no difficulty in identifying who the actual referent is, given this particular context. In general, therefore, the rigidity of proper names can be maintained. Concluding, incomplete temporal locutions can be assimilated to referential ones, as far as the properties discussed in this chapter are concerned. See also Giorgi and Pianesi (2003) and Bertinetto and Bianchi (1993).

[5] The use of a referential temporal locution with a present tense is slightly odd:

i. ?Gianni ha detto che il 26 dicembre Maria è felice
    Gianni said that on 26 December Maria is happy

The reason for this oddness is presumably a pragmatic redundancy. The sentence becomes more natural if the temporal expression is used as an appositive to the indexical one:

ii. Gianni ha detto che oggi, 26 dicembre, Maria è felice
     Gianni said that today, 26 December, Maria is happy

I do not consider this issue in this work. Another question that I am not going to address concerns the sentence initial or sentence final position of the temporal adverb. Though important for the interpretation of the sentences, it does not seem to me to be relevant here.

(9)   Gianni ha detto che Maria è partita il 26 dicembre
       Gianni said that Maria left on 26 December

(10)   Gianni ha detto che Maria partirà il 26 dicembre
       Gianni said that Maria will leave on 26 December

(11)   Gianni ha detto che Maria sarebbe partita il 26 dicembre
       Gianni said that Maria would leave on 26 December

In these examples the main verb is a past form. The temporal locution is available with an embedded past, a future, and a future-in-the-past. An embedded imperfect gives rise to the same result:

(12)   Gianni ha detto che il 26 dicembre Maria era a Parigi
       Gianni said that on 26 December Maria was(IMPF) in Paris

(13)   Gianni ha detto che Maria era partita il 26 dicembre
       Gianni said that Maria had(IMPF) left on 26 December

If the main verb selects a subjunctive in the embedded clause, like a verb of *belief*, the result does not change:

(14)   Gianni credeva che Maria partisse il 26 dicembre
       Gianni believed that Maria left(SUBJ) on 26 December

(15)   Gianni credeva che Maria fosse partita il 26 dicembre
       Gianni believed that Maria had(SUBJ) left on 26 December

Finally, the referential locution is available with *credere* (believe) and the future-in-the-past as well:

(16)   Gianni credeva che Maria sarebbe partita il 26 dicembre
       Gianni believed that Maria would leave on 26 December

It is not surprising, therefore, that it is available when the main verbal form is a future tense:

(17)   Gianni dirà che Maria è partita il 26 dicembre
       Gianni will say that Maria left on 26 December

(18)   Gianni dirà che Maria partirà il 26 dicembre
       Gianni will say that Maria will leave on 26 December

Consistently with what has been observed in the previous section, the locution must be compatible with Sequence of Tense properties. For instance, if we add in example (19) a temporal specification on the superordinate clause, it must refer to a time following the one of the embedded clause:

(19)   Il 28/*24 dicembre Gianni ha detto che Maria è partita il 26
On the 28th/*24th of December Gianni said that Maria left on the 26th

Given that the embedded event must precede the utterance event, the locution *on the 24th of December* is not available in the main clause. A case such as the following is analogous:

(20)   Il 24/*28 dicembre Gianni ha detto che Maria partirà il 26
On the 24th/*28th of December Gianni said that Maria will leave on the 26th

This case is the mirror image of the one given above, so that the time of the saying must precede that of the leaving.

Notice, finally, that everything must be compatible with the utterance time. Namely, for a sentence such as (19) to be felicitous, the utterance event must be located after the 28th of December. For (20) to be felicitous, the utterance event must be located in between the saying, on the 24th, and the leaving, on the 26th, and therefore for instance on the 25th.

The same computations hold in the case of the dependencies from a main future. Therefore, it is possible to add to sentence (17) the following temporal specifications:

(21)   Il 28/*24 dicembre Gianni dirà che Maria è partita il 26
On 28/*24 December Gianni will say that Maria left on the 26th

As observed above, the time of the leaving must precede the time of the saying. Therefore, the 28th of December is a possible temporal specification, whereas the 24th is not. Consider now the following example, corresponding to the sentence given in (20) above:

(22)   Il 24 dicembre Gianni dirà che Maria partirà il 26
On 24 December Gianni will say that Maria will leave on the 26th

In this case, the leaving event must follow the saying, and therefore given that the saying takes place on the 24th of December, the leaving can occur on the 26th.

Consider now the location of the utterance event. With respect to the example (22), trivially, it must precede the saying and therefore the leaving. Consequently, it must occur prior to the 24th of December.

With respect to the example in (21), the situation is more interesting. The saying event must follow the utterance event, being with future morphology. The location of the embedded event—i.e., of the leaving—is only relative to the saying. Therefore, the utterance event can either be placed in between the two, for instance on the 27th of December—i.e., before the saying and after the leaving—or before both events. For instance, if today is the 25th of December, I can still place the saying on the 28th and the leaving on the 26th. This is coherent with the observations on example (3) above, repeated here for simplicity:

(23)   (Domani, quando gli porterai il caffè,) Gianni dirà che ci hai messo poco zucchero
       (Tomorrow, when you will take him the coffee,) Gianni will say that you put(PRES PERF) in it too little sugar

5.3.2 *Indexical temporal locutions*

Indexical temporal locutions, like all indexicals, are taken to be *rigid* (see Kaplan 1989)—namely, to identify always the same items independently of the semantic and syntactic domain in which they are used. Here I sketch the distribution of these elements in main and embedded clauses.

In main clauses indexical temporal locutions must be coherent with the verbal form:

(24)   Gianni è partito ieri/*domani
       Gianni left yesterday/*tomorrow

(25)   Gianni partirà domani/*ieri
       Gianni will leave tomorrow/*yesterday

Indexical temporal locutions can appear in embedded clauses both with indicative and subjunctive verbal forms. Let's consider the indicative first:

(26)   Questa mattina Gianni ha detto che Maria è partita ieri/*domani
       This morning Gianni said that Maria left yesterday/*tomorrow

In this sentence, the embedded event precedes the saying, which in turn precedes the utterance event. Trivially, therefore, an indexical placing the embedded event in the future, such as *domani* (tomorrow), cannot be compatible with the embedded clause.

Furthermore, a locution appearing in the superordinate clause must be compatible with the correct sequencing of the events. For instance, the following sentence is not felicitous:

(27) *Ieri Gianni ha detto che Maria è partita stamattina
      Yesterday Gianni said that Maria left this morning

Due to the obligatoriness of temporal anchoring, as discussed in Chapter 2, a past under a past yields the interpretation according to which the embedded event precedes the main one and *both* precede the utterance event. The same considerations apply to the embedded future:

(28) Questa mattina Gianni ha detto che Maria partirà domani/*ieri
      This morning Gianni said that Maria will leave tomorrow/*yesterday

(29) *Domani Gianni ha detto che Maria partirà questa mattina
      *Tomorrow Gianni said that Maria will leave this morning

In these cases, the leaving event must follow both the saying and the utterance event in this sequencing: saying event > utterance event > leaving event and the temporal locutions must be coherent with this intepretation.

An embedded *futurate*—i.e., a present tense with a future interpretation—exhibits the expected properties as well:

(30) Questa mattina Gianni ha detto che Maria parte domani/*ieri
      This morning Gianni said that Maria leaves tomorrow/*yesterday

(31) *Domani Gianni ha detto che Maria parte questa mattina
      *Tomorrow Gianni said that Maria leaves this morning

Sentences (30) and (31) parallel examples (28) and (29).

Note that in all the cases listed above, ungrammaticality is due to syntax, in particular to the requirement concerning the obligatoriness of anchoring in attitude contexts. If such a requirement did not exist, all the sentences above would be well formed.

The future-in-the-past does not raise any special problem, given that the embedded event might either precede or follow the utterance event:

(32) Questa mattina Gianni ha detto che Maria sarebbe partita ieri/domani
      This morning Gianni said that Maria would leave yesterday/tomorrow

When the embedded verbal form is a subjunctive one, all indexicals are available for locating the embedded event, as discussed in Chapter 2:[6]

(33)   Gianni credeva che Maria partisse ieri/oggi/domani
       Gianni believed that Maria left (PAST SUBJ) yesterday/today/tomorrow

Recall that in these cases, the embedded event does not need to be located with respect to the utterance time, in that subjunctive contexts do not enforce the DAR, contrasting with the indicative ones.

In the same vein, if the embedded form is an imperfect, all indexicals are equally available:[7]

(34)   Gianni ha detto che Maria partiva ieri/oggi/domani
       Gianni said that Maria left(IMPF) yesterday/today/tomorrow

Therefore, it is possible to conclude that indexical temporal locutions can appear both in DAR and in non-DAR contexts.

Consider now what happens when a past tense is embedded under a future:

(35)   Gianni dirà che Maria è partita ieri
       Gianni will say that Maria left yesterday

As expected, this sentence is grammatical, and does not raise any special problem. The leaving occurs before the saying and, as specified by the indexical adverb *ieri* (yesterday), also before the utterance time. However, the embedded event does not necessarily have to precede the utterance one. Compare example (36) with example (21):

(36)   Il 28 dicembre Gianni dirà che Maria è partita il 26
       On 28 December Gianni will say that Maria left on the 26th

---

[6] Note that for aspectual reasons *partisse oggi* is interpreted as a futurate. However, if the embedded eventuality is a state, such an interpretation disappears:

i.   Gianni credeva che oggi Maria fosse felice
     Gianni believed that today Maria(PAST SUBJ) is happy

In this case, the state of happiness overlaps with the time of Gianni's belief.

[7] In this example the imperfect conveys a *modal* meaning, to the effect that *Maria intended to leave*, or *was supposed to leave*. A discussion of this topic would lead me too far away, therefore I will abstract here from these interpretive properties, which however do not seem to have any consequence for the specific question discussed in this chapter.

I pointed out above that this sentence can be uttered on the 25th of December—namely at a time preceding both the saying and the leaving, which in turn is past with respect to the saying. The ordering of the events is therefore utterance event > leaving > saying.

Interestingly, the following example is totally unacceptable, even if *today* is the 25th:[8]

(37) *Il 28 dicembre Gianni dirà che Maria è partita domani
       *On 28 December Gianni will say that Maria left tomorrow

On the one hand, *tomorrow* rigidly refers to the day after the utterance. On the other, the embedded past locates the leaving event in the past with respect to the saying event, but does not locate it anywhere with respect to the utterance one, as illustrated above. That is, in the sentence *Il 28 dicembre Gianni dirà che Maria è partita* (On the 28th of December, Gianni will say that Maria left) the leaving does not necessarily precede the utterance time, but must only be located prior to the saying. Consequently, the sentence should in principle be possible, *tomorrow* in the above scenario being compatible with such a reading. This reading, however, is not available.

In other words, the leaving *is* placed *tomorrow*—i.e., in the day after the utterance according to the speaker's point of view—but this meaning can be expressed by means of sentence (36), but not by means of sentence (37).

One might claim that this is due to the simple fact that, for whatever reason, the sequence *past tense + tomorrow* yields ungrammaticality, as happens in main clauses:

(38) *Gianni è partito domani
       Gianni left yesterday

Yet it is far from clear why this should be the case, i.e., why (37) should be ungrammatical for the same reason as (38). After all, (38) is

---

[8] In the following chapter about Free Indirect Discourse, I will consider some cases in which the sequence *past tense + tomorrow* is perfectly acceptable. Consider for instance the following case, discussed in Chapter 6:

i. **Tomorrow was** Monday, Monday, the beginning of another school week!

The very existence of this example shows that the sequence is indeed available, provided that there is a suitable context. See below for discussion.

ungrammatical because *tomorrow* places the event in the future of the speaker, whereas the verbal form places it in her past, yielding a contradiction. But this is not the case with respect to (37).

One might answer to this that the phenomenon in question might be regarded as a simple mismatch of features, *left* being marked as [+past] and *tomorrow* being marked as [−past]. However, this explanation cannot hold either. Consider in fact that the same evidence can be reproduced with nominal constructions, as in the following example:

(39)   Dopodomani Gianni dirà che [la tua partenza di domani] è stata necessaria
       The day after tomorrow Gianni will say that your leaving tomorrow was necessary

(40)   Gianni dirà che [la tua partenza di domani] è necessaria
       The day after tomorrow Gianni will say that your leaving tomorrow is necessary

(41)   *Dopodomani Gianni dirà che [la tua partenza di domani] è necessaria
       The day after tomorrow Gianni will say that your leaving tomorrow is necessary

In these examples the indexical *tomorrow* refers to a leaving event, which is expressed by means of a nominal, *partenza* (the leaving). These examples show that the impossibility of *tomorrow* in sentences such as (41) is not just a matter of trivial *incompatibility* between a certain verbal form and an indexical adverb, but that it depends on the specific configuration and its properties. I will consider these sentences again below. Consider now the following cases:

(42)   *Dopodomani Gianni dirà che Maria partirà domani
        The day after tomorrow Gianni will say that Maria will leave tomorrow

(43)   Gianni dirà che Maria partirà domani
       Gianni will say that Maria will leave tomorrow

(44)   Dopodomani Gianni dirà che Maria partirà
       The day after tomorrow Gianni will say that Maria will leave

Sentence (44) expresses the following meaning: *the day after tomorrow Gianni will announce the leaving of Maria*, which in turn lies in the future with respect to the saying—and, consequently, the utterance event. The sequence obtained is the following: utterance event > saying (on the day after tomorrow) > leaving. Sentence (43) means that at some point, placed between the utterance event and tomorrow, Gianni will announce Maria's leaving, which lies in the future with respect to the saying and the utterance event. The sequence is therefore: utterance event > saying > leaving (tomorrow). The generalization holding in this case seems to be that *partirà* must be a future with respect both to the saying event and the utterance event. Consequently, it cannot be located between the two.[9]

Concluding, in this section I pointed out two sources of unacceptability. The first one concerns the distribution of embedded indexicals, as illustrated by means of the distribution of *domani* (tomorrow). The second one concerns the relative location of events, as illustrated by the examples (42)–(44). In section 5.4 I address these issues and propose an explanation.

5.3.3 *Anaphoric temporal locutions*

In this section I briefly sketch the main phenomena having to do with the distribution of this kind of locution. I will consider the topic in greater detail in section 5.4.2.2.

In general, these locutions need an antecedent in the previous discourse or in the sentence. Consider the following discourse:

(45)   A: Maria è partita il 23 marzo B: Ma no! È partita il giorno prima
      A: Maria left on 23 March B: No! She left the day before

Without the background provided by A, the sentence in B would be unacceptable. This might be considered as a trivial case of anaphoricity: if there is no antecedent for x in 'e before x'—where e is the given event, and x is the variable to be saturated—the structure is not acceptable.

---

[9] The same effects are found with an embedded futurate-present:

i.   Dopodomani Gianni dirà che Maria parte
    The day after tomorrow Gianni will say that Maria leaves

ii. Gianni dirà che Maria parte domani
    Gianni will say that Maria leaves tomorrow

In this case as well, the leaving event cannot be located in between the utterance event and the main event of saying. That is, the ordering cannot be: utterance event > leaving > saying, but must be: utterance event > saying > leaving.

However, consider again the simple unacceptable case, uttered *out of the blue*:

(46)   # Maria è partita il giorno prima
        Maria left the day before

The claim that in the out of the blue situation the context provides no antecedent for *x* is not totally correct, however. The utterance event is in fact in principle available, as we know given the interpretation of the tense on the verb, which locates the leaving in the past with respect to the utterance. Giorgi and Pianesi (2003) addressed this question and proposed that the utterance event, though available, is incompatible with these expressions.[10]

These considerations will prove relevant in the analysis I propose in the following sections, and I address this issue again below. For the time being, let me point out that sentence (46) cannot mean *Maria left the day before the day of utterance*. If the speaker wants to express precisely this meaning, she must use the indexical expression:

(47)   Maria è partita ieri
        Maria left yesterday

One might claim that the anaphoric locution is disfavoured because the indexical one is available. Therefore, sentence (47) is favoured over (46) and chosen when possible.[11]

Consider now the dependencies from a future, in particular, the structure expressing the sequence of events given in examples (36) and (37): utterance event > leaving > saying. I have already shown that the presence of an indexical for placing the embedded event of leaving is impossible—cf. example (37), repeated here:

(48)   *Il 28 dicembre Gianni dirà che Maria è partita domani
        On 28 December Gianni will say that Maria left tomorrow

---

[10] For a discussion of the reason of the incompatibility, see Giorgi and Pianesi (2003).

[11] This, however, is not the case, but only a simplification for the sake of the present argument. See the text below for an analysis. See also Giorgi and Pianesi (2003) for a comprehensive discussion of the phenomena involved with this kind of temporal locution.

One might expect the anaphoric locution to be available, contrary to facts:

(49)   *Il 28 dicembre/dopodomani Gianni dirà che Maria è partita il giorno prima
On 28 December/the day after tomorrow Gianni will say that Maria left the day before

The impossibility holds whether we find a referential temporal locution in the main clause—*il 28 dicembre*—or an indexical one-*dopodomani*.

If the embedded verbal form is an imperfect, then the anaphoric locution becomes available:

(50)   Il 28 dicembre/dopodomani Gianni dirà che Maria era partita il giorno prima
On 28 December/the day after tomorrow Gianni will say that Maria had(IMPF) left the day before

This sentence clearly contrasts with the one given above. Contrasts of this sort are found systematically, even with main past forms. Consider the following examples, where a past verbal form is embedded under a past:

(51)   *Ieri Gianni ha detto che Mario è partito il giorno prima
Yesterday Gianni said that Mario left the day before

(52)   *Il 23 maggio Gianni ha detto che Mario è partito il giorno prima
On 23 May Gianni said that Mario left the day before

In these cases the judgement is as in (49). Analogously to what we saw above, the presence of the imperfect makes the sentence grammatical:

(53)   Ieri/il 23 maggio Gianni ha detto che Mario era partito il giorno prima
Yesterday/on 23 May Gianni said that Mario left the day before

The same pattern obtains with a future embedded under a future:

(54)   *Il 28 dicembre/dopodomani Gianni dirà che Maria partirà 2 giorni dopo/da lì a due giorni
On 28 December/the day after tomorrow Gianni will say that Maria will leave two days after

(55)   Il 28 dicembre/dopodomani Gianni dirà che Maria sarebbe partita 2
       giorni dopo/da lì a due giorni
       On 28 December/the day after tomorrow Gianni will say that Maria
       would leave two days after[12]

Again, in this case the verb embedded under a future tense behaves
on a par with a verb embedded under a past tense:

(56)   *(Ieri) Gianni ha detto che Mario partirà due giorni dopo
       (Yesterday) Gianni said that Mario will leave two days after

(57)   *Il 23 maggio Gianni ha detto che Mario partirà 8 giorni dopo (oggi è il
       26 maggio)
       On 23 May Gianni said that Mario will leave 8 days after (today is 26 May)

The sentence becomes grammatical if a future-in-the-past appears in
the embedded clause:[13]

(58)   (Ieri) Gianni ha detto che Mario sarebbe partito due giorni dopo
       (Yesterday) Gianni said that Mario would leave two days after

(59)   Il 23 maggio Gianni ha detto che sarebbe partito 8 giorni dopo
       On 23 May Gianni said that he would leave 8 days after

As I briefly discussed in section 5.2, the imperfect and the future-in-
the-past do not require the embedded event to be located with respect
to the utterance event, whereas the 'normal' indicative forms do. Simplifying somehow, Giorgi and Pianesi's (2003) generalization concerning
the distribution of anaphoric temporal locutions is the following:

(60)   Anaphoric temporal locutions cannot be used for locating events
       which are in a direct relation R with the utterance event

This generalization captures both the observation in main clauses
and the data concerning the clauses depending on a past.

Concluding this section, a (non-imperfect) indicative form
embedded under a future follows the 'normal' pattern. That is, the
form *è partita* (has left/left) embedded under a future behaves with

---

[12] The locution *da lì a due giorni* (lit: from then to two days after, 'after two days'), is
an anaphoric locution identifying the moment in which the event can possibly occur. In
some sense it is equivalent to 'not earlier than'.

[13] Higginbotham (p.c.) pointed out that the temporal locutions with *ago*—as for
instance *two months ago* –are for some speakers anaphoric, whereas for others they are
indexical. For this reason, I avoid using this kind of locution here.

respect to anaphoric temporal locutions exactly like *è partita* (has left/left) under a past tense.

This fact is surprising, given that *è partita* depending from a future does not need to be located with respect to the utterance event—cf. section 5.2. Therefore, it should not fall under generalization (60) and should be compatible with an anaphoric temporal locution. The distribution of anaphoric temporal locutions is expected to parallel the one found with the imperfect and the future-in-the-past, contrary to facts. In the next section I propose a solution to this puzzle.

5.4 Towards an explanation

The hypothesis I develop in this section capitalizes on the last consideration of the preceding section: *è partita* under a future behaves like *è partita* under a past. Coherently with this observation, it might be worth exploring the idea that, contrary to appearances, the context created by a main future has the same properties as the context created by a main past. On the other hand, DAR effects are not the same in the two cases, as shown in section 5.2, and therefore something must account for this fact.

5.4.1 *DAR effects*

As discussed in Chapters 2 and 3, in Italian all the embedded (non-imperfect) indicative verbal forms—and not just the present tense—are evaluated twice. The evaluation takes place with respect to two sets of temporal coordinates: the coordinate of the subject—or better to say, the bearer of the attitude—and the coordinate of the speaker. Let me briefly summarize the relevant points.

The starting observation, discussed in Chapter 2, is that typologically there are no languages in which the embedded verbal form is evaluated exclusively indexically. That is, in no language might a sentence such as *Gianni said that Maria is pregnant* mean that Maria is pregnant *now*, but *not* at the time of Gianni's saying it. There are only two types of languages: the Italian (English)-like ones—with

DAR—and the Chinese-like ones—non-DAR languages, where the embedded eventuality is only anchored to the superordinate clause. Therefore anchoring to the superordinate event is obligatory, as a property of UG. On the other hand, the anchoring of the embedded eventuality to the utterance event only obtains with DAR.

In the preceding chapters I proposed a syntactic implementation of this view, and argued that in the syntactic structure itself there are two projections that are read off at the interface as pointers to the respective set of coordinates. The anchoring with the superordinate event—i.e., the evaluation of the embedded event with respect to the subject's temporal coordinate—takes place in the projection T where the verbal tense appears. Tense moves then to C, where the embedded event is evaluated with respect to the speaker's temporal location. Under the present approach, in fact, the highest projection in the C-layer contains the features that, at the interface, are interpreted as pointing to the utterance event itself. Consider again the sentence discussed above in Chapter 2:

(61)   Gianni ha detto [$_{\text{Cspeaker}}$ che$_{\text{C}}$ Maria [$_{\text{T-subject}}$ è incinta]]
    Gianni said that Maria is pregnant

The eventuality of *being pregnant* overlaps—henceforth notated as '$\approx$'—with the *saying* event. When T moves to C, it enters into a relation with the speaker's coordinate—i.e., with the utterance event. The relation to be interpreted at the interface is the following: $e_{\text{being pregnant}} \approx e_{\text{utterance}}$. The eventuality *being pregnant* is therefore overlapping with the utterance event as well, hence the DAR. In the previous chapters I proposed that this relation between T and C is instantiated when the embedded verbal form is an indicative. In a sense, it might be said that this is what being an indicative amounts to—cf. also the discussion of the Italian imperfect and the English past in Chapter 4.

A verbal form embedded under a future of a saying predicate is an indicative and therefore is expected to be subject to the same generalizations concerning the indicative. The point in question is exactly this: it does not. There are two possible ways out: either we deny that a verbal form embedded under a future maintains the general properties of indicative verbs, or we demonstrate that, contrary to appearances, the DAR holds in these contexts as well.

This latter hypothesis has the advantage that it could also provide a solution to the problem concerning the distribution of anaphoric temporal locutions. As I remarked above, such locutions do not occur in DAR contexts. In fact, as illustrated above, they do not occur in future embedded contexts either. Therefore the assimilation of future embedded contexts to DAR ones would yield the correct results.

The hypothesis I discuss in this section runs as follows. The projection of the high Complementizer C of the future embedded clause contains the speaker's coordinate, like the other indicative contexts. The difference with a main future is that in these contexts the speaker assumes the perspective of the subject—i.e., of the attitude bearer. The *meaning* of the future is therefore the shifting of the temporal coordinate of the speaker to the temporal location of the subject.

In other words, interpretively the temporal location of the main event becomes the (new) temporal location of the speaker, who therefore, with respect to the subordinate event, ends up having the same temporal location as the subject. Importantly, in this way the *syntax* of the embedded clause is computed exactly as in all the other cases: there is no difference at all between a clause depending on a main past and a clause depending on a main future with respect to the syntactic properties. The difference only resides in the specific value assigned to the speaker's coordinate at the interpretive interface.

Here I will work out the cases presented above, to show that this is exactly what happens. Consider now an embedded past:

(62) Gianni dirà [$_{\text{Cspeaker=subject}}$ che$_{\text{C}}$ Maria [$_{\text{T-subject}}$ è partita]]
      Gianni will say that Maria left

In T, the embedded event is interpreted as a past with respect to the temporal location of the subject. Consequently, the leaving precedes the saying. When in C, it is interpreted as a past with respect to the speaker's coordinate. The speaker's coordinate, however, has been reset to the subject coordinate—i.e., the saying event again. Therefore, the Double Access Reading of these contexts locates the embedded event twice with respect to the saying. It never locates it with respect to the utterance event. The resetting operation is an interface one, as part of the meaning assigned to the future. Syntactically, everything is as described in Chapter 2. Namely, C-speaker is projected out of the numeration, but its *value* is not *now*, but Gianni's temporal location.

Let's consider the interpretive process in more detail. The first step proceeds on a par with the contexts depending from a past: the anchoring procedure locates the embedded event with respect to the main event. In the second step, when T moves to C, the leaving is located with respect to the event defining the temporal coordinate of the speaker. Again, this move parallels the interpretation of tenses depending from a past. In the case of a main future, however, the event defining the speaker coordinate is a different one. In the main clauses—as in clauses depending from a past—the event defining the temporal coordinate of the speaker is the utterance event, *u*. By contrast, when the embedded context depends from a future, the event defining the speaker's coordinate is not *u*, but coincides with the main event. Let's call it *u'*. In other words, the main event provides a new set of coordinates for the speaker. In section 5.5 I briefly address the question of the *resetting* of the speaker's coordinate.

This hypothesis can explain how it is possible for an embedded indicative verbal form not to manifest DAR effects—as if it were a subjunctive or an imperfect—while maintaining the properties of an indicative. The peculiarity of future contexts is not constituted by the fact that the anchoring procedures are *different*—they are not—but by the *resetting* of the speaker's coordinate. Namely, the speaker looks at the embedded event from the perspective of the bearer-of-attitude.[14]

---

[14] Higginbotham (p.c.) notes that in some cases the speaker's coordinate is actually not reset. In these examples a strong context must be provided to ensure that the salient event locating the speaker is the utterance event *u* and no shifting to *u'* is possible. Consider the following examples (Higginbotham p.c.):

i.   Guarda come balla bene Maria! Domani dirai che sta ballando bene
     Look how well Maria is dancing! Tomorrow you will say that she is dancing well

The embedded verbal form is interpreted with respect to *u* and there is no resetting to *u'*. This interpretation, however, must be *forced* by the context. It is impossible to have in an out-of-the-blue sentence, such as the following:

ii. Domani Gianni dirà che Maria sta ballando bene
     Tomorrow Gianni will say that Maria is dancing well

In the absence of a strong context, it is impossible to interpret the embedded dancing as simultaneous to the utterance time *u*. The only possible interpretation makes it simultaneous with the saying by Gianni, which lies in the future with respect to *u*.

The derivation of an embedded present proceeds along the same lines:

(63)   Gianni dirà [$_{\text{C speaker=subject}}$ che$_\text{C}$ Maria [$_{\text{T-subject}}$ è incinta]]
       Gianni will say that Maria is pregnant

The pregnancy must only hold at the time Gianni speaks about it and does not have to hold at the utterance time u. The same process I described above yields the correct interpretation in this case as well. The future introduces a temporal location u', relocating the speaker coordinate at the time of Gianni's *saying*. Therefore u' coincides with e_{saying}. The pregnancy is therefore taken to hold at the time of e_{saying} and, once T moves to C, at u'—i.e., the reset temporal location of the speaker. However, u' is nothing else than the saying event. Therefore, even if the embedded eventuality is temporally evaluated twice, it turns out to overlap only with the saying and not with the utterance event u. Note that, as above, syntactically everything works as described in the normal cases discussed in Chapter 2.

Interestingly, the following sentence sounds odd:

(64)   Fra due anni Gianni dirà che Maria adesso è incinta
       In two years Gianni will say that now Maria is pregnant

The state of pregnancy is specified as holding *now*, i.e., at u. the embedded present must be anchored to the saying and therefore it must also coincide with it: $e_{being\ pregant} \approx e_{saying}$. Then it is located with respect to u' (the saying, again), i.e., the reset speaker's coordinate. The e_{saying} however is located *fra due anni* (in two years). Given what we know about human beings, this is not a sound reading.

To conclude, the presence of the indexicals in this case induces an evaluation of the embedded eventuality with respect to *now*. The oddity of sentence (64), however, is entirely due to the presence of the temporal adverbs and not to the fact that the embedded event must be evaluated with respect to *now* as a rule.

The interpretation of the embedded future follows, trivially:

(65)   Gianni dirà [$_{\text{Cspeaker=subject}}$ che$_\text{C}$ Maria [$_{\text{T-subject}}$ partirà]]
       Gianni will say that Maria will leave

The leaving is located after the saying, which is itself in the future. Consequently, the relocating of the speaker coordinate does not affect the interpretation of the embedded event.

5.4.2 *Towards an explanation of the distribution of temporal locutions*

5.4.2.1 *Indexical temporal locutions*   In this section I apply my proposal to the distribution of the temporal locutions. Consider the following example:

(66)   Oggi è il 25 dicembre. Il 27, Gianni dirà che Maria è partita il 26/*domani/*il giorno prima
Today is 25 December. On the 27th, Gianni will say that Maria left on the 26th/*tomorrow/*the day before

As illustrated above, in the past contexts depending from a future, both the anaphoric and the indexical temporal location have an anomalous distribution, in that neither one is acceptable. Only the referential one is grammatical. Consider also the following case, with an embedded imperfect:

(67)   Oggi è il 25 dicembre. Il 27, Gianni dirà che Maria era partita il giorno prima
Today is 25 December. On the 27th, Gianni will say that Maria left(IMPF) the day before

The imperfect in the embedded clause sharply contrasts with the corresponding example in (66), in that the anaphoric temporal locution is grammatical.

Let us consider sentence (66). An indexical such as *domani* (tomorrow) places the event in the future with respect to the speaker's coordinate: $u > t_{domani}(e_{leaving})$. The utterance time precedes the time of the leaving, which is *tomorrow*. When the temporal predicate in T is interpreted, the leaving is located before the saying: $e_{leaving} > e_{saying}$. At this point *therefore*, the event $e_{leaving}$ is in the future with respect to the speaker and in the past with respect to bearer of attitude. Then, T moves to C where the speaker's coordinate u is reset to u', i.e., the time of the saying. The leaving at this point must be located in the past with respect to the speaker's coordinate u'. As a consequence, a problem arises: the leaving has already being located by means of *tomorrow* in the *future* of the speaker, and now, by virtue of the resetting of u to u', it should be located in her *past*. This is impossible and the sentence turns out unacceptable. Ultimately, therefore, the reason *domani* is not admitted in these contexts is the same as in main clauses: *Gianni left tomorrow*. If something is located in the future with respect to the speaker, by means of *domani*, then it cannot simultaneously be located in her past, by means of verbal morphology. The difference is that in this case this result is obtained indirectly, by virtue of the resetting of u to u'.

The same reasoning holds even when *domani* locates an event expressed in a nominal structure—cf. examples (39)–(41) above, repeated here:

(68) *Dopodomani Gianni dirà che [la tua partenza di domani] è necessaria
    The day after tomorrow Gianni will say that your leaving tomorrow is necessary

(69)   Dopodomani Gianni dirà che [la tua partenza è stata necessaria]
    The day after tomorrow Gianni will say that your leaving tomorrow was necessary

(70)   Gianni dirà che [la tua partenza di domani] è necessaria
    The day after tomorrow Gianni will say that your leaving tomorrow is necessary

In sentence (68), the saying event is located in the future by means of the temporal locution *the day after tomorrow*, so that the leaving is located in the past with respect to it, being specified as taking place *tomorrow*. *Tomorrow* also locates the leaving event in the future of the speaker. But then in the embedded clause u is reset to u', i.e., the saying event. Therefore, the event of leaving should be simultaneously located in the future of the speaker—by means of *tomorrow*—and in her past, given that the leaving has to *precede* the saying. This is impossible, and the structure is unacceptable.

Examples (69) and (70) are both grammatical. In sentence (69) the leaving is located in the past with respect to the saying, and we do not know whether it is also located in the past with respect to the utterance event u or not. All we know is that $e_{leaving} > e_{saying}$.

Consequently, when u is reset to u', nothing changes and the sentence is grammatical.

In sentence (70) the leaving is specified as occurring in the future with respect to the speaker, by means of *tomorrow*: $u > e_{leaving}$. When u is reset to u', then the leaving must follow u', the saying, as well. In this case this is possible, contrasting with (68), given that there is no specification forcing the location of the saying to be posterior to the leaving. In (70), therefore, the leaving follows both the utterance time *and* the saying, as in the following case:

(71)   Fra un'ora Gianni dirà che la tua partenza di domani è necessaria
        In one hour Gianni will say that your leaving tomorrow is necessary

The same pattern can be found in infinitival complements:

(72)   Gianni dirà di essere partito (*domani)
        Lit: Gianni will say to have left (tomorrow)
        Gianni will say he left tomorrow

The leaving must precede the saying: $e_{leaving} > e_{saying}$. It is also located by means of *tomorrow* in the future of the speaker: $u > e_{leaving}$. When u is reset to u', i.e., the saying, then it ends up being located both before and after the saying: $u'(e_{saying}) > e_{leaving}$. This yields unacceptability.

Let us consider now the distribution of the futurate present and of the future:

(73)   *Dopodomani Gianni dirà che Maria parte/partirà domani
        The day after tomorrow Gianni will say that Maria leaves/will leave tomorrow

(74)   Dopodomani Gianni dirà che Maria parte/partirà
        The day after tomorrow Gianni will say that Maria leaves/will leave

(75)   Gianni dirà che Maria parte/partirà domani
        Gianni will say that Maria leaves/will leave tomorrow

The embedded form in (73) must be located in the future with respect to the saying, like *partirà* (will leave): $e_{saying} > e_{leaving}$. The presence of *tomorrow* locates the event after u: $u > e_{leaving}$. Then u is reset to u', yielding $u' > e_{leaving}$. So far everything works, and the sentence is acceptable—as is the case with example (75)—having the same indexical specification in the embedded clause. However, the presence of *dopodomani* in the main clause of (73) gives rise to unacceptability, given that it forces an ordering between the saying and the leaving such that $e_{leaving} > e_{saying}$, contrasting with the ordering obtained through temporal anchoring. As expected, if the temporal adverb *domani* does not appear in the sentence, as in (74), no problem arises.

Notice also that in sentence (75), in order to preserve the interpretation in which the saying precedes the leaving, *tomorrow* turns out to be both *the day after u* and *the day after u'*. In other words, the acceptable interpretation implies that Gianni spoke *today*, and that therefore the day identified as *tomorrow* by the speaker is also identifiable as *tomorrow* by Gianni. In this case, therefore, the time span identified by *domani* is preserved both with respect to *u* and with respect to *u'*.

Let us consider briefly the distribution of *ieri* (yesterday), i.e., the temporal mirror image of *tomorrow*. Consider the following examples:

(76) Gianni dirà che Maria è partita ieri
      Gianni will say that Maria left yesterday

The adverb *ieri* locates the leaving event in the past with respect to *u*: $e_{leaving} > u$. The anchoring process locates the leaving before the saying: $e_{leaving} > e_{saying}$. Finally, *u* is reset to *u'*—the saying again—and therefore $e_{leaving} > u'$. No problem arises and the sentence is therefore acceptable.

Now the question arises concerning the precise interpretation of the time span identified by *ieri* (yesterday)—i.e., the day before the day of the utterance event. It seems to me that it does not have to be preserved, in that the only requirement to be met is the relative ordering of the events. In other words, the day of the event is identified only on the basis of the time of *u*. The relative ordering requirement—i.e., $e_{leaving} > e_{saying}$, $e_{leaving} > u$ and $e_{leaving} > u'$—can be met even if the utterance event and the saying event occur in different days, as for instance in the following case:

(77) Dopodomani Gianni dirà che Maria è partita ieri
      The day after tomorrow Gianni will say that Maria left yesterday

The speaker's *yesterday* in this case does not coincide with Gianni's *yesterday*, but the sentence is nevertheless acceptable. On the other hand, this is the case even in the past under past clauses:

(78)   Ieri Gianni ha detto che Maria è partita l'altro ieri
      Yesterday Gianni said that Maria left the day before yesterday

The day before yesterday is such only with respect to the speaker, and not to the subject Gianni.[15]

In other words, even in those cases where there is no resetting of the temporal coordinate, the combined result of the temporal anchoring and of the location of the events according to the indexical locutions must be coherent. Consider in fact that a sentence inverting the temporal specification given in (78)—i.e., where the embedded event is located *ieri* (yesterday) and the main one *l'altro ieri* (the day before yesterday)—yields the opposite ordering of the events and is consequently unacceptable:

(79)   #L'altro ieri Gianni ha detto che Maria è partita ieri
      The day before yesterday Gianni said that Maria left yesterday

In (79) the anchoring process orders the leaving before the saying. This result contrasts with the relative ordering induced by the temporal locutions, hence the oddity of the sentence.

In Italian, the coherence of the relative ordering is the only condition to be met, whereas in English, and maybe in other languages as

---

[15] For some English speakers these sentences turn out to be unacceptable. It might be the case that in English the time span identified by the indexical has to be preserved throughout the sentence. That is, the indexical not only places the event in the past or in the future of the speaker, but also establishes a specific temporal relation with the other events (Higginbotham, p.c.). In this perspective, in sentence (78) a locution such as *the day before yesterday* would locate the event in the past of the speaker *and* in the day before the day preceding the utterance event, when evaluated with respect to *u*. When the embedded event is evaluated with respect to the saying of *Gianni*, the temporal locution locates it in the past of *Gianni*, and also in the day preceding the day before *Gianni's saying*. In Italian the process would not take place in the same way. The temporal locution only locates the event in the past, or in the future of the speaker. As I have shown in this chapter, its temporal location must be coherent with the anchoring process, so that if *u* is reset to *u'* the relative order of the events can be maintained.

well, it looks likely that every time the event is temporally evaluated, the time span identified by the indexical is also interpreted. Consider the following example:

(80)   John said that Mary left yesterday

In English this sentence is acceptable only if John said it *today*.

To conclude, it is possible that the indexical temporal locutions behave in slightly different ways across languages, so that the status of (79), for instance, might vary from one language to another. However, what all languages, at least all DAR languages, have in common, is that the temporal anchoring and the locating of the event in time by means of temporal adverbs interact with each other in ways which are grammatically, and syntactically, defined.

5.4.2.2 *Anaphoric temporal locutions*   Let us now consider the distribution of anaphoric temporal locutions such as *il giorno prima/dopo* (the day before/after). As I remarked in section 5.3.3, Giorgi and Pianesi (2003) showed that the temporal variable x, necessary for interpreting *before* and *after*, cannot pick up its reference from u. Therefore, as pointed out above, an out-of-the-blue sentence such as (81) is infelicitous:

(81)   #Gianni è partito il giorno prima
       Gianni left the day before

If no possible antecedent for x, in *the day before (the day x)*, is present in the context, the sentence is ill-formed. The point of interest here is that example (81) cannot mean *Gianni left the day before the day of the utterance*. Recall that u on the other hand is available as an anchoring point for the past tense, as shown by the fact that the leaving is located in the past with respect to it: $e_{leaving} >$ u. On the other hand, antecedenthood can be provided by the context external to the sentence, as in example (45), here repeated for simplicity:

(82)   A: Maria è partita il 23 marzo B: Ma no! È partita il giorno prima
       A: Maria left on 23 March B: No! She left the day before

The contrast between (81) and (82) shows that anaphoric temporal locutions are not *per se* incompatible with the indicative forms; the incompatibility is specifically between x and u.

In embedded clauses, this incompatibility extends to all DAR contexts, which necessarily involve evaluation of the embedded event with respect to u. The way out is to substitute the 'normal' indicative, with the imperfect, which does not require such an evaluation. Consider the following contrasts (examples (49) and (50) given above, here repeated):

(83) *Il 28 dicembre/dopodomani Gianni dirà che Maria è partita il giorno prima
      On 28 December/the day after tomorrow Gianni will say that Maria left the day before

(84) Il 28 dicembre/dopodomani Gianni dirà che Maria era partita il giorno prima
      On 28 December/the day after tomorrow Gianni will say that Maria had(IMPF) left the day before

The sentence in (84) is not subject to the DAR, in that the imperfect does not need to be evaluated in C with respect to the speaker's coordinate. The fact that u is reset to u' does not matter, given that the reasons for the original incompatibility between the anaphoric temporal locution and the speaker's coordinate persist in spite of its relocation.

This contrast is a strong argument in favour of the analysis proposed here. Even if a sentence such as (83) is not at first sight a *double* access sentence, it still exhibits a DAR pattern. The idea I am advocating here is that this is a DAR context *in disguise*, given that the speaker's and the subject's coordinates are made to coincide. Therefore, the distribution of the items that are sensitive to the presence of the speaker's coordinate does not vary.

The example in (84) gives rise to the same temporal interpretation as (83) with respect to the location of the events: $u > e_{leaving} > e_{saying}$. The only difference is that the embedded event is not re-evaluated with respect to u' in C. This makes it possible for the anaphoric locution to appear in this context.

5.5 Further speculations and conclusions

Note that all the examples I discussed in the preceding section are not syntactically marked. The basic idea of this chapter is that, even if this does not seem to be the case, the syntactic computation in these contexts is exactly as described for 'normal' cases. The only difference is that interpretively, and once again *not* syntactically, the speaker's temporal coordinate takes over a peculiar value—a resetting—due to the meaning of the main verbal form. Now, the issue concerns the precise implementation, at the interpretive level, of this resetting idea. Here I do not have a definite answer, and actually this book is mostly about syntax, but I do have a suggestion: whatever happens in these contexts has some property in common with certain kinds of counterfactuals.

More precisely, in this section I address the following question: why are the contexts created by a future different from those created by a past verbal form?

As I said above, I am not able to provide an exhaustive answer, but I try to show that the contexts in question have something in common, in the relevant respect, with counterfactuals. Therefore one might expect that whatever accounts for the peculiar properties of counterfactuals might also account for these cases.

According to the proposal sketched above, the crucial properties, from which all the others follow, is the peculiarity of the future of resetting u to u', so that the speaker assumes the subject's perspective with respect to the embedded event.

As far as I can see, besides these contexts, the resetting of indexicals is possible in sentences like the following one:[16]

(85)   If I were you, I would marry me

The value of *I*, which is indexically identified, is reset in this context, by means of the *if*-clause, to the value of another individual, *you*. In the main clause, the two instances of the first person pronoun,

---

[16] A reviewer points out that this sentence is acceptable only in a semi-humorous deviation from the norm. What is interesting here, however, is the possibility for this sentence to exist at all. In the next chapter I will analyse some stylistic devices which produce various narrative effects.

allegedly referring to the speaker, must be kept distinct, as shown by the oddness of the following sentence:

(86)   #If I were you, I would marry myself

The reflexive pronoun *myself* must refer back to *I* and cannot take a reference distinct from that of its antecedent. Note that the reason for the unacceptability of (86) does not lie in the syntax. Principles A and B of the Binding Theory are computed in exactly the way we expect them to be: *me*, as a pronoun in sentence (85), is disjoint from *I*, since the latter is in the same local domain. Analogously, in sentence (86), *myself* must be locally bound, hence it is bound by *I*. The anomaly of the judgement, which is exactly the reverse of what seems to be predicted by the Binding Theory, is due to the presence of the preceding *if*-clause, which intervenes on the reference of the first person pronoun. Since *I* does not refer to *speaker* any more, but to *hearer*, it is as a matter of fact disjoint from *me* in (85), and, conversely, cannot be a suitable antecedent for *myself* in (86).

The similarities between this context and those discussed in the preceding sections concern the fact that the future operates the same sort of resetting as is illustrated above. It does not operate on the reference of pronouns, but on temporal coordinates. Tentatively, one could propose that the future introduces a counterfactual operator, which has the effect of shifting the temporal coordinate of the speaker from u to u'. In the superordinate clause the coordinate to be taken into account is u; in the subordinate clause u' must be considered as the relevant coordinate. In a sense, therefore, they must both be present, but kept distinct.

In conclusion, in this chapter I have argued that the contexts created by a future are DAR contexts, and therefore do not constitute an exception to the generalization discussed in the preceding chapters. DAR effects show up once the phenomena are considered in greater detail and in particular when investigated with respect to the distribution of temporal locutions. Giorgi and Pianesi (2003) in fact argued that anaphoric temporal locutions, as opposed to indexical and referential ones, cannot appear in those contexts where anchoring to the speaker's coordinate is required. By using this as a test, it is possible to observe that future contexts are indeed incompatible with anaphoric temporal locutions. Under the hypothesis that the contexts embedded under a future are DAR ones, the distribution of the indicative verbal forms is no longer an exception.

The only additional hypothesis required concerns the resetting of the speaker's coordinate: the speaker assumes the perspective of the subject by virtue of its intrinsic meaning, perhaps as a counterfactual-like element.

6

When *Somebody Else* is Speaking: Free Indirect Discourse

6.1 Introduction

In this chapter I will consider the properties of the so-called Free Indirect Discourse, henceforth FID, which is a peculiar literary style—hence, something 'artificial'—created with the precise purpose of giving rise to a particular narrative effect. The aim of this chapter is to show that it is possible to assign the correct interpretation to these contexts without resorting to *ad hoc* hypotheses having the sole purpose of describing this style.

I will show that FID sentences can be interpreted by means of the same grammatical apparatus needed in 'normal' sentences, once we understand and describe the grammar underlying this literary device. I will show that the semantics of these contexts can be read directly off their syntax, as in the other cases discussed in this book. I argue that, in a way, FID sentences constitute the mirror image of the dependencies from the future discussed in the previous chapter. In that case, the future has the role of relocating the speaker in the subject's (temporal) location, so that the speaker's coordinate is no longer provided by the utterance event but by the superordinate, future, event. The FID device, conversely, might be taken to *promote* the subject, that is, the character of the story, to speaker. Consequently, an embedded eventuality must be located twice—Italian and English being DAR languages—with respect to the subject's coordinate: once in T and once in C. This shifting, however, will be shown to have effects on the distribution of the embedded verbal forms. According to this proposal, in fact, the embedded verb cannot explicitly require anchoring to the speaker, given that the latter in FID contexts has disappeared from the embedded clause and been substituted by the subject.

Finally, I will posit an additional root syntactic layer, the *informational layer*—already briefly discussed in Chapter 3—which accounts for word order phenomena observed in the distribution of what I call here the *introducing predicate*. The presence of this layer is also justified on the basis of observations concerning a variety of root phenomena, such as vocatives (Moro 2003) and exclamatives (Zanuttini and Portner 2003).

6.2 Free Indirect Discourse: properties

In the FID the narration, in the third person, proceeds from a source internal to the narrated text, i.e., one of the characters. The result of this technique, as will be clear from the examples, is that the reader has the impression of listening directly to the character's thoughts or speech. As an illustration, consider the following example:

(1)   It was, he now realized, because of this other incident that **he** had suddenly decided to come home and begin the diary today (Orwell, *1984*, ch. 1)

Consider also the following example, discussed in the previous literature (Banfield 1982: 98; Schlenker 2004):

(2)   Where was he this morning, for instance? Some committee, **she** never asked what (Woolf, *Mrs Dalloway*)

In this example the narrating character is identified by means of the third person pronouns *he* and *she* and we are listening to this character's thoughts. Consider also the following case in Italian:[1]

(3)   Lo ricordò dopo uno sforzo di memoria anzi di ragionamento: [*pro*] doveva essere passata per quella via essendo giunta a quell'altra da casa **sua**. Il giovinotto era un **suo** cugino ritornato dagli studii. Un ragazzo

---

[1] All the translations of the Italian examples are mine. Sources of literary examples are listed on p. 210.

cui non bisognava dare importanza (Italo Svevo, *La novella del buon vecchio e della bella fanciulla*, ch. 8)

She remembered it with an effort of memory, or better to say of reasoning: she should have passed through that street to reach that other one from her home. The young man was her cousin, who had come back from school. A young man who should not be given importance (Svevo, *The short story of the old man and the pretty girl*, ch. 8)

In this case, analogously to the previous one, we are listening to a speech by one of the characters—the 'pretty girl'. The character is identified by means of third person pronominal forms—in this case the null pronoun, *pro*, and the possessive pronouns *suo/sua* (her).

In what follows, therefore, I will distinguish the *internal source*— i.e., the character whose thoughts are being expressed—from the *external source*—i.e., the writer or speaker, in other words, the *creator* of the text. I will also dub phrases such as *he now realized* in example (1), or *Lo ricordò dopo uno sforzo di memoria anzi di ragionamento* (She remembered it with an effort of memory, or better to say of reasoning) in (3), *introducing predicates* (for a discussion see section 6.4 below).

These contexts exhibit several interesting peculiarities, which I will analyse shortly. The most striking one concerns the distribution of indexical temporal (and spatial) adverbials.

As noted in the linguistic literature on the topic, in the FID, temporal indexicals refer to the time coordinate of the internal source. In example (1), for instance, the indexical *now* is interpreted on the basis of the temporal coordinates of the character and not of the utterer, in this case the *writer*. Consider also in the following example:

(4)   The thing that **now** suddenly struck Winston was that his mother's death, **nearly thirty years ago**, had been tragic and sorrowful in a way that it was no longer possible. Tragedy, he perceived, belonged to the ancient time [...]. Such things, he saw, could not happen **today. Today** there were fear, hatred, and pain, but no dignity of emotion (Orwell, *1984*, ch. 3)

In this example, *now* and *today,* as well the indexical locution *thirty years ago,* take their reference from the temporal coordinates of

Winston—i.e., from the internal source of the narration. Consider now the following example (already discussed in Banfield 1982, Doron 1991, and Schlenker 2004):

(5) **Tomorrow** was Monday, Monday, the beginning of another school week!
(Lawrence, *Women in Love*, p. 185)

This characteristic concerning the interpretation of temporal indexicals can be found in Italian as well:

(6) Ah, Ecco perchè era così, **oggi**. Piangeva (Deledda, *Le colpe altrui*, p. 76)
Ah, this was why she was like that, today. She was crying

(7) Era la sua forza—commentava Baudolino a Niceta—e in questo modo lo aveva menato per il naso una prima volta, lo stava menando **ora** e lo avrebbe menato per alcuni anni ancora
This was his strength—Baudolino was commenting to Niceta—and in this way he had taken him by the nose once, he was leading him by the nose now, and he would take him by the nose for some years still (Eco, *Baudolino*, p. 264)

The properties of the temporal indexical forms show that the FID is not just a variant of indirect discourse. In indirect discourse, indexical temporal locutions take their value from the temporal coordinate of the speaker:

(8) Gianni disse che sarebbe partito domani/il giorno dopo
Gianni said that he would leave the next day/**tomorrow**

In indirect discourse, the interpretation of the indexical *tomorrow* is crucially different from the interpretation of *the next day*. The anaphoric temporal locution *il giorno dopo* (the next day) identifies the day after Gianni's speech, whereas *tomorrow*—an indexical temporal location—only identifies the day after the day of the utterance—i.e., it takes its value from the speaker's coordinates. This is the 'normal' behaviour of temporal indexical expressions.

I will consider this point in more detail below. For the time being, let me point out that FID phenomena on the one hand could be analysed from a purely stylistic point of view—namely, one could consider when and why an author should use FID and exactly what narrative nuances it produces.[2] On the other hand, one could wonder what exactly creates this particular effect in the syntax of these sentences. Native speakers have very clear and consistent intuitions, as discussed also in Guéron (2006a, 2007), about the syntax of these sentences and know exactly how they should be structured and what their grammar is. For instance, an Italian speaker finds a very clear contrast between a sentence such as (7) above and the following one:

(9)   #È/ È STATA la sua forza [commentava Baudolino a Niceta] e in questo modo lo HA MENATO per il naso una prima volta, lo STA MENANDO ora e lo MENERÀ per alcuni anni ancora.

This is/has been (PRES/PRES PERF) his strength—Baudolino was commenting to Niceta—and in this way he has(PRES/PERF/PAST) taken him by the nose once, he is(PRES) leading him by the nose now, and he will(FUT) take him by the nose for some years still

In sentence (9) the imperfect indicative verbal forms have been substituted by other indicative verbal forms. While the result of such a substitution is otherwise not particularly problematic in normal contexts, in this case it gives rise to a deviant sentence. Compare the contrast between (7) and (9) with the following pair:

(10)   Gianni ha detto che Maria è partita
         Gianni said that Maria left(PRES PERF)

(11)   Gianni said that Maria era partita
         Gianni said that Maria had left(IMPF)

With respect to Sequence of Tense, in both (10) and (11) the leaving is located before the saying and, as far as this simple case goes, the two sentences are more or less equivalent.[3]

---

[2] Note, however, that FID is not only a narrative *literary* style, but it is also sometimes adopted in normal *everyday* speech. I recommend the reader to try an experiment and keep notice of its occurrences in his/her own conversation: the outcome might be surprising! For instance, one might reproduce somebody's speech using the third person, but making gestures and using a tone of voice resembling the person's. This actually happens quite frequently and the properties of the sentences so produced are those observed in the FID.

[3] The issue—i.e., the usage of the present perfect/past vs. the imperfect—in Romance is actually quite a complex one. See Giorgi and Pianesi (2004b) and references cited there for a discussion. See also Chapter 4 above.

This does not happen with examples (7) and (9), however. In particular, for instance, *lo sta menando ora per il naso* (he is leading him by the nose now) can be temporally interpreted only with respect to the external source's coordinates, meaning that at the time the writer is writing Baudolino is being taken by the nose. Analogously, *lo menerà* (he will lead him by the nose) can only mean that at a time lying in the future with respect to time of the writing, Baudolino will be taken by the nose.

The fact that native speakers have intuitions and grammaticality judgements in relation to these contexts is important because it contributes to dismantling a prejudice we might have with respect to written texts. The prejudice can be more or less stated as follows: an author *creates* her language *and* grammar; therefore we cannot expect grammatical rules to be *obeyed* as they are in non-literary everyday language. All sorts of violations are permitted. The language of literary texts is therefore qualitatively different from *real* language and a theoretical, formal linguist has nothing to say about it.

On the contrary, linguists have shown, as a basic *tenet* of a Theory of Grammar, that it is possible to give a formal account of the various phenomena of FID. In other words, FID facts follow from the rules of grammar as they are established for non-literary contexts. The aim of this chapter therefore is to provide a grammar for FID and to show that the hypothesis illustrated in previous chapters concerning the syntactic representation of the speaker's coordinate provides an explanation for native speakers' intuitions in these cases as well.

As I briefly illustrated in the previous examples, in these contexts it is possible to observe a sort of dissociation between the interpretation of pronouns, indexicals, and tenses. In what follows I introduce these properties one by one.

6.2.1 *Pronouns*

In the previous section I already pointed out the peculiarity concerning the distribution of the third person pronoun. Summarizing the observations proposed above, it is possible to say that *normally* a sentence expresses the thoughts of the speaker, and when the speaker introduces herself in the sentence in languages such as Italian and English she does so by means of a first person pronoun. A third person pronoun identifies *somebody else*. This is not the case in FID, where a third person pronoun identifies the thinker or *internal source*.[4]

In this section I consider the properties of the first person pronoun in such contexts. The basic observation is that when a first person pronoun appears in a FID text, it *must* refer to the external source. Consider for instance the following example, built on example (3) above:

(12) Lo ricordò dopo uno sforzo di memoria anzi di ragionamento: [***pro***] doveva essere passata per quella via essendo giunta a quell'altra da casa **mia**

      She remembered it with an effort of memory, or better to say of reasoning: (she) should have passed through that street to reach that other one from **my** home

In this example, I substituted the first person possessive form *sua* (his/her) from example (3) above with a first person possessive *mia* (my). This sentence can only be understood as expressing the following meaning: the main character in the story—the *internal source*—is telling something that identifies the owner of the house as the *external source*. Notice, incidentally, that the same effect arises when using second person pronouns:

(13) Lo ricordò dopo uno sforzo di memoria anzi di ragionamento: [***pro***] doveva essere passata per quella via essendo giunta a quell'altra da casa **tua**

      She remembered it with an effort of memory, or better to say of reasoning: (she) should have passed through that street to reach that other one from **your** home

In this case the presence of a second person possessive suggests that the external narrator is telling the story, adopting the FID style, to another

---

[4] Notice that it is not always true that a third person pronoun identifies somebody other than the speaker. There are several cases in the literature where the speaker might refer to herself in the third person. Consider for instance the following sentence, where the speaker is Maria:

i. Chi ha detto che Maria non vincerà la gara? Vincerò sicuramente invece!

    Who said that Maria will not win the race? I will certainly win, on the contrary!

There are several questions connected to this issue, which however are not crucial to the present investigation and I will not discuss them further.

external participant.[5] This is relevant because it shows that the internal source is identified as a third party *from the outside*. This peculiarity has already been noted in the literature and discussed by Banfield (1982) and Schlenker (2004). I will return on this property in section 6.3 below.

Recall also that a first person pronoun does not necessarily identify the actual utterer. For instance, it identifies a third party in direct speech:

(14) Gianni **mi** ha detto: '**Io** voglio comprare quella casa'
      Gianni told **me**: 'I want to buy that house'

In this example the two occurrences of the first person pronoun identify two different speakers—the *actual* speaker, and the *reported* speaker—in the course of the same speech act.

In literary contexts, first person narration constitutes another obvious case:

(15) Oggi [*pro*] scopro subito qualche cosa che piú non [*pro*] ricordavo. Le prime sigarette ch'**io** fumai non esistono piú in commercio (Svevo, *La coscienza di Zeno*, ch. 3)[6]

      Today I immediately find out something that I did not remember anymore. The first cigarettes that I smoked are no longer sold.

The first person pronouns here identify the character, *Zeno*, and not the actual writer, Svevo.

This observation leads us to conclude that a first person pronoun refers to the *speaker*; the speaker in most cases is the actual utterer, but in some cases it is not. The two examples given above, where the first person pronoun does not identify the *utterer*, illustrate this view:

---

[5] The same happens with plural pronouns:

i. Lo ricordò dopo uno sforzo di memoria anzi di ragionamento: [*pro*] doveva essere passata per quella via essendo giunta a quell'altra da casa **nostra/vostra**.
    She remembered it with an effort of memory, or better to say of reasoning: (she) should have passed through that street to reach that other one from our/your home.

The effect given by means of the plural pronouns is the same as the one discussed in the text.

[6] Note that in this example the temporal indexical expression *oggi* (today) appears. From the passage of the novel it is clear that it identifies the day in which the author is writing that particular chapter, since the whole novel is conceived as a day-by-day diary. In this sense therefore, *oggi* (today) takes its value from the same context that assigns the correct interpretation to the first person subject.

in these sentences the first person pronoun, though not the *utterer,* is the *speaker,* namely, the person performing the speech act reported in the sentence.

In conclusion, these observations show that it is necessary to distinguish the *utterer* from the *speaker.* The first person pronoun must always refer to a speaker/writer, who might or might not be the utterer as well.[7]

6.2.2 *Indexical temporal expressions*

6.2.2.1 *The internal source*   As I briefly pointed out above, temporal indexicals in FID texts take their reference from the internal source. Examples (1) and (4) above illustrate this point with respect to past and present indexical expressions—such as *thirty years ago, today, now.* The following example illustrates it with respect to a future temporal indexical, *tomorrow:*

(16)   The new ration did not start till **tomorrow** and **he** had only four cigarettes left (Orwell, *1984,* ch. 5)

---

[7] When the speaker is identified by means of a first person pronoun and the utterer is not the speaker—as in the examples given—then the utterer is not identifiable by means of a pronoun, but only by means of a set of spatial and temporal coordinates. This might be viewed as a lexical gap, or as a principled property of language. If a lexical gap, we expect languages to exist with a different pronoun for the two cases: one for the speaker and one for the utterer, to be used at least in those contexts where the two do not overlap. If the second option is the correct one, then a principled explanation should be found for this fact. So far, I do not have suggestions on this particular issue.

Consider also that, trivially, in languages like Italian and English, not all the speakers are identified by means of first person pronoun—namely all first person pronouns identify speakers, but not vice versa. This might not be the case in languages like Amharic, though, if the data discussed in Schlenker (2003, 2004) are consistent. Here I report Schlenker's example (2003, ex. 3):

i.   Situation to be reported: John says: 'I am a hero'.

ii.   Amharic (lit.): John$_i$ says that I$_i$ am a hero.

iii. English: John$_i$ says that he$_i$ is a hero / *John$_i$ says that I$_i$ am a hero

Moreover, an analysis of languages having logophoric pronouns with respect to their usage in these contexts would also be relevant to the present discussion. For an introduction to phenomena concerning logophoric pronouns see, among others, Clements (1975) and Hagège (1974). I will not discuss this issue any further and I refer the reader to the quoted reference.

In sentence (16), we understand the eventuality of having only four cigarettes left as holding at the internal source's *now*. The indexical *tomorrow* refers to the day following the day in which the subject *he*, the internal source, is located. With respect to the temporal coordinate of the internal source, the eventuality of having four cigarettes is interpreted as holding presently, and the starting of the new ration is understood as being located in the future.

In other words: in this example, as well as in those given above, the temporal coordinates permitting the interpretation of the indexical temporal expressions are those pertaining to the internal source, identified by means of a third person pronoun. Consistently, the various eventualities appearing in the sentence are understood as located along the temporal continuum on the basis of the internal source's coordinates.

In this sense, the interpretation of example (16) would not differ from the interpretation of the corresponding sentence given in the normal, non-FID style:

(17)   The new ration will not start till **tomorrow** and **I** have only four cigarettes left

In (17), as is usually the case, the speaker refers to himself by means of a first person pronoun, *I*, and the indexical *tomorrow* identifies the day which follows the day of the utterance—i.e., the day in which the speaker is temporally located. The future tense and the present tense order the events with respect to each other and with respect to the speaker's coordinates.

Concluding these brief remarks: the interesting property of the FID exemplified by the examples given above is that temporal indexicals do not identify a temporal location of the event with respect to the external source—the writer/speaker—but with respect to the internal one—the thinker. In this sense, therefore, it looks like they cease to be real *indexicals*, in that the context that is relevant for their interpretation is not provided by the actual utterance event, but by the literary, created context.

6.2.2.2 *Indexical temporal expressions and pronouns*   In the light of the discussion in the previous section and in section 6.2.1 above, consider now what happens by adding an introducing predicate with a first person pronoun to example (17):

(18)   The new ration did not start till **tomorrow** and **he** had only four cigarettes left, *I thought*

The first person refers to the internal source—i.e., to the person thinking. As a result, the indexical *tomorrow* refers to the day after the day of the thinking.[8]

The same happens in Italian. Consider the following translation of the example in (17):

(19)   Il nuovo razionamento sarebbe cominciato **domani** e **(egli)** aveva solo altre quattro sigarette, *pensai*
The new ration did not start till **tomorrow** and **he** had only four cigarettes left, *I thought*

In these cases the internal source and the external one coincide, in that the *thinker* must also be the *speaker*. Therefore, it is not surprising that temporal indexicals and events are interpreted on the basis of the coordinates of the speaker/thinker. The only interpretation for this sentence is the following one: *I, the speaker, thought that tomorrow the new ration would start and he had only four cigarettes left*. Therefore, for the sentence to hold—that is, in order to interpret *tomorrow* correctly—the thinking must be located *today* in both English and Italian, as exemplified by the following examples:[9]

(20)   The new ration did not start till **tomorrow** and **he** had only four cigarettes left, *I thought this morning*

(21)   Il nuovo razionamento sarebbe cominciato **domani** e **(egli)** aveva solo altre quattro sigarette, *pensai questa mattina*

In these examples the speaker is explicitly identified with the thinker and the behaviour of the temporal indexical does not exhibit any special features.

---

[8] The speaker might be the *writer* of the story, or a first person narrator. Since the specific interpretation is not particularly relevant to the point I am making here, I will leave it unspecified.

[9] For observations in the same vein, see also Banfield (1982), who talks about the *priority of the speaker*, and Schlenker (2004).

Let's consider, however, some cases in which the first pronoun appears as a participant in the FID context. I discuss here an example proposed in Schlenker (2004, ex. 16):[10]

(22) Oh how extraordinarily nice I was, she told my father, without realizing that I was listening to the conversation

Let's consider now what happens in this case when we add a temporal indexical, both in English and Italian:

(23) Oh how extraordinarily nice I was **yesterday morning**, she told my father **last night**, without realizing that I was listening to the conversation

(24) Oh, come ero (stato) meraviglioso **ieri mattina**, Maria disse a mio padre **ieri sera**, senza rendersi conto che io stavo ascoltando la conversazione

In these sentences, which are examples of the FID style, the first person *I* refers to the speaker—namely, the *external source*, the person uttering the sentence. The intuition of native speakers, both in English and Italian, is that the days in question cannot be two different ones—namely, the two temporal indexicals refer to the morning and the night of the same day. Moreover, the specific day is identified on the basis of the location of the speaker—the first person *I*—and not of the location of the internal source, Maria.

For the same reason, the following sentences are infelicitous:

(25) Oh how extraordinarily nice I was **yesterday night**, she told my father **last morning**, without realizing that I was listening to the conversation

(26) Oh, come mi ero comportato bene **ieri sera**, Maria disse a mio padre **ieri mattina**, senza rendersi conto che io stavo ascoltando la conversazione

---

[10] Schlenker (2004) proposes this example while discussing a similar one by Banfield (1982). Here I am not pursuing the same line of reasoning, so I will not summarize that particular discussion. Let me only point out that I am proposing this example because it permits us to analyse the properties of the first person in an FID context, making the first person character a participant in the *situation*, though not a participant in the actual *conversation*, thanks to the phrase *without realizing that I was listening to the conversation*. This *escamotage* is important to avoid side issues which might invalidate the discussion, as remarked in Schlenker (2004).

This is due to the fact that the temporal reference of *yesterday night* and *yesterday evening* in these cases is not compatible with the requirement that the day be the same.

It seems therefore that a first person attracts the indexical: when a first person appears in FID contexts, the temporal indexicals must be interpreted according to the coordinates associated with it.

Note that the same is true with spatial interpretation:

(27)   **I** showed **her this** room, Maria told my father without realizing that I was listening to the conversation

(28)   **Io le** avevo mostrato **questa** stanza, Maria disse a mio padre, senza rendersi conto che io avevo sentito la conversazione

The room in question is the one where the first person speaker is, and not the one where the referent of the third person is.

Given these considerations, it is possible to formulate the following generalization:

(29)   When the speaker is introduced in a given context, her temporal and spatial coordinates determine the interpretation of spatial and temporal indexicals.

In normal, non-FID contexts this generalization applies as a *default*, in the sense that it might seem to be a property of indexicals in themselves and not of a peculiar context.

The first person's coordinates—i.e., in this case the speaker's—constitute the reference set which permits the interpretation of the indexicals. The hypothesis I will develop below is that the value of the temporal and spatial coordinates is set in the C-layer. Once they refer to the speaker, they cannot be modified by means of the resetting operation I will discuss in section 6.3 below.[11]

Several scholars have studied the double perspective of these contexts—namely, the presence of a centre of indexicality differing from the first person speaker. In order to account for the observations above, Schlenker (2004), elaborating on proposals by Banfield (1982) and Doron (1991), argues in favour of a distinction between

---

[11] In section 6.4 below I will show that the informational layer, the INF-layer, also plays an important role in accounting for these phenomena.

the context of utterance—i.e., an uttering event—and a context of thought—i.e., an event of thinking. He suggests that, whereas in everyday speech the two contexts are perfectly overlapping, because the thinker and the speaker are the same person, in FID they are dissociated.[12]

The result of the dissociation is that part of the sentence is interpreted according to one context and part according to the other. Schlenker (2004) argues that, given the peculiarities of FID sentences, indexicals are interpreted with respect to the context of thought—i.e., they identify temporal and spatial locations according to the coordinates of the thinker—in my terminology, the internal source. Pronouns, by contrast, take their reference from the context of utterance—i.e., in my terminology, the external source. Finally, tenses in FID are interpreted in the context of utterance, along with pronouns.

Schlenker's main argument to this effect follows the proposal originally suggested by Partee (1973), who argued that tenses behave as *temporal* pronouns. In this sense, therefore, Schlenker suggests that pronouns and tenses form a natural class.

In the next section I will show that a more fine-grained analysis of verbal morphology appearing in these contexts permits a better understanding of FID phenomena, leading to a different, and perhaps simpler, account.

6.2.3 *The past tense*

As noted in the literature on the topic, in English FID verbs consistently appear in the past form, even when combined with future or present indexicals. This is illustrated in examples (16) and (4), repeated here for simplicity:

(30)   The new ration **did** not start till **tomorrow** and he **had** only four cigarettes left (Orwell, *1984*, ch. 5)

(31)   The thing that **now** suddenly **struck** Winston was that his mother's death, nearly thirty years ago, had been tragic and sorrowful in a way that it was no longer possible. Tragedy, he perceived, belonged to the

---

[12] For development of a proposal in the same vein, see also Sharvit (2004, 2008).

ancient time [...]. Such things, he saw, **could** not happen **today. Today** there **were** fear, hatred, and pain, but no dignity of emotion (Orwell, *1984*, ch. 3)

In these examples the verb bears past morphology, irrespective of the location that the indexical temporal locutions assign to the events. For instance, in (30) the first event, *the starting of the ration*, has a future location, provided by *tomorrow*, whereas the verb is in the past form, *did start*.

These facts constitute a puzzle, given that in normal language indexicals must agree with the verbal tense:

(32)   **Tomorrow**/*Yesterday Mary will leave

(33)   Yesterday/***Tomorrow** Mary left

The solution proposed in the literature so far (Banfield 1982; Doron 1991; Schlenker 2004) is that tenses receive their interpretation according to the speaker's coordinates. Namely, there is a dissociation between indexicals on one side and tenses and pronouns on the other, so that indexicals are interpreted with respect to the subject's temporal location, whereas tenses and pronouns are centred in the speaker's *here* and *now*.

As it turns out, all the sentences in question feature a past tense. Therefore, according to this approach, all the eventualities are placed in the past with respect to the utterance time. Why are they located in the past? The authors mentioned above do not provide a clear-cut answer to this question. However, pursuing their line of reasoning, one might say that for stylistic reasons the narrator demotes the action to some unspecified past because people think of a narrated event as an event which has *already* occurred some-time somewhere. In other words, from this point of view there is no interesting theoretical reason concerning the selection of the verbal form.

On the other hand, however, given that according to this account the choice of the past form is not determined by grammar, but is a mere stylistic device, a different choice should not give rise to ungrammaticality, but should simply be an instantiation of a different literary style.

As pointed out in section 6.1 for Italian—cf. example (9)—the adoption of a different verbal form does determine ungrammaticality. The same holds in English. Consider for instance the following example:

(34)   It **was**, he *now* **realized**, because of this other incident that he **had** suddenly **decided** to come home and begin the diary *today* (Orwell, *1984*, ch. 1)

(35)   *It **is**, he *now* **realizes**, because of this other incident that he **has** suddenly **decided** to come home and begin the diary *today*

In principle, sentence (35) should be a variant of the FID example in (34), in which the external source decided not to demote the action to the past. Sentence (35) cannot be interpreted as an FID example, but only as a normal assertion, where the pronoun *he* refers to a third person, different from the speaker (and hearer).

In other words, if the explanation of the presence of the past tense is just that the external narrator wants to demote the action from her present, we would expect a possible variant of this style to exist, in which no such a demotion takes place. In other words, if it were just a stylistic choice, one would expect it not to be *obligatory* and hence sentence (35) to be grammatical.

There is another observation concerning examples like (30) above. In that example, two past forms appear—*did start* and *had*. According to the theory I am reviewing here, the past tenses are the grammatical effect of the location of the corresponding eventualities in the past of the external narrator. However, in the example in question the two events are ordered with respect to each other: the event expressed in the first part of the sentence follows the event in the second one, as made clear by the presence of *tomorrow*. The two events, however, are not ordered with respect to the temporal coordinates of the external source, but with respect to the coordinates of the internal one: the second event—the starting of the ration—is future with respect to the temporal location of the internal source and the first one—having only four cigarettes left—is simultaneous with it. This means that there must be somehow an anchoring of the events with respect to the internal source. Note also that this ordering could be obtained even without the intervention of indexical temporal expressions. Consider for instance the following sentence, based on Orwell's example above:

(36)   The new ration would start soon and he had only four cigarettes left, he thought

In this case, the future orientation of the first sentence is provided by the presence of the future-in-the-past *would start*. The same holds in Italian:

(37)   Il nuovo razionamento sarebbe iniziato presto e lui aveva solo quattro sigarette, pensò
The new ration would start soon and he had only four cigarettes left, he thought

The first sentence contains a future-in-the-past, *sarebbe iniziato* (would start), and the English simple past verbal form *had* is translated by means of the Italian imperfect form *aveva* (see section 6.3.1 below).

In a way, therefore, the analysis provided so far in the literature is unsatisfactory. According to that view, the verbal morphology appearing in FID sentences locates the eventualities only with respect to the temporal location of the external source. In the examples illustrated above, on the contrary, the eventualities do not seem to be temporally located with respect to the external source, but with respect to the internal one. Their temporal location can be achieved by means of temporal indexicals, but also, importantly, by means of verbal morphology—for instance, future-in-the-past vs. simple past.

To solve this puzzle, I will argue that FID sentences are not different from the other contexts analysed so far, in that they resort to two sets of coordinates. In non-FID texts the two sets of coordinates pertain to the subject and the speaker. In FID texts the two sets are identified by the internal source—analogous to the subject—and the external one—analogous to the speaker.

As in all the other contexts, the internal source/subject is identified by means of a third person pronoun and the external source/speaker by means of a first person one. This is true in both normal prose and FID.[13]

I also propose, contrary to the previous accounts, that there is no dissociation between indexicals on one side and tenses on the other. A cross-linguistic analysis of FID sentences might shed some light on these questions.

6.3 A theoretical proposal for Free Indirect Discourse

6.3.1 *Italian*

On one hand, Schlenker and the other scholars are certainly correct in proposing that the verbal forms appearing in FID texts have the stylistic effect of locating the action in some *unspecified* temporal point. I want to argue however that this point is *not* in the *past* and certainly not in the past with respect to the external source/speaker's coordinates.

My proposal is that the tense is not an ordinary past, but is the form used in fictional contexts, among which there are *dreams*, as discussed in Chapter 4. As should be clear at this point, the main idea of this work is to distinguish the *subject's* coordinates from the *speaker's* coordinates. Both sets play a role in the syntax and interpretation of sentences.

The first important consideration, drawn on the basis of the examples given above, is that in Italian in FID contexts the verb never appears with simple past morphology, and not even with the present perfect one, but always appears in the imperfect form.

---

[13] The *subject* can either be a second or third person, as in the following examples:

i. You believed that Mary had left

ii. He believed that Mary had left

In the FID second person pronouns cannot work as *subjects* for reasons that will be made clear below.

As I pointed out above in section 6.1, in fact, in Italian FID contexts it is not possible to substitute the imperfect with other tenses of the indicative. I reproduce here the relevant examples:[14]

(38)   Era la sua forza [commentava Baudolino a Niceta] e in questo modo lo
        aveva menato per il naso una prima volta, lo stava menando **ora** e lo
        avrebbe menato per alcuni anni ancora (Eco, *Baudolino*, p. 264)
            This was(IMPF) his strength—Baudolino was commenting to Niceta—
        and in this way he had(IMPF) taken him by the nose once, he was(IMPF)
        leading him by the nose now, and he would(FUT-IN-PAST) take him by
        the nose for some years still

(39)   # È/ È STATA la sua forza [commentava Baudolino a Niceta] e in questo
        modo lo HA MENATO/ MENÒ per il naso una prima volta, lo STA
        MENANDO ora e lo MENERÀ per alcuni anni ancora
            This is/has been (PRES/PRES PERF) his strength—Baudolino was
        commenting to Niceta—and in this way he has(PRES/PERF/PAST) taken
        him by the nose once, he is(PRES) leading him by the nose now, and he
        will(FUT) take him by the nose for some years still

The impossibility of having other indicative tenses is reminiscent of the contrast illustrated in English between the sentences (34) and (35).

Giorgi and Pianesi (2001b, 2004a) pointed out that the imperfect of the indicative is the form used in peculiar contexts such as narration and dreams. I proposed in Chapter 4 that the imperfect is marked as a [−speaker] tense. Here I will develop this proposal and show that the imperfect, due to this property, fits the requirements posed by FID.[15]

The starting point is the idea that FID is characterized by the resetting of the speaker's coordinates to those of the subject. In FID sentences the internal source/subject provides the coordinates that permit the temporal location of events, whereas in non-FID sentences, as illustrated in the previous chapters, this role is played by the speaker's coordinates. In other words, the external source decides, as a

---

[14]   The sentence cannot appear with the subjunctive either, given that the subjunctive in whatever context cannot be a main, independent verbal form. For an analysis of tense in fiction, see also Zucchi (2001).

[15]   On the usage of the imperfect as a narrative non-past, see also Kamp and Rohrer (1983) and Vet (1985).

literary device, to use the subject's coordinates as the centre of indexicality. The first person, however, both in Italian and English, is reserved to the external source, hence it cannot be used to refer to the subject.

If we look at the facts in this perspective, there is no need to hypothesize a double set of coordinates and a dissociation between tenses and indexicals, as in the previous literature.

Let's consider how this idea applies to actual examples. Consider for instance the following FID sentence:[16]

(40) Era finalmente partita, pensò
      She had(IMPF) finally left, she thought

For simplicity, let's hypothesize that in this sentence, the person *thinking* is the same person who *left*—though this is not necessary. In non-FID clauses, the coordinates represented in C are the speaker's; in FID clauses, according to my hypothesis, they are reset to the subject/internal source's. After resetting the temporal coordinates in C, example (40) corresponds to the following structure:

(41) $[C_{INT\ SOURCE} \cdots [T_{[-speaker]} \cdots V\,]\,]$

The features in T are then raised to C. Recall that the imperfect bears the feature [−speaker], but in this case the speaker is no longer represented in C. Therefore, the imperfect can be anchored to the temporal location of the internal source, giving rise to a reading in which resultant state of being left is simultaneous with the thinking.[17]

The same happens with a stative predicate:

(42) Finalmente era felice, pensò
      Finally she was happy, she thought

In this case, the state of happiness overlaps with the thinking. As in the example considered above, the left-most position in the C-layer contains the *internal source's* coordinates, due to the resetting of the speaker's coordinates to those of the internal source.

[16] I will discuss the role of the introducing predicate, *pensò* (she thought), in section 6.4.

[17] Therefore, as illustrated above in Chapter 4, the event is interpreted as preceding the thinking.

Consider now what happens when the sentence also contains a temporal indexical:

(43)   Era partita solo ieri e già le sembrava un secolo, pensò
        She had(IMPF) left only yesterday and it already seemed a century, she
        thought

The indexical *ieri* (yesterday), analogously to what I discussed in Chapter 5, must combine with the event. This locates it in the past of the speaker, and precisely in the day before the day of the speaking event. However, in this case the temporal coordinate of the speaker is reset to the temporal coordinate of the internal source. Consequently, the temporal indexical locates the resultant state of the leaving event in the past of the internal source, and precisely in the day before the thinking event.

The imperfect verb then moves to C, as illustrated above, giving rise to the following interpretation: there is a resultant state of a leaving event—which took place the day before the day in which the internal source is thinking—holding at the time of the thinking by the internal source.

The future-in-the-past has the same property as the imperfect, under the hypothesis sketched in Chapter 4. Consider the following example:

(44)   Finalmente domani sarebbe partita, pensò
        Finally **tomorrow** she would leave, she thought

The temporal indexical locates the event in the future of the internal source and the verbal morphology instantiates a modality, expressing futurity, holding at the internal source's temporal location. The interpretation then obtains as above.

Other tenses, such as the past, present perfect, and future indicative, are incompatible with FID, because in that case the event *must* be located with respect to the speaker's coordinate and no resetting is allowed. In other words, in FID contexts, the speaker's coordinate disappears and its role is played by the subject's, repeated twice—once in T and once in C. If the verbal form explicitly encodes reference to the speaker's coordinate, then its presence causes ungrammaticality. On the contrary, the presence of the imperfect, specified as [−speaker] as discussed in Chapter 4, does not yield ungrammaticality.

Consider now the distribution of the temporal topic. As discussed above, with an imperfect the presence of the temporal topic, either realized in the sentence or present in the context, is obligatory. Consider for instance the following case:

(45) #Gianni era in giardino
         Gianni was (IMPF) in the garden

A sentence such as (45) uttered out of the blue is unacceptable, because the imperfect cannot be properly anchored. The only available anchor in fact would be the utterance time. If anchored to this point, however, the anti-speaker requirement of the imperfect would not be satisfied. As a consequence, an additional anchoring point must be introduced by means of a temporal topic:

(46) Alle 4, Gianni era in giardino
         At four, Gianni was in the garden

If however a sentence such as (45) is a FID sentence, the topic is not necessary:

(47) Gianni era in giardino, pensò
         Gianni was in the garden, she thought

This fact is predicted by my hypothesis. As I said above, in this case the eventuality is interpreted as simultaneous with the temporal coordinate of the internal source. Given that the internal source is not the speaker, the anti-speaker requirement posed by the imperfect is satisfied, even in absence of a temporal topic.

Notice that the same situation arises when the imperfect appears in an embedded clause in non-FID contexts:

(48) Maria ha detto che Gianni era in giardino
         Maria said that Gianni was (IMPF) in the garden

In this case no embedded temporal topic is present and the sentence is felicitous. The reason is that the anchor is provided by the superordinate predicate *ha detto* (said) and therefore it does not coincide with the temporal coordinate of the speaker.

These observations constitute a strong argument in favour of the hypothesis developed in this book with respect to the feature specification of the imperfect in Italian.

6.3.2 *English*

In this section I consider the fact that in English the past tense appears. The explanation is quite trivial at his point, given the analysis provided in Chapter 4 above. In English the past tense can either be a two-place predicate form—i.e., e > e', where e' in main clauses is interpreted as *u*—or can be a temporal form like the imperfect, namely a one-place predicate which needs to be anchored to a context. The difference between the Italian imperfect and the English past is that the latter does not bear the [−speaker] specification and therefore never needs a temporal topic. Therefore, the English form compatible with FID contexts is the past tense. Moreover, in both languages, the only kind of future that can appear is the future-in-the-past, being the only one not requiring the presence of the speaker's temporal coordinate. Descriptively, the past tense—i.e., the two-place predicate—needs to be anchored in a way analogous to the Italian past, as briefly illustrated in Chapter 4 (see also Giorgi and Pianesi 1997, 2001a). This process is sensitive to the aspectual nature of the predicate—i.e., eventive vs. stative—whereas in dream and FID contexts it is not. This consideration also fits well with what I said so far: in FID contexts there is no anchoring to a superordinate predicate, or to the utterance event. The eventuality in question is simply interpreted as the content of the thought, in a way analogous to dream contexts.

6.4 The syntax of FID sentences

6.4.1 *The distribution of the* introducing predicate

As illustrated by Banfield (1982), FID sentences do not have the syntax of subordinate sentences. For instance they are never introduced by an overt Complementizer:

(49) (*che) era la sua forza—commentava Baudolino a Niceta
(That) this was his strength—Baudolino was commenting to Niceta
(Eco, *Baudolino*, p. 264)

Moreover, FID sentences show the presence of items that could not appear in embedded contexts:

(50) Ah, Ecco perchè era così, oggi (Deledda, *Le colpe altrui*, p. 76)
Ah, this was why she was like that, today

(51) *Pensò che ah, ecco perchè era così, oggi
He thought that ah, this was why she was like that, today

I am not going to reproduce here the relevant discussion by Banfield (1982)—which I think is quite convincing—but will take for granted that the sentences in question cannot simply be considered syntactically subordinate clauses.

On the other hand, they admit the presence of a main predicate in post-sentential position, as shown in the examples above and in the following one:

(52) Sarebbe partita domani, pensò
She would leave **tomorrow**, she thought

The verbal predicate *pensò* (she thought) cannot appear in pre-sentential position, with an FID interpretation:

(53) #Pensò sarebbe partita domani
She thought she would leave **tomorrow**

In this case, the indexical temporal expression can only be understood as the day after the utterance time—i.e., it is evaluated with respect to the external source's coordinates—and the embedded clause is interpreted as a normal complement clause, with no Complementizer, i.e., where Complementizer Deletion phenomena take place (see Chapter 2). In this sense, it is analogous to the following example, where *domani* (tomorrow) is substituted by an anaphoric expression:

(54) Pensò sarebbe partita l'indomani/il giorno dopo
She thought she would leave the next day/the day after

Both *l'indomani* (the next day) and *il giorno dopo* (the day after) are anaphoric temporal locutions. In that case the clause is simply interpreted as a subordinate one, with CD.

Notice that among the examples above only in example (3) does the introducing predicate precede the FID sentences. In that case, however, it is separated by a long pause, represented in the written text by a semicolon. The issue at this point concerns the syntactic position of the introducing predicate, when realized.[18]

Consider first that the realization of such a predicate is a root phenomenon, in the sense that, more generally, FID clauses cannot be embedded:

(55) Gianni, pensò, sarebbe partito domani
      Gianni, she thought, would leave **tomorrow**

(56) *Luigi disse che Gianni, pensò, sarebbe partito domani
      Luigi said that Gianni, she thought, would leave **tomorrow**

Example (55) has a FID interpretation; example (56) does not. In other words, a FID structure cannot be embedded under another predicate.

Consider now the nature of the phrases preceding the introducing predicate. It is possible to have the whole sentence, the subject, an adverb, or whatever other constituent from an internal position. Therefore, besides (55) above, the following word orders are available:

(57) Gianni sarebbe partito domani, pensò
      Gianni would leave **tomorrow**, (she) thought

(58) Francamente/sicuramente/probabilmente, pensò, Gianni sarebbe partito domani
      Frankly/surely/probably, she thought, Gianni would leave **tomorrow**

(59) Domani, pensò, Gianni sarebbe partito
      Tomorrow, she thought, Gianni would leave

(60) A Maria, pensò, Gianni non avrebbe più fatto regali
      To Maria, (she) thought, Gianni would give no more presents

In all the cases listed above, the phrase preceding the introducing predicate is interpreted as a topic—i.e., as given information, *with respect to the context relevant to the internal source*. This observation

---

[18] Recall that the introducing predicate is not obligatory, even if in literary texts it is most often expressed, as exemplified by the examples provided above.

is important, because it shows that the setting of the context with respect to the coordinates of the internal source affects the whole interpretive process, including the phrases appearing linearly on the left of the introducing predicate.

Notice that if the preposed phrase is a focus, the FID sentence is still possible but quite marginal:

(61)   ??A MARIA (non a Luisa), pensò, Gianni non avrebbe fatto più regali
       TO MARIA (not to Luisa), (she) thought, Gianni would give no more
       presents

Even in this case, for those who accept the sentence, the only possible interpretation is that the focused phrase is new information *in the context relevant to the internal source.*

Finally, the introducing predicate can be simultaneously preceded and followed by a topic or multiple topics:

(62)   Domani, pensò, quel libro, l'avrebbe finalmente venduto
       Tomorrow, (she) thought, that book, (she) it-CL would eventually sell

(63)   Domani, a Gianni, pensò, quel libro, gliel'avrebbe finalmente venduto
       Tomorrow, to Gianni, (she) thought, that book, (she) to him-it-CL
       would eventually sell

Consider that the introducing predicate can be a complex expression, as in the literary examples given above: *he now realized*, in example (1); *Lo ricordò dopo uno sforzo di memoria anzi di ragionamento* (she remembered it with an effort of memory, or better to say of reasoning), in example (3); *he perceived, he saw*, in example (4), etc. Therefore, it is not a simple head, but a whole phrase. The issue is to establish what syntactic position it occupies. In the next section I address this issue.

6.4.2 *The syntactic structure*

Let me summarize the properties observed so far:

- The syntactic realization of the introducing predicate appears to be a root phenomenon.
- When preceding the FID sentence, the introducing predicate is followed by a long pause.

- It can follow a topic phrase—and more rarely and marginally a focus phrase. This, however, is interpreted in the scope of the introducing predicate—i.e., as pertaining to the context created around the internal source.

These characteristics closely resemble the properties observed for exclamative sentences—see Zanuttini and Portner (2003)—and vocative structures—see Moro (2003).[19]

In particular, Moro (2003: examples (12b) and (13b)) observes the following contrast in vocative sentences between topic and focus:

(64)   ?I ragazzi, o Maria, li aiuta Gianni
        The boys, o Maria, them-CL helps Gianni
        The boys, o Maria, Gianni helps, not the rabbits

(65)   *I RAGAZZI, o Maria, Gianni aiuta, non i conigli
        The boys, o Maria, Gianni helps

This contrast is reminiscent of the one illustrated above between the sentences (60) and (61).

In all these cases, it seems reasonable to hypothesize a position external to the C-layer of the clause, therefore accounting for the root properties of these phenomena.

In particular with respect to FID sentences, I propose that there is a root layer, at the left of the C-layer, which can be characterized as an

---

[19] Zanuttini and Portner (2003) actually conclude that to characterize exclamative clauses, the notion of *illocutionary force* is not appropriate, whereas the notion of *semantic force* is. Their crucial point is that according to their analysis no single element is present in all and only exclamative clauses, but that instead this clause type is defined by the co-occurrence of two distinct semantic characteristics. In general, the authors question the basic assumption of whether a *syntactic* representation of sentential—root—force is necessary, or whether it just comes out as an implementation from the semantic and pragmatic component.

The perspective of my work is of course different: the central hypothesis, in its strongest formulation, of this monograph is that the semantic interpretation is directly read off the syntax.

Following this perspective, based on their observations, it seems to me that it can safely be concluded that the component(s) marking exclamative clauses are very high in the C-layer, preceding all other items which can appear there. Further investigation would be necessary, however, to reach a final assessment of this clause type according to the point of view developed here.

informational layer, let's call it INF-layer. The phrase containing the introducing predicate occurs in this layer—say, in the projection of the head INF—and the FID clause follows. INF has the role of resetting the context coordinates to those pertaining to the internal source. It might be the case that Vocatives and Exclamatives have components involving this layer as well, but in this work I will not pursue this particular issue.[20]

The fact that topics—and only topics—can precede the introducing predicate giving rise to a fully grammatical sentence can be explained exploiting Rizzi's (2002) suggestion that *topics are special*, being neither argumental, quantificational, or modificational. In a sense, therefore, they might appear freely in various contexts, without showing intervention effects. This suggestion might also explain the contrast between topics and focus.[21]

6.5 Conclusion

The proposal developed in this chapter follows the main lines illustrated through the book. Namely, the semantics of indexicality is read off the syntax, which contains all the information relevant to the interpretation.

The literary device of FID consists precisely in a manipulation of the temporal coordinates, in a way analogous to what I illustrated in Chapter 5 with respect to the dependencies from a future. The difference is that in this case the manipulation is *intended* by the narrator, the external source, to create a peculiar stylistic effect. The external

---

[20] Notice that in English the *introducing predicate* can undergo inversion, as discussed by Guéron (2007), as for instance in the following example:

i.   He had never seen a thing like that, *said John*

This might be taken as evidence that the level in question precedes the sentence, as hypothesized here, and that the final word order is due to movement of the whole clause to the left. Further analysis is required, however.

[21] Actually, Rizzi (2002) advances this proposal only tentatively, among other suggestions, to explain the immunity of topics from locality effects. The proposal seems promising to me, however, and I think it might be interesting to investigate it further.

source decides to substitute the speaker's temporal coordinate with the subject's. The distribution of all indexical items is affected by this modification.

Theoretically, the starting point of my analysis is the observation that the use of this artificial device is *possible*, which in generative grammar reasoning implies that *its results must be compatible with Universal Grammar and compatible with the speaker's competence.* Hence, the manipulation in question must yield as a final result something which is recognized by the native speaker as belonging to her language. This is actually the case, as already explicitly recognized in the literature, and as discussed above, because native speakers do make grammaticality judgements about these sentences, even if the FID is the effect of a literary manipulation.

The other important conclusion from this analysis of FID contexts is that it is necessary to hypothesize a further layer—the *informational layer*—realized only at root level. This layer hosts the introducing predicate, which defines what set of spatial and temporal coordinates will be relevant for the interpretation of the following sentence. In FID structures, the introducing predicate identifies as relevant the spatial and temporal coordinates of its subject. I have already pointed out in Chapter 3 the need for such a level, hosting items such as *frankly*, but here I think that the evidence to this end is even more compelling.

Note that I follow Banfield (1982) in claiming that these structures are not subordinate clauses, and as a matter of fact, they do not exhibit any of the syntax of subordinate contexts. On the other hand, however, in a way they are subordinate to *something*, because it must be clear to the native speaker—in this case the *recipient* of the literary work—that the FID device is at work and that the coordinate shift must take place.

Literary sources

Grazia Deledda, *Le colpe altrui*, Nuoro, Ilisso, Bibliotheca Sarda, 2008.
Umberto Eco, *Baudolino*, Florence, Bompiani, 2000.
D. H. Lawrence, *Women in Love*, London, Heinemann, 1971.

George Orwell, *1984*, New York, Penguin, 1962.

Italo Svevo, *La coscienza di Zeno*, Florence, Giunti Editore, 1994.

Italo Svevo, *La novella del buon vecchio e della bella fanciulla*, Rome, Tascabili Economici Newton, 1993.

Virginia Woolf, *Mrs Dalloway*, Ware, Herts, Wordsworth Editions, 1996.

7

Concluding Remarks

In this book I have argued in favour of the following hypothesis: the left-most position of the C-layer is devoted to representation of the speaker's temporal and spatial coordinates. I have shown that this position is required both by the superordinate predicate and by the embedded verbal form.

In certain cases, as for instance in the dependencies involving a subjunctive in Italian, such a position is not required and the speaker's coordinates are not relevant, either syntactically or interpretively. An important argument in favour of the complex interactions between syntax and interpretation is constituted by the clauses depending from *ipotizzare* (hypothesize), where the representation of the speaker can still be there, giving raise to a typical pattern.

I also argued that in certain cases this *interface* position is overtly realized in Italian by means of a first person head, with epistemic value, namely, *credo* (I think). I proposed that the Italian imperfect indicative can also be analysed in the framework discussed here, providing insights into some anomalous distribution of the English past.

Following my proposal, certain structures, which have traditionally been considered problematic, such as the dependencies from future verbal forms and the narrative style called Free Indirect Discourse, do not have to be treated as special cases any more, because their properties follow from a simple manipulation of the value assigned to the speaker's coordinates. The syntax and the interpretive device remain exactly the same as in 'normal' cases.

The advantages of this hypothesis are twofold. On one side, it can explain several empirical observations, such as the occurrence of the Double Access Reading in certain contexts but not in others,

Complementizer Deletion phenomena in Italian, the distribution of the various kinds of temporal locutions, the properties of Chinese Long Distance anaphors, etc. It can also explain more specific facts. For instance, in Italian the DAR is mostly found with the indicative, but not with the subjunctive; the imperfect and the future-in-the-past exhibit anomalous behaviour; the dependencies from a main future and FID sentences apparently exhibit contradictory properties.

On the other, the hypothesis highlights an important point: the relation between the context and the syntax cannot be a one-way relation. The presence of the speaker's coordinates in C is determined by the syntax and conversely, their presence determines syntactic phenomena.

In other words, I have shown that in Italian certain predicates require an indicative or a subjunctive in their complement clause, defining a certain syntactic structure with respect to the Complementizer layer and consequently yielding a certain interpretation of the sentence with respect to the context.

Conversely, given a certain context, which might or might not be a literary one, a given syntax is fixed, with precise consequences for the usage of tenses, temporal locutions, pronouns, etc.

Independently of the specific implementation I propose in this work, I hope that the results of this particular way of thinking about the relationships between syntax and context might prove heuristically useful for further investigation in this fascinating empirical realm.

References

Abusch, Dorit, 1997, Sequence of Tense and Temporal De Re. *Linguistics and Philosophy*, 20, pp. 1–50.

Banfield, Ann, 1982, *Unspeakable Sentences*, London, Routledge.

Beninca', Paola, 2001, Syntactic Focus and Intonational Focus in the Left Periphery, in Guglielmo Cinque and Gianpaolo Salvi (eds.), *Current Studies in Italian Syntax: Essays Offered to Lorenzo Renzi*, Amsterdam, Elsevier, pp. 9–64.

—— and Cecilia Poletto, 1994, *Bisogna* and its Companions: The Verbs of Necessity, in Guglielmo Cinque, Jan Koster, Jean-Yves Pollock, Luigi Rizzi, and Raffaella Zanuttini (eds.), *Paths Towards Universal Grammar: Studies in Honor of Richard S. Kayne*, Washington, Georgetown University Press, pp. 35–58.

—————— 2004, Topic Focus and V2: Defining the CP Sublayers, in L. Rizzi (ed.), *The Structure of CP and IP*, New York, Oxford University Press, pp. 52–75.

Bertinetto, Pier Marco, 1986, *Tempo, Aspetto e Azione Nel Verbo Italiano: Il Sistema dell'indicativo*, Florence, Accademia della Crusca.

—— 1997, *Il Dominio Tempo-Aspettuale: Demarcazioni, Intersezioni, Contrasti*, Turin, Rosenberg and Sellier.

—— and Denis Delfitto, 2000, Aspect vs. Actionality: Why They Should Be Kept Apart, in Östen Dahl (ed.), *Tense and Aspect in the Languages of Europe*, Berlin, Mouton de Gruyter, pp. 189–225.

—— and Valentina Bianchi, 1993, Temporal Adverbs and the Notion of 'Perspective Point', *Quaderni del Laboratorio di Linguistica* 7, Scuola Normale Superiore di Pisa, pp. 11–21.

Bianchi, Valentina, 2003, On Finiteness as Logophoric Anchoring, in Jacqueline Guéron and Liliane Tasmovski (eds.), *Temps et Point de Vue/Tense and Point of View*, Université Paris X Nanterre, pp. 213–46.

—— 2006, On the Syntax of Personal Arguments, *Lingua*, 116, pp. 2023–67.

Calabrese, Andrea, 1984, Una differenza sintattica fra il salentino e l'italiano: la complementazione frasale, *Rivista Italiana di Dialettologia*: Scuola, Società, Territorio, VIII, pp. 195–203.

—— 1993, The Sentential Complementation of Salentino: A Study of a Language without Infinitival Clauses, in Adriana Belletti (ed.), *Syntactic Theory and the Dialects of Italy*, Turin, Rosenberg & Sellier, pp. 28–98.

Cappelen, Herman and Ernie Lepore, 2002, Indexicality, Binding, Anaphora and *a priori* Truth, in *Analysis*, 64.2, pp. 271–81.

Cecchetto, Carlo and Gennaro Chierchia, 1999, Reconstruction in Dislocation Constructions and the Syntax/Semantics Interface, in Susan Blake et al. (eds.), *Proceedings of WCCFL XVII*, Stanford, CSLI, pp. 132–46.

Clements, George, 1975, The Logophoric Pronoun in Ewe: Its Role in Discourse, *Journal of West African Languages*, 10, pp. 141–77.

Chierchia, Gennaro, 1995, Individual-Level Predicates as Inherent Generics, in Greg N. Carlson and Francis Jeffry Pelletier (eds.), *The Generic Book*, Chicago, University of Chicago Press, pp. 176–222.

Chomsky, Noam, 1995, *The Minimalist Program*, Cambridge, Mass., MIT Press.

—— 2001, Derivation by Phase, in Michael Kenstowicz (ed.), *Ken Hale: A Life for Language*, Cambridge, Mass., MIT Press, pp.1–52.

—— 2005, On Phases, unpub. m.s., Massachusetts Institute of Technology.

Cinque, Guglielmo, 1999, *Adverbs and Functional Heads*, New York, Oxford University Press.

—— 2004, Issues in Adverbial Syntax, *Lingua*, 114, pp. 683–710.

Cole, Peter, Gabriella Hermon, and James Huang (eds.), 2001, *Long-Distance Reflexives*, New York, Academic Press.

Coene, Martine, Yves D'Hulst and Larisa Avram, 2004, Future and Future in the Past Readings in Romanian, in Olga Tomic (ed.), *Balkan Linguistics*, Amsterdam, John Benjamins, pp. 355–74.

Costantini, Francesco, 2005, On Obviation in Subjunctive Clauses, unpub. Ph.D. thesis, University of Venice.

—— 2006, Obviation in Subjunctive Argument Clauses and the First Personal Interpretation, in Mara Frascarelli (ed.), *Phases of Interpretation*, Berlin, Mouton de Gruyter, pp. 213–319.

DeGraff, Michel, 2005, Morphology and Word Order in 'Creolization' and Beyond, in Guglielmo Cinque and Richard Kayne (eds.), *The Oxford Handbook of Comparative Syntax*, Oxford, Oxford University Press, pp. 293–372.

Delfitto, Denis, 2004, On the Logical Form of Imperfective Aspect, in Jacqueline Guéron and Jacqueline Lecarme (eds.), *The Syntax of Tense*, Cambridge, Mass., MIT Press, pp. 115–42.

Delfitto, Denis, and Pier Marco Bertinetto, 2000, Word Order and Quantification over Time, in James Higginbotham, Fabio Pianesi, and Achille Varzi (eds.), *Speaking of Events*, New York, Oxford University Press, pp. 207–43.

Demirdache, Amida and Miriam Uribe-Extebarria, 2006, On the Temporal Syntax of Non-root Modals, in Jacqueline Guéron and Jacqueline Lecarme (eds.), *Time and Modality*, New York, Springer, pp. 79–114.

Dobrovie Sorin, Carmen, 1994, *The Syntax of Romanian*, Berlin and New York, Walter de Gruyter.

Doron, Edit, 1991, Point of View as a Factor of Content, in S. Moore and A. Wyner, *Proceedings of SALT II*, Ithaca, NY, Cornell University Press, pp. 51–64.

Enç, Murvet, 1986, Towards a Referential Analysis of Temporal Expressions, *Linguistics and Philosophy*, 9, pp. 405–26.

—— 1987, Anchoring Conditions for Tense, *Linguistic Inquiry*, 18, pp. 633–57.

Farkas, Donca, 1985, *Intensional Descriptions and the Romance Subjunctive Mood*, New York, Garland Publishers.

—— 1992a, On the Semantics of Subjunctive Complements, in P. Hirschbühler (ed.), *Romance Languages and Modern Linguistic Theory*, Amsterdam, John Benjamins, pp. 69–105.

—— 1992b, On Obviation, in Ivan A. Sag and Anna Szabolcsi (eds.), *Lexical Matters*, Stanford, Stanford University, CSLI, pp. 85–109.

von Fintel, Kai and Sabine Iatridou, 2006, How to Say *Ought* in Foreign: The Composition of Weak Necessity Modals, in Jacqueline Guéron and Jacqueline Lecarme (eds.), *Time and Modality*, New York, Springer, pp. 115–41.

Fleischman, Suzanne, 2009, *The Future in Thought and Language*, Cambridge, Cambridge University Press.

Franconi, Enrico, Alessandra Giorgi, and Fabio Pianesi, 1994, A Mereological Characterization of Temporal and Aspectual Phenomena, in Carlos Martin-Vide (ed.), *Current Issues in Mathematical Linguistics*, Amsterdam, Elsevier, North-Holland Linguistic Series, pp. 269–278.

Giorgi, Alessandra, 2006, From Temporal Anchoring to Long Distance Anaphors, *Natural Language and Linguistic Theory*, 24.4, pp. 1009–47.

—— 2007, On the Nature of Long Distance Anaphors, *Linguistic Inquiry*, 38.2, pp. 321–42.

—— 2008, Reflections on the *Optimal Solution*: On the Syntactic Representation of Indexicality, paper presented at the Biolinguistics: Language Evolution and Variation conference, Venice, June 2007.

—— 2009, Toward a Syntax of the Subjunctive Mood, *Lingua*, special issue on Mood, ed. Josep Quer (in press).

—— and Fabio Pianesi, 1991, Toward a Syntax of Temporal Representations, *Probus*, 2, pp. 187–213.

———— 1996, Verb Movement in Italian and Syncretic Categories, *Probus*, 8, pp. 137–60.

———— 1997, *Tense and Aspect: From Semantics to Morphosyntax*, New York, Oxford University Press.

———— 1998, Present Tense, Perfectivity and the Anchoring Condition, in Adam Wyner (ed.) *Proceedings of the 13th Annual Conference of the Israel Association for Theoretical Linguistics* (IATL-5), pp. 75–95.

———— 2000, Sequence of Tense Phenomena in Italian: A Morphosyntactic Analysis, *Probus*, 12, pp. 1–32.

———— 2001a, Tense, Attitudes and Subjects, in R. Hastings, B. Jackson, and Z. Zvolenszky (eds.), *Proceedings of SALT XI*, CLC Pub., Ithaca, NY, Cornell University Press, pp. 212–30.

———— 2001b, Imperfect Dreams: The Temporal Dependencies of Fictional Predicates, *Probus*, 13, pp. 31–68.

———— 2003, The Day After: Anaphoric Temporal Locutions, in Jacqueline Guéron and Liliane Tasmosky (eds.), *Perspective and Point of View*, Paris, University of Paris X Press, pp. 128–71.

———— 2004a, The Temporal Perspective of the Speaker and the Subject: From Semantics to Morphosyntax, in Jacqueline Guéron and Jacqueline Lecarme (eds.), *The Syntax of Time*, Cambridge, Mass., MIT Press, pp. 129–52.

———— 2004b, Complementizer Deletion in Italian, in L. Rizzi (ed.), *The Syntax of CP and IP*, New York, Oxford University Press.

———— 2004c, *Credo* (I Believe): Epistemicity and the Syntactic Representation of the Speaker, unpub. m.s., University of Venice and IRST.

Greenberg, Joseph, 1966, *Language Universals*, The Hague, Mouton.

Guéron, Jacqueline, 1993, Sur la syntaxe du temps, *Langue française*, 100, pp. 102–22.

—— 2000, From Need to Necessity: A Syntactic Path to Modality, *Belgian Journal of Linguistics, Modal Verbs in Germanic and Romance Languages*, 17, pp. 89–114.

—— 2004, Tense Construal and the Argument Structure of Auxiliaries, in Jacqueline Guéron and Jacqueline Lecarme (eds.), *The Syntax of Time*, Cambridge, Mass., MIT Press, pp. 299–328.

Guéron, Jacqueline, 2006a, Point of View in Literary and Non-Literary Texts: On Free Indirect Discourse, unpub. m.s., Paris 3.

—— 2006b, On the Temporal Function of Modal Verbs, in Jacqueline Guéron and Jacqueline Lecarme (eds.), *Time and Modality*, New York, Springer, pp. 143–72.

—— 2007, Remarks on the Grammar of Unspeakable Sentences, unpub. m.s., University of Paris X.

—— and Teun Hoekstra, 1995, The Temporal Interpretation of Predication, in Anna Cardinaletti and Maria Teresa Guasti (eds.), *Syntax and Semantics*, 28, Small Clauses, New York, Academic Press, pp. 77–107.

—— and Jacqueline Lecarme (eds.), 2008, *Time and Modality*, New York, Springer.

Hagège, Claude, 1974, Les Pronoms Logophoriques, *Bulletin de la Société de Linguistique de Paris*, 69, pp. 287–310.

Higginbotham, James, 1995, Tensed Thoughts, *Mind and Language*, 10.3, pp. 226–49.

—— 2002, Why is Sequence of Tense Obligatory? in G. Preyer and G. Peter (eds.), *Logical Form and Language*, Oxford, Clarendon Press, pp. 207–227.

—— 2003, Remembering, Imagining and the First Person, in A. Barber (ed.), *Epistemology of Language*, Oxford, Oxford University Press, pp. 496–533.

—— 2004, The English Progressive, in Jacqueline Guéron and Jacqueline Lecarme (eds.), *The Syntax of Time*, Cambridge, Mass., MIT Press, pp. 329–58.

—— 2006, The Anaphoric Theory of Tense, in M. Gibson and J. Howell (eds.), *Proceedings of SALT XVI*, Ithaca, NY, Cornell University Press, pp. 59–76.

d'Hulst, Yves, Martine Coene, Larisa Avram, and Liliane Tasmowsky, 2003, Morphology and Tense Anchoring in the Romanian Tense System, in J. Guéron and L. Tasmowski (eds.), *Tense and Points of View*, Paris, Université Paris X, pp. 167–84.

Huang, James, 1984, On the Distribution and Reference of Empty Pronouns, *Linguistic Inquiry*, 15, pp. 531–74.

—— and Jane Tang, 1991, The Local Nature of the Long-Distance Reflexive in Chinese, in Jan Koster and Lars Hellan (eds.) *Long Distance Anaphora*, Cambridge, Cambridge University Press, pp. 263–82.

—— and Luther Liu, 2001, Logophoricity, Attitudes, and *ziji* at the Interface, in Peter Cole, Gabriella Hermon, and James Huang (eds.), *Long-Distance Reflexives*, New York, Academic Press, pp. 141–95.

Iatridou, Sabine, 2000, The Grammatical Ingredients of Counterfactuality, *Linguistic Inquiry*, 31.2, pp. 231–70.

—— and Kai von Fintel, 2007, Anatomy of a Modal Construction, *Linguistic Inquiry*, 38.3, pp. 445–83.

Ippolito, Michela, 2001, Temporal Subordinate Clauses: The Syntax of Tense, *MIT Working Papers in Linguistics*, 39, pp. 127–49.

—— 2004, Imperfect Modality, in Jacqueline Guéron and Jacqueline Lecarme (eds.), *The Syntax of Time*, Cambridge, Mass., MIT Press, pp. 359–87.

Jackendoff, Ray, 1972, *Semantic Interpretation in Generative Grammar*, Cambridge, Mass., MIT Press.

Kamp, Hans and Christian Rohrer, 1983, Tense in Texts, in Reiner Bauerle, Christoph Schwarze, and Arnim von Stechow (eds.), *Meaning, Use and Interpretation of Language*, Berlin, de Gruyter, pp. 250–69.

Kaplan, David, 1989, Demonstratives, in Joseph Almog, John Perry, and Howard Wettstein, *Themes from Kaplan*, New York, Oxford University Press, pp. 481–563.

Kayne, Richard, 1994, *The Antisymmetry of Syntax*, Cambridge, Mass., MIT Press.

Kempchinsky, Paula, 1985, The Subjunctive Disjoint Reference Effect, in Carol Neidle and Rafael Nuñez Cedeño (eds.), *Studies in Romance Linguistics*, Dordrecht, Foris, pp. 123–40.

—— 2009, The Subjunctive Disjoint Reference Effect, Again, *Lingua*, special issue on Mood, ed. Josep Quer (in press).

Legendre, Geraldine, 1997, Secondary Predication and Functional Projections in French, *Natural Language and Linguistic Theory*, 15.1, pp. 1–45.

Lin, Jo-Wang, 2003, Temporal Reference in Mandarin Chinese, *Journal of East Asian Linguistics*, 12, pp. 259–311.

—— 2006, Time in a Language without Tense: The Case of Chinese, *Journal of Semantics*, 23, pp. 1–53.

Molinelli, Piera, 2000, Sequence of Tenses and Mood Selection in Late Latin, in Gualtiero Calboli (ed.), *Papers on Grammar, Vol. V*, Amsterdam, John Benjamins, pp. 125–50.

Moro, Andrea, 2003, Notes on Vocative Case: A Case Study in Clause Structure, in Josep Quer, Jan Schroten, Mauro Scorretti, Petra Sleeman, and Els Verheugd (eds.), *Romance Languages and Linguistic Theory*, Amsterdam, John Benjamins, pp. 247–61.

Ogihara, Toshiyuki, 1995a, The Semantics of Tense in Embedded Clauses, *Linguistic Inquiry*, 26, pp. 663–79.

Ogihara, Toshiyuki, 1995b, Double-Access Sentences and Reference to States, *Natural Language Semantics*, 3, pp. 177–210.

—— 1996, *Tense, Attitudes, and Scope*, Dordrecht, Kluwer Academic Publishers.

Parsons, Terence, 1990, *Events in the Semantics of English*, Cambridge, Mass., MIT Press.

Partee, Barbara, 1973, Some Structural Analogies between Tenses and Pronouns, *Journal of Philosophy*, 70.18, pp. 601–9.

Pesetsky, David and Ester Torrego, 2001, T-to-C Movement: Causes and Consequences, in Michael Kenstowicz (ed.), *Ken Hale: A Life in Language*, Cambridge, Mass., MIT Press, pp. 355–425.

—————— 2004a, The Syntax of Valuation and the Interpretability of Features, in Simin Karimi, Vida Samiian, Wendy K. Wilkins, and Joseph E. Emonds (eds.), *Phrasal and Clausal Architecture: Syntactic Derivation and Interpretation*, Amsterdam, John Benjamins, pp. 262–93

—————— 2004b, Tense, Case and the Nature of Syntactic Categories, in Jacqueline Guéron and Jacqueline Lecarme (eds.), *The Syntax of Time*, Cambridge Mass., MIT Press, pp. 435–537.

—————— 2006, Probes, Goals and Syntactic Categories, in Yukio Otsu (ed.), *Proceedings of 7th Annual Tokyo Conference on Psycholinguistics*, Tokyo, Keio University.

Poletto, Cecilia, 1995, Complementiser Deletion and Verb Movement in Italian, *Working Papers in Linguistics*, University of Venice.

—— 2000, *The Higher Functional Field*, New York, Oxford University Press.

—— 2001, Complementizer Deletion and Verb Movement in Standard Italian, in Guglielmo Cinque and Giampaolo Salvi (eds.), *Current Studies in Italian Syntax*, Amsterdam, Elsevier, pp. 265–86.

Pollard, Carl and Ivan Sag, 1992, Anaphors in English and the Scope of Binding Theory, *Linguistic Inquiry*, 23.2, pp. 261–303.

—— and Ping Xue, 1998, Chinese Reflexive *Ziji*: Syntactic Reflexives vs. Nonsyntactic Reflexives, *Journal of East Asian Linguistics*, 7, pp. 287–318.

—————— 2001, Syntactic and Nonsyntactic Constraints on Long-Distance Reflexives, in Peter Cole, Gabriella Hermon, and James Huang (eds.), *Long-Distance Reflexives*, New York, Academic Press, pp. 317–42.

Portner, Paul, 1997, The Semantics of Mood, Complementation, and Conversational Force, *Natural Language Semantics*, 5, pp. 167–212.

Quer, Josep, 1998, *Mood at the Interface*, The Hague, HAG.

Quer, Josep (ed. and introd.), 2009, *Lingua*, special issue on Mood (in press).

Ramchand, Gillian, 1997, *Aspect and Predication*, Oxford, Oxford University Press.

Ritter, Elizabeth and Martina Wiltschko, 2004, The Lack of Tense as a Syntactic Category: Evidence from Blackfoot and Halkomelem. *Papers for the 39th International Conference on Salish and Neighbouring Languages*, pp. 341–70.

———— 2005, Anchoring Events to Utterances without Tense, in John Alderete, Chung-hye Han, and Alexei Kochetov (eds.), *Proceedings of the 24th West Coast Conference on Formal Linguistics*, Somerville, Mass., Cascadilla Press, pp. 343–51.

———— 2008, Varieties of INFL: Tense, Location and Person, in Jeroen Van Craenenbroeck (ed.), *Alternatives to Cartography*, Berlin, Walter de Gruyter, pp. 347–73.

Rizzi, Luigi, 1997, The Fine Structure of the Left Periphery, in Liliane Haegeman (ed.), *Elements of Grammar*, Amsterdam, Kluwer, pp. 281–337.

—— 2001, On the Position of Int(errogative) in the Left Periphery of the Clause, in Guglielmo Cinque and Giampaolo Salvi (eds.), *Current Studies in Italian Syntax*, Amsterdam, Elsevier, pp. 287–96.

—— 2002, Locality and Left Periphery, in Adriana Belletti (ed.), *Structures and Beyond: The Cartography of Syntactic Structures*, vol. 3, Oxford, Oxford University Press.

Rooryck, Jan, 2001a, Evidentiality, Part I, *Glot International*, 5.4, pp. 125–33.

—— 2001b, Evidentiality, Part II, *Glot International*, 5.5, pp. 161–68.

Roussou, Anna, 2009, In the Mood for Control, *Lingua*, special issue on Mood, ed. Josep Quer (in press).

Schlenker, Philippe, 2003, A Plea for Monsters, *Linguistics and Philosophy*, 26, pp. 29–120.

—— 2004, Context of Thought and Context of Utterance: A Note on Free Indirect Discourse and Historical Present, *Mind and Language*, 19.3, pp. 279–304.

—— 2005, The Lazy Frenchman Approach to Subjunctive: Speculations on Reference to Worlds and Semantics Defaults in the Analysis of Mood, in Twan Geerts, Ivo van Ginneken and Haike Jacobs (eds.), *Romance Languages and Linguistic Theory*, Amsterdam, John Benjamins, pp. 269–309.

Scorretti, Mauro, 1994, Complemetizer Deletion, unpub. Ph.D. thesis, University of Amsterdam.

Sharvit, Yael, 2004, Free Indirect Discourse and De Re Pronouns, in Kazuha Watanabe and Robert Young (eds.), *Proceedings of SALT XIV: Semantics and Linguistic Theory*, Ithaca, NY, Cornell University Press, pp. 305–22.

—— 2008, The Puzzle of Free Indirect Discourse, *Linguistics and Philosophy*, 31, pp. 353–95.

Sigurðsson, Halldor, 2004, The Syntax of Person, Tense, and Speech Features, *Italian Journal of Linguistics*, 16.1, pp. 219–51.

—— 2007, Argument Features, Clausal Structure and the Computation, in Eric Reuland, Tanmoy Bhattacharya, and Giorgos Spathas (eds.), *Argument Structure*, New York, John Benjamins, pp. 121–57.

Smith, Carlota, 1997, *The Parameter of Aspect*, New York, Springer.

—— 2007, Reference Time without Tense, in Jacques Moeschler, Louis De Saussure, and Genoveva Puskas (eds.), *Recent Advances in the Syntax and Semantics of Tense, Aspect and Modality*, Berlin and New York, Mouton de Gruyter, pp. 229–47.

—— and Mary Erbaugh, 2005, Temporal Interpretation in Mandarin Chinese, *Linguistics*, 43.4, pp. 713–56.

Squartini, Mario, 2001a, Filogenesi e Ontogenesi del Futuro Italiano, *Archivio Glottologico Italiano*, 86, pp. 194–225.

—— 2001b, The Internal Structure of Evidentiality in Romance, *Studies in Language*, 25, pp. 97–334.

—— 2004, La Relazione Semantica tra Futuro e Condizionale nelle Lingue Romanze, *Revue Romane*, 39, pp. 68–96.

Stowell, Timothy, 1993, The Syntax of Tense, unpub. m.s., UCLA.

—— 1996, The Phrase Structure of Tense, in Jan Roorick and Laurie Zaring (eds.), *Phrase Structure and the Lexicon*, Dordrecht, Kluwer Academic Publishers, pp. 277–91.

—— 2008, The English KII, in Jacqueline Guéron and Jacqueline Lecarme (eds.), *Time and Modality*, New York, Springer, pp. 251–72.

Tang, Jane, 1989, Chinese Reflexives, *Natural Language and Linguistic Theory*, 7, pp. 93–121.

Tsoulas, George, 1996, The Nature of the Subjunctive and the Formal Grammar of Obviation, in Karen Zagona (ed.), *Linguistic Theory and Romance Languages*, Amsterdam, John Benjamins, pp. 295–306.

Vet, Co, 1985, Univers de discours et univers d'enonciation: les temps du passé et du futur, *Langue française*, 67, pp. 38–58.

Williams, Edwin, 1980, Predication, *Linguistic Inquiry*, 11.1, pp. 203–38.

Xue, Ping, Carl Pollard, and Ivan Sag, 1994, A New Perspective on Chinese *ziji*, in Aranovich Raul et al. (eds.), *Proceedings of WCCFL 13*, CSLI Pub., pp. 432–47.

Zagona, Karen, 1988, *Verb Phrase Syntax: A Parametric Study of English and Spanish*, New York, Springer.

—— 1994, Perfectivity and Temporal Arguments, in Michael L. Mazzola (ed.), *Issues and Theory in Romance Linguistics*, Washington, DC, Georgetown University Press, pp. 523–46.

—— 1995, Temporal Argument Structure: Configurational Elements of Construal, in Pier Marco Bertinetto, Valentina Bianchi, James Higginbotham, and Mario Squartini (eds.), *Temporal Reference, Aspect, and Actionality, Vol. I, Semantic and Syntactic Perspectives*, Turin, Rosenberg and Sellier, pp. 397–410.

—— 1999, Structural Case and Tense Construal, in Jean-Marc Authier, Barbara E. Bullock, and Lisa A. Reed (eds.), *Formal Perspectives on Romance Linguistics: Selected Papers From the 28th Linguistic Symposium on Romance Languages (LSRL XXVIII)*, Amsterdam, John Benjamins, pp. 305–27.

—— 2007, On the Syntactic Features of Epistemic and Root Modals, in Luis Eguren and Olga Fernández Soriano (eds.), *Coreference, Modality, and Focus*, Amsterdam, John Benjamins, pp. 221–36.

—— 2008, Phasing in Modals: Phrases and the Epistemic/Root Distinction, in Jacqueline Guéron and Jacqueline Lecarme (eds.), *Time and Modality*, New York, Springer, pp. 273–91.

Zanuttini, Raffaella and Paul Portner, 2000, The Characterization of Exclamative Clauses in Paduan, *Language*, 76.1, pp. 123–32.

———— 2003, Exclamative Clauses: At the Syntax-Semantics Interface, *Language*, 79.1, pp. 39–81.

Zucchi, Alessandro, 1999, Incomplete Events, Intensionality and Imperfective Aspect, *Natural Language and Semantics*, 7, pp. 179–215.

—— 2001, Tense in Fiction, in Carlo Cecchetto, Gennaro Chierchia, and Maria Teresa Guasti, *Semantic Interfaces: Reference, Anaphora and Aspect*, Stanford, CSLI Publications, pp. 320–56.

Index of Subjects

Index of Names

OXFORD STUDIES IN THEORETICAL LINGUISTICS

Printed and bound by CPI Group (UK) Ltd, Croydon, CR0 4YY